B. B. WARFIELD

Essays on His Life and Thought

B. B. WARFIELD

Essays on His Life and Thought

EDITED BY GARY L. W. JOHNSON

FOREWORD BY DAVID B. CALHOUN

INTRODUCTION BY MARK A. NOLL

P&R
PUBLISHING
P.O. BOX 817 • PHILLIPSBURG • NEW JERSEY 08865-0817

Chapter 2 appeared as "B. B. Warfield's Apologetical Appeal to 'Right Reason': Evidence of a 'Rather Bald Rationalism'?" in *Scottish Bulletin of Evangelical Theology* 16 (Autumn 1998): 156–77. Adapted and used by permission.

Chapter 3 appeared as "Old Princeton, Westminster, and Inerrancy" in *Westminster Theological Journal* 50 (1988): 65–80. Used by permission.

Chapter 4 appeared as "Old Princeton and the Doctrine of Scripture" in William A. Dembski and Jay Wesley Richards, eds., *Unapologetic Apologetics: Meeting the Challenges of Theological Studies* (Downers Grove, Ill.: InterVarsity, 2001), 111–30. Substantially revised and updated, and used by permission.

Chapter 5 appeared as "B. B. Warfield on the Apologetic Nature of Christian Scholarship: An Analysis of His Solution to the Problem of the Relationship between Christianity and Culture" in *Westminster Theological Journal* 62 (2000): 89–111. Adapted and used by permission.

Printed in the United States of America

Library of Congress Control Number: 2007927141

FOR

RICHARD A. MULLER
DAVID F. WELLS

and in memory of

S. LEWIS JOHNSON JR.

all scholars and Christian gentlemen
after the Warfieldian model

Contents

Contributors

David B. Calhoun (Ph.D., Princeton Theological Seminary), professor of church history, Covenant Theological Seminary, St. Louis, Missouri.

Raymond D. Cannata (Th.M., Princeton Theological Seminary; D.Min. cand., Westminster Theological Seminary), pastor, Redeemer Presbyterian Church (Presbyterian Church in America), New Orleans, Louisiana.

Bradley J. Gundlach (Ph.D., University of Rochester), associate professor of history, Trinity International University, Deerfield, Illinois.

Paul Kjoss Helseth (Ph.D., Marquette University), associate professor of Christian thought, Northwestern College, St. Paul, Minnesota.

Gary L. W. Johnson (Th.M., Westminster Theological Seminary; D.Th. cand., University of South Africa), senior pastor, Church of the Redeemer, Mesa, Arizona.

Stephen J. Nichols (Ph.D., Westminster Theological Seminary), professor of biblical and theological studies, Lancaster Bible College and Graduate School, Lancaster, Pennsylvania.

Mark A. Noll (Ph.D., Vanderbilt University), professor of history, University of Notre Dame, Notre Dame, Indiana.

Moisés Silva (Ph.D., University of Manchester), Litchfield, Michigan; visiting professor of New Testament, Westminster Theological Seminary, Philadelphia, Pennsylvania.

Barry Waugh (Ph.D., Westminster Theological Seminary), Glenside, Pennsylvania.

Foreword

David B. Calhoun

Prayer and Work

Said one, one day: "My cause is good,
The Lord will prosper it."
Said Luther: "Take it to Him, then;
That were provision fit."

Trust in the Lord, not in thy cause,
However good it be;
Take it forthwith in faithful hands
And lay it on His knee.

The best of causes go amiss;
The Lord will never fail:
Commit thy ways into his care,
And then—shake out thy sail.

—*B. B. Warfield*

The year 2001 marked the one hundred and fiftieth anniversary of the birth of Benjamin Breckinridge Warfield. That this milestone passed largely unnoticed merely underscores the fact that the most serious omission in the study of American Christianity and theology is the neglect of Princeton Theological Seminary's greatest professor. It was in Italy, surprisingly enough, that the Warfield anniversary was commemorated. Meetings in Naples and Padova both dealt with "this man of God." "In the evangelical theology of the twentieth century," the Italians asserted, "Benjamin Warfield has had disciples, but he has never had equals." Francis Landey Patton, in a memorial address for Dr. Warfield given at the First Presbyterian Church in Princeton on May 2, 1921, described his departed colleague as "preeminently a scholar [who] lived among his books." "I may be pardoned perhaps for saying somewhat extravagantly," Patton continued, "that his line has gone out into all the earth and his words to the end of the world."

If scholarly attention has largely passed Warfield by (there are some able dissertations and articles), he has by no means been forgotten by serious Christians worldwide. His writings (including collections of articles, essays, and reviews of English, German, French, and Dutch books) have remained in print.

In a visit to Toronto in 1932, D. Martyn Lloyd-Jones discovered in the library of Knox Seminary the recently published ten volumes of the works of B. B. Warfield. Lloyd-Jones's feelings at that moment, he was later to write, were like those of "stout Cortez," as described by Keats, when he first saw the Pacific. For many days Lloyd-Jones reveled in those ten volumes. There he found, according to Iain Murray, "theology anchored in Scripture, but with an exegetical precision more evident than in the older [Reformed] authors, and combined with a devotion which raised the whole above the level of scholarship alone." (Lloyd-Jones, introducing a collection of Warfield's writings published in 1958 as *Biblical Foundations*, wrote, "No theological writings are so intellectually satisfying and so strengthening to faith as those of Warfield.")

Dr. Warfield was above all a theologian, and the key to his theology was his unfaltering belief in the inspiration of the Old and New Testaments. He labored diligently to defend the authority and authenticity of the Bible (what he and others called the "inerrancy" of Scripture) against growing criticism and unbelief. In doing so he did not, as some have claimed, create a new doctrine of biblical inspiration. He inherited the doctrine that he so ably defended—from Charles Hodge and Archibald Alexander, from Francis Turretin and the Reformed Confessions, from Calvin and Augustine. And, most important, he found in the Bible itself the claim that God's Word is truth. In a recent interview, British preacher and Christian statesman John Stott was asked: "What are the top five most influential books in your life?" Stott began with *Revelation and Inspiration* by B. B. Warfield—a collection of essays concerning biblical authority. Stott said, "This book is marked by the careful exegesis for which Warfield was renowned, and lays a solid foundation for an acceptance of biblical authority. The argument is compelling; I do not believe that it has ever been answered."

Warfield (like his mentor Charles Hodge) came to theology from biblical studies. He was a theologian, but he was a theologian who based the content of his teaching on the plain and obvious meaning of the inspired Word of God. It does not take a student of Warfield long to discover that he was a master of Scripture's meaning.

Warfield also excelled in historical theology, amply demonstrated by his major studies of Tertullian, Augustine, Calvin, and the Westminster Assembly. (Warfield's student and colleague J. Gresham Machen spoke of Warfield as "one of the greatest masters in the field of the history of doctrine.") Recently, in my Ancient and Medieval Church History class at Covenant Theological Seminary, I ended my comments on the creation of the New Testament canon in the early church by quoting Warfield on the subject, and then adding, "You will find that when I don't know what else to say about something, I will quote Warfield!"

Warfield needs to be studied seriously because of the value and lasting solidity of his teaching. He also needs to be studied to correct the false impressions that have been created about him: that he was a rigid scholastic theologian who hardened the doctrine of inspiration into a new concept of inerrancy; that he was a rationalist who minimized the noetic effects of sin and the supernatural work of the Holy Spirit; that he was an evidentialist who could not appreciate the importance of Christian presuppositions; and that he was an intellectualist without spiritual fervor. (One of Warfield's students characterized him as "the most Christ-like man that I have ever known.")

If Warfield the scholar has been ignored, so has Warfield the man. His was not an exciting life. He seldom traveled beyond Princeton, staying at home to care lovingly for his invalid wife until her death.

He rarely preached outside Princeton. He was not active in the courts of the church, except to attend sessions of the local presbytery. But the life of this man, who, according to Francis Patton, "bore the marks of a gentleman to his finger-tips," is not without interest. He was called to be a teacher—and he was punctilious in the discharge of his duties as a teacher. Patton reported that "the manner of his death was in keeping with the habits of his life. He met his class on the day he died. The lecture was over, he returned to his lonely dwelling: there came a few sharp shocks of pain—and he had left the work that had been his joy, to be with the Saviour whom he loved."

When I was a student at Princeton Seminary twenty-five years ago, Warfield's picture hung in the student center with other Princetonians, but he was neither read nor greatly respected. One of my professors belittled him as "a sophisticated fundamentalist." It is time that modern Christians come to know the real Warfield. Andrea Ferrari, in his preface to the book of addresses on Warfield given by Italian Protestants in 2001, stated that "more than a scholar with an amazing intellectual capacity, Warfield was a believer deeply attached to Christ and to the faith passed on to the saints once and for all . . . a man whose heart was on fire for Christ's truth and for the triumph of God's kingdom in the world." This Warfield we need to know.

Acknowledgments

A number of people were instrumental in getting "the Warfield project" off the drawing board and into print. Allan Fisher, who now serves in a similar capacity at Crossway Books, sought approval for the project and oversaw its earliest stages. Marvin Padgett, who came from Crossway to P&R, oversaw the remaining stages. Associate editor Barbara Lerch proved to be both cheerful and patient. Louise Brown, Jean Johns, Autumn Frey, and Nancy Lindsay proved invaluable in preparing the manuscript for submission.

Many thanks to all of you.

Gary L. W. Johnson

Introduction

MARK A. NOLL

As one of the last great expositors of orthodox and classical Calvinism in the modern world, B. B. Warfield faced a double burden. It was obvious in nearly all his work that he was trying to present the doctrines of sovereign grace and gracious sovereignty with faithfulness to the traditions of high Calvinist theology that he had learned at Princeton Theological Seminary from Charles Hodge and, even before that, in his own household through the influence of his grandfather, Robert Breckinridge. But it was also obvious that Warfield was trying to articulate those doctrines as exactly what his contemporaries needed for both a proper foundation of Christian piety and a proper framework of Christian thinking. Despite his formidable gifts as biblical exegete, biblical theologian, and biblical apologist, it is not clear that Warfield's dual effort has been appreciated as it should have been. To modern thinkers he has seemed old-fashioned, to active revivalists overly Calvinistic, to some Calvinists too much a rationalist. Yet Warfield has never lacked readers who appreciated the clarity with which he maintained traditional Calvinist doctrines or ventured forth from his Calvinist foundations to address new problems, and the numbers of those readers seem to be growing. It is, thus, all to the good that this book is being published in order to stimulate closer attention to who Warfield was and what his theological contributions actually mean.

Among the following chapters, several attempt to resuscitate one aspect or another of Warfield's theology. Readers who follow in Warfield's train will read these chapters carefully, critically, and charitably, but they will also be making up their own minds about the success of those efforts. At the very least, all who follow the authors as they

1

track Warfield through thickets of theological complexity will be amply rewarded for their efforts.

Other chapters in what follows are more strictly biographical, and from these all readers will benefit. Warfield's reputation as a thinker is well deserved, but that reputation has also obscured how interesting the life of this thinker actually was. As that life is brought alive by the biographical studies in this book, new dimensions will open into the significance of this theological champion as well as the character of what he championed.

But first, as an introduction to both theological and biographical considerations, it may help to present a brief overview of the man and his main concerns. Such a sketch, if only an aperitif, should help prepare the way for the solid and nutritious fare found in the chapters themselves.

Benjamin Breckinridge Warfield was the most widely known advocate of confessional Calvinism in the United States at the end of the nineteenth and the beginning of the twentieth centuries.[1] Warfield continues to exert an influence today mostly through his defense of biblical inerrancy, although, as chapters below by Paul Helseth indicate, his convictions about the role of reason in apologetics also stimulate ongoing discussion. Now nearing a century after his death, many of his works remain in print. And his opinions continue to count, not only among conservative Presbyterians and modern advocates of biblical inerrancy, where such attention could be expected, but also with Southern Baptists, Wesleyans, some neoorthodox theologians, and still others whose interest in Warfield's views might be regarded as a surprise.

Warfield was born on November 5, 1851, at Grasmere, his family's estate in the vicinity of Lexington, Kentucky. His father, William

---

1. This introduction adapts and abridges material on Warfield by Mark A. Noll in *Handbook of Evangelical Theologians*, ed. Walter Elwell (Grand Rapids: Baker, 1993), 26–39; and by Noll and David N. Livingstone in "Introduction: B. B. Warfield as Conservative Evolutionist," in B. B. Warfield, *Evolution, Science, and Scripture: Selected Writings* (Grand Rapids: Baker, 2000), 13–44.

Warfield, a prosperous gentleman farmer, served as a Union officer in the Civil War. It was pertinent for Warfield's later writings on scientific questions that his father bred livestock and was the author of *The Theory and Practice of Cattle Breeding* (1888). It is also significant for his later epistemological and ethical views that Warfield's entrance into the sophomore class at the College of New Jersey (later Princeton University) in 1868 coincided with the installation of James McCosh as president. McCosh had been called to Princeton from his post as professor of moral philosophy at the Queen's University of Belfast in Ireland, where he was one of the last great exponents of the Scottish philosophy of common sense. Even more significantly, McCosh also advocated full and frank dialogue between traditional Christian faith and the best modern science, philosophy, and ethics.

After graduating from college in 1871, traveling in Europe for a year, and serving briefly as an editor for the *Farmer's Home Journal* in Lexington, Warfield entered Princeton Seminary to prepare for the ministry. During his time at the seminary, he was particularly impressed with the piety and theological comprehension of the elderly Charles Hodge. After graduating from the seminary, Warfield married, once again visited Europe, served for a short time as an assistant minister in Baltimore, and then in 1876 accepted a call to teach New Testament at Western Theological Seminary near Pittsburgh. In 1887, upon the death of Archibald Alexander Hodge, son of his own teacher, Warfield returned to Princeton Seminary as professor of didactic and polemic theology. During thirty-four years in that position, he instructed more than 2,700 students. Warfield died at Princeton late in the evening of February 16, 1921, after meeting his classes earlier that day.

Warfield's incredibly prolific output of books, learned essays, and reviews (which were frequently sophisticated monographs in their own right) was a product of his devotion to the confessional standards of Presbyterianism and, behind those standards, to his conception of classic Christian faith. Even in the long line of outstanding conservative theologians from "old Princeton" that stretched from Archibald Alexander (the founding professor in 1812) to J. Gresham Machen (who left Princeton Seminary in 1929), Warfield stands out. In that distinguished company, he was the most widely read, had the greatest skill in European languages, displayed the most patience in

3

unpacking arguments, and wrote more clearly on a wider range of subjects. Some of Warfield's convictions—especially his conception of the inerrancy of Scripture in its original autographs—have generated a great quantity of polemical attack and defense. Yet despite helpful work by John E. Meeter, Roger Nicole, and now the authors who contribute to this volume, there exists no comprehensive account of Warfield's theology.[2] Bradley Gundlach's contributions to this book are the first real steps to an adequate biography.

One reason for the absence of such work may be directly related to Warfield's conception of his task. He was, in the strictest sense of the terms, a polemical and a conserving theologian. Despite comprehensive learning, he never attempted a full theological statement, primarily because he found Charles Hodge's *Systematic Theology* generally satisfactory for himself and his students. Because he was content with the positions of the Westminster Confession and Catechisms, he devoted an enormous amount of patient writing to explicating traditional Calvinism, fending off misreadings, and defending it against the modernizing, enthusiastic, or naturalistic tendencies of his day.

Warfield was also content with what had been handed down to him by his Princeton predecessors on questions concerning the larger framework of thought. He did not delight in speculation (and so would mildly criticize Jonathan Edwards for his "individualisms," while praising Edwards for being "a convinced defender of Calvinism").[3] Rather, he gave himself wholeheartedly to Princeton's deeply ingrained commitment to theology as a scientific task (with "science" defined in conventional terms). In so doing, he thus shared fully in Princeton's equally long-standing confidence in a philosophy of common-sense realism. That philosophy owed something to its formal statement by the cautious savants of the Scottish Enlightenment such as Thomas Reid and Dugald Stewart. But it owed even more to a concrete, antispeculative turn of mind that the "old Princeton" theologians liked to describe as a simple inductivist Anglo-Saxon inheritance. From the

2. See especially John E. Meeter and Roger Nicole, *A Bibliography of Benjamin Breckinridge Warfield, 1851–1921* (Nutley, N.J.: Presbyterian and Reformed, 1974).

3. B. B. Warfield, "Edwards and the New England Theology" (1912), in *Studies in Theology*, vol. 9 of *The Works of Benjamin Breckinridge Warfield* (1932; repr., Grand Rapids: Baker, 1981), 530–31.

perspective of the late twentieth century, the philosophy of common sense at Princeton looks mostly like a gentlemanly, Victorian, and dignified Presbyterian adaptation of the practical bent so common at all levels in nineteenth-century American culture. Again, chapters below represent some of the best work on how Warfield approached such basic philosophical questions.

Warfield's stance as an ardent defender of confessional Calvinism, combined with his positions on the issues that engaged Presbyterians around the turn of the century, have led to a curiosity. Warfield seems to have regarded his work as a coherent effort to maintain the theology of Calvin and the Westminster divines. Later attention, however, has focused more on his exposition of individual topics, like the inerrancy of Scripture, counterfeit miracles, or the place of apologetics in theology more generally. The result has been that, although several of Warfield's positions continue to exert considerable influence among theological conservatives, the defense of Calvinism that loomed large in his own work receives far less attention today.

By the early 1880s, American Presbyterians were being drawn more directly into European debates over the Bible.[4] Presbyterian leaders realized that new higher critical proposals touched the heart of their faith as it had developed in Britain and America. They also knew that the controversies raging over modern criticism in Scotland during the 1870s, especially concerning the work of William Robertson Smith of the Free Church, would soon arrive in America. Smith's acceptance of Old Testament higher criticism was especially significant for Princeton Seminary because Princetonians had championed the Free Church since its founding in 1843. So it came about that A. A. Hodge of Princeton and Charles Briggs of Union Seminary in New York agreed that the journal they jointly edited, the *Presbyterian Review*, should consider these matters. Briggs, who was predisposed toward the newer opinions, enlisted several colleagues to write in favor of adjusting traditional views. Hodge too sought assistance in supporting his conviction that the new views were mostly a threat to the church. For this purpose

---

4. See Mark A. Noll, *Between Faith and Criticism: Evangelicals, Scholarship, and the Bible in America*, 2nd ed. (Grand Rapids: Baker, 1991), 27–31.

his first recruit was B. B. Warfield, then still a young New Testament professor at Western Theological Seminary.

The essay, titled simply "Inspiration," which Hodge and Warfield published in the April 1881 issue of the *Presbyterian Review*, both recapitulated many of the themes that had been prominent in previous Princeton writing and anticipated most of the points about the Bible that Warfield would make over the next forty years in a wealth of publications. What was new about the doctrine of Scripture in this essay was its precision of statement and its detailed response to modern theories. The essay's burden was to show that proper scholarship on Scripture and its background supported, rather than undercut, a high view of verbal inspiration. The doctrine this essay defended was the belief that "God's continued work of superintendence, by which, his providential, gracious and supernatural contributions having been presupposed, he presided over the sacred writers in their entire work of writing, with the design and effect of rendering that writing an errorless record of the matters he designed them to communicate, and hence constituting the entire volume in all its parts the word of God to us."[5]

Throughout the essay, as indeed throughout his entire career, Warfield took great care to qualify the doctrine of plenary verbal inspiration. Hodge and Warfield stated, almost at the outset, that this doctrine was not "a principle fundamental to the truth of the Christian religion" as such, nor was it the case "that the truth of Christianity depends upon any doctrine of inspiration whatever."[6] They also maintained at length that such a view of inspiration did not rule out a full, active participation of Scripture's human authors in its production. They held that these biblical authors "were in large measure dependent for their knowledge upon sources and methods in themselves fallible, and that their personal knowledge and judgments were in many matters hesitating and defective, or even wrong."[7] They insisted that the Bible must be interpreted after the intent of its authors, an intent that often required careful study to discover. They held that supposed errors in Scripture

5. Archibald A. Hodge and Benjamin B. Warfield, *Inspiration*, ed. Roger R. Nicole (Grand Rapids: Baker, 1979), 17–18.
6. Ibid., 8.
7. Ibid., 28.

must be located in "some part of the original autograph,"[8] rather than haphazardly drawn from what might be corrupted transmissions of the text. And they acknowledged that this doctrine, which they held to be the plain teaching of many scriptural passages themselves, needed to be confirmed by full attention to all possible objections arising from the study of the Bible itself (e.g., questions concerning mistaken history or geography, inaccurate quotations from the Old Testament in the New, internal lack of harmony, and the like). Yet once having made these qualifications, Hodge and Warfield insisted that the Bible was fully inspired, absolutely without error, and legitimately to be regarded not just as a bearer of the Word of God but as that Word itself.

As critics responded to this position paper, and as the Princeton theologians themselves fleshed out their conception of biblical inerrancy in scores of works, Warfield made crucial statements about Scripture that would also shape his response to questions of science. Of particular importance was his response to the charge that his view of inspiration amounted to a mechanical view of divine dictation. In response, Warfield repeatedly argued that he was advocating not dictation, but what he called "concursus." For example, in an 1894 article on "The Divine and Human in the Bible," Warfield was at pains to defend the fully human character of the Bible *in addition to* its fully divine character. As he phrased it in this discussion of the Bible, "concursus" meant that "the Scriptures are the joint product of divine and human activities, both of which penetrate them at every point, working harmoniously together to the production of a writing which is not divine here and human there, but at once divine and human in every part, every word and every particular."[9] The importance of this way of thinking for Warfield's scientific views was great. In simple terms, the products of natural history could be the consequence—at the same time—of both natural forces and divine action.

The main points of Warfield's defense of an inerrant Bible, if not necessarily the details of his position, eventually became major

8. Ibid., 36.
9. B. B. Warfield, "The Divine and Human in the Bible" (1894), in Benjamin B. Warfield, *Selected Shorter Writings*, 2 vols., ed. John E. Meeter (Nutley, N.J.: Presbyterian and Reformed, 1970, 1973), 2:547.

guideposts for the American fundamentalist movement.[10] The rise of fundamentalism, however, placed Warfield and other confessional conservatives in an ambiguous situation. While they applauded the fundamentalists' adherence to biblical infallibility and their defense of a supernatural faith, they found fundamentalism theologically eccentric and methodologically suspect. Many later fundamentalists would employ Warfield's formulation of biblical inerrancy as a definition of their own beliefs about Scripture, but Warfield himself maintained several important positions that set him apart from fundamentalism. In the first instance, Warfield held that fundamentalist proof-texting represented a retrograde step in studying the Bible.[11] In addition, Warfield was unimpressed by the dispensationalism that became so important in American fundamentalism. Modern theologies associated with John Nelson Darby, C. I. Scofield, or other promoters of dispensationalism were suspect to Warfield for faulty exegesis, questionable theological construction, and errors on the work of the Holy Spirit.[12] Finally, like his college teacher James McCosh and his senior colleague, A. A. Hodge, Warfield found little difficulty in thinking that, if scientific facts called for such a move, it would be a straightforward theological task to align historic confessional Calvinism with non-naturalistic forms of evolution.[13] This, of course, was a move that fundamentalists were unwilling to make.

In his views on dispensationalism, evolution, and the use of the Bible, therefore, Warfield was not a fundamentalist as the label came to be used. A carefully qualified view of biblical inerrancy, like the one Warfield developed, did not necessarily entail the particulars of fundamentalist theology, but could in fact ground judgments on nature, the

10. See George M. Marsden, *Fundamentalism and American Culture* (New York: Oxford University Press, 1980); Ernest R. Sandeen, *The Roots of Fundamentalism: British and American Millenarianism, 1800–1930* (Chicago: University of Chicago Press, 1970); George W. Dollar, *A History of Fundamentalism in America* (Greenville, S.C.: Bob Jones University Press, 1973).

11. See, for example, his review of *What the Bible Teaches* (1899), by R. A. Torrey, *Presbyterian and Reformed Review* 39 (July 1899): 562–64.

12. See, for example, B. B. Warfield, "The Millennium and the Apocalypse" (1904), in *Biblical Doctrines*, vol. 2 of *The Works of Benjamin Breckinridge Warfield* (1929; repr., Grand Rapids: Baker, 1981), 643–64.

13. See, for example, A. A. Hodge, review of *Natural Science and Religion*, by Asa Gray, *Presbyterian Review* 1 (July 1880): 586–89; or his "Introduction" to Joseph S. van Dyke, in *Theism and Evolution* (New York: A. C. Armstrong & Son, 1886), xv–xxiii.

character of biblical theology, and approaches to biblical scholarship very different in tone, and significantly different in substance, from what was found among fundamentalists.

Important as Warfield felt it was to contend for the truthfulness of the Bible, he exerted even more energy throughout his long career expounding the truths of the Bible. Warfield, in other words, was concerned to secure the Bible as the ground of theology and to protect reason as a prime theological tool, but he was characteristically more interested in the theology he felt the Bible taught and reason supported.

Warfield was not embarrassed to say what that theology was and where he felt it had been best represented in the history of the church. Time and again throughout his historical, exegetical, and polemical works (and it was never easy to disengage these categories from each other), Warfield defined true Christianity as the pure religion of the Reformation; or, in phrases that to him meant the same thing, as the Augustinian grasp of human sin and divine grace recovered by Luther and especially Calvin; or, even more fully, as the Pauline summation of the biblical gospel passed on especially to Augustine and then renewed by the magisterial Reformers. "Calvinism," he wrote in 1904, "is just religion in its purity. We have only, therefore, to conceive of religion in its purity, and that is Calvinism."[14]

Five years later Warfield spelled out explicitly what he meant by Calvinism—"a profound apprehension of God in His majesty, with the inevitably accompanying poignant realization of the exact nature of the relation sustained to Him by the creatures as such, and particularly by the sinful creature." In the same place, Warfield suggested that he was not using "Calvinism" as a narrow label for those holding a certain theological position. Rather, "Calvinism" meant a way of life before God that, in the course of history, had been most satisfactorily described by the Protestant Reformers, who recovered an Augustinian understanding of the biblical message. If Warfield's theological labeling was narrow, his conception of the thing for which the label spoke was broadly catholic.

14. B. B. Warfield, "What Is Calvinism?" (1904), in *Selected Shorter Writings*, 1:389.

He who believes in God without reserve, and is determined that God shall be God to him in all his thinking, feeling, willing—in the entire compass of his life-activities, intellectual, moral, spiritual, throughout all his individual, social, religious relations—is, by the force of that strictest of all logic which presides over the outworking of principles into thought and life, by the very necessity of the case, a Calvinist.[15]

The comprehensiveness of this kind of Calvinism—its picture of a God who pervaded all aspects of existence—was critical for Warfield's stance in general.

Although Warfield is today better known for his views on the Bible, a solid case can be constructed on the basis of his own works that his commitment to classic Protestantism was deeper and more comprehensive than even his commitment to biblical inerrancy as such. By this classic Protestantism, Warfield meant commitment to an Augustinian view of God, the sinful human condition, and salvation in Christ, but also a broadly open acceptance of the world as the arena of God's creative activity. For Warfield, the heart of both theology and active religion was the glory of God, who rescued sinful humans from self-imposed destruction and who enabled them to share his work of the kingdom in every sphere of life, including the natural world.

Even Warfield's defense of biblical inerrancy, which often seems to be undertaken on behalf of a bare notion of biblical veracity, was also a product of his overarching Calvinism. The point of defending traditional views of the Bible was not so much the Bible itself as what the Bible taught. When Warfield in 1910 reviewed the autobiography of William Newton Clarke, a Northern Baptist who over the course of a long career moved from believing in the Bible as inerrant revelation from God to considering it a refined record of religious encounter with God, Warfield rehearsed the arguments he had made many times before concerning Jesus' own testimony to the infallibility of Scripture. But in the end the critical matter was not just Scripture: "He who no longer holds to the Bible of Jesus—the word of which cannot be broken—will be found on examination no longer to hold

15. B. B. Warfield, "Calvinism" (1908), in *Calvin and Calvinism*, vol. 5 of *The Works of Benjamin Breckinridge Warfield* (1931; repr., Grand Rapids: Baker, 1981), 354–56.

to the Jesus of the Bible." This Jesus, who communicates forgiveness to needy sinners, is the one "to whom it [Scripture] bears consentient witness."[16] Historian L. Russ Bush has made the important observation that Warfield's understanding of the Bible follows his more general conception of theology as a whole.[17]

It is that theology, and the man who held it, that are opened up in an unusually helpful way by the chapters that follow.

16. B. B. Warfield, review of *Sixty Years with the Bible*, by William Newton Clarke, *Princeton Theological Review* 8 (Jan. 1910): 167.

17. L. Russ Bush, "The Roots of Conservative Perspectives on Inerrancy (Warfield)," in *Proceedings of the Conference on Biblical Inerrancy, 1987* (Nashville: Broadman, 1987), 280–81.

"B" Is for Breckinridge: Benjamin B. Warfield, His Maternal Kin, and Princeton Seminary

BRADLEY J. GUNDLACH

When the news spread of B. B. Warfield's call to the most vener-able professorship in the Presbyterian church in early 1887, letters of congratulation arrived from all over the country, as well as from Great Britain. Princeton and the Hodge family were delighted. "My sister says who should succeed A. A. but B. B.!" quipped Caspar Wistar Hodge, Warfield's mentor in New Testament. From San Francisco, Warfield's uncle Josie, a beefy officer in the U.S. Army, exulted, "I could chirp like the bird upon the bough except that I am too old & large and the bough would be sure to break." Some British cor-respondents seemed less enthralled with the name of Princeton and the task of dogmatic theology. W. R. Nicoll, editor of the London *Expositor*, tempered his well-wishes with an expression of regret that the church would lose an important New Testament exegete when Warfield changed departments, and William Sanday of Oxford wrote tactfully of the appointment, "I presume it is in accordance with your tastes & wishes." David Brown, aged principal of the Free Church College in Aberdeen, with whom Warfield enjoyed a long and rich collegial correspondence on topics of New Testament interpretation,

13

said, "Well, you'll do real good, I believe, by bringing your woof across their warp (if that is a right figure of your relation to them) at Princeton," where till now "the Dogmatics of two Hodges has probably over-Hodged it."[1]

Some of the British reserve over Warfield's call to Princeton derived from a methodological preference for exegesis and criticism over systematics, and some from doctrinal differences with the Princeton theology. But as Brown's remarks suggest, it arose also from a sense that Warfield was not just another specimen from the Princetonian hot-house—that his advent in Princeton in the chair of the Hodges would bring something qualitatively new. Some of Warfield's own relatives concurred. Uncle George Morrison declared, "Nothing can be grander for Princeton than that the Breckinridge Warfield Blood shall be infused into Princeton."[2]

Warfield was not in fact the first man from the Breckinridge line to teach at Princeton, nor were the Breckinridges unknown there—far from it. This family had a long and tangled history with Princeton already; their relationship was intimate yet often oppositional. For that very reason Uncle George was right: in view of the past record of unstable relations, the call of a Breckinridge to the hallowed chair at Princeton was worth remarking.

Warfield's great-uncle John Breckinridge served as professor of pastoral theology at Princeton Seminary in the 1830s, and was a close friend of Professors Charles Hodge (at the seminary) and James Waddell Alexander (then at the college). Hodge and Breckinridge had been classmates at Nassau Hall. Both men experienced conversion in the college revival of 1815. After John's untimely death the Princetonians revered him as "the personification of all that is noble and gentle in his humanity, and all that is fearless and self-sacrificing in the work of his Master"—so much so that the index volume of the *Biblical Repertory and Princeton Review* devoted five pages to a fulsome biographical

---

1. Caspar Wistar Hodge to B. B. Warfield (hereafter BBW for correspondence), February 6, 1887 (Warfield Papers, Princeton Theological Seminary [hereafter PTS], box 17); Joseph Cabell Breckinridge to BBW, undated (early 1887) (Warfield Papers, PTS, box 6); W. R. Nicoll to BBW, February 5, 1887 (Warfield Papers, PTS, box 17); William Sanday to BBW, March 20, 1887 (Warfield Papers, PTS, box 17); David Brown to BBW, February 15, 1887 (Warfield Papers, PTS, box 17).

2. George Morrison to BBW, January 29, 1887 (Warfield Papers, PTS, box 6).

sketch of this man who contributed only two articles to the journal. Perhaps in explanation of this disproportionate honor, the author acknowledged that "a romantic interest is now associated with his name."[3]

John was just one of four Breckinridge brothers whose lives were tied to Princeton. He, older brother Cabell, and younger brother Robert all attended college there.[4] John and Robert went on to study at the seminary as well. In those early days the college faculty numbered a mere handful, and the seminary faculty only three.[5] In that cozy environment three of the four brothers married wives from the leading families of both Princeton institutions. Cabell and the fourth brother, William, married into the already interconnected families of Princeton College presidents John Witherspoon and Samuel Stanhope Smith. John married Margaret Miller, the eldest daughter of seminary professor Samuel Miller. Thus the mingling of Princeton and Breckinridge blood had occurred in actual fact, well in advance of Uncle George's metaphor.[6]

The joining of families thus far had brought an infusion of Princeton blood into the Breckinridge line. Uncle George now triumphantly looked forward to an infusion in the other direction, and this time in metaphorical—that is, theological and churchly—form. Hitherto the theological meeting of the two lineages had taken place in the eccle-

3. "Breckinridge, John," *Biblical Repertory and Princeton Review*, index volume, 111. On John's relationship with Charles Hodge, see Hodge's letters to him, 1819–41 (Hodge Family Papers, Princeton University, box 14).

4. The father, John Breckinridge Sr.—attorney general for Thomas Jefferson—sent his sons to Princeton on the recommendation of James Madison. Ethelbert Dudley Warfield, "The Breckinridges of Kentucky: A Chronicle of Loyalty," *Independent*, May 22, 1890 (clipping among the Warfield Papers at the University of Kentucky).

5. Cabell graduated from Princeton College in 1810. John was one of twenty-five students in the Princeton Seminary class of 1822. Among them were Charles Clinton Beatty, who, as a director of Western Seminary, would offer Warfield his first academic job; and John Maclean, president of Princeton College at the time of Warfield's admittance. Robert technically belonged to the class of 1834, but pursued his theological studies under an independent-study arrangement with Samuel Miller. *Biographical Catalogue of the Princeton Theological Seminary, 1815–1932*, comp. Edward Howell Roberts (Princeton, 1933).

6. On Joseph Cabell Breckinridge, see James C. Klotter, *The Breckinridges of Kentucky, 1760–1981* (Lexington: University Press of Kentucky, 1986), 95–96. Cabell was the father of U.S. vice president, presidential candidate, and Confederate General John C. Breckinridge. Cabell's wife was Mary Clay Smith, daughter of Samuel Stanhope Smith and granddaughter of John Witherspoon. William's wife was her niece, Frances Caroline Prevost, Smith's granddaughter and Witherspoon's great-granddaughter.

siastical debates of the Presbyterian church, and these were often far from amicable. At times involving John and William, they centered on Warfield's grandfather, Robert Jefferson Breckinridge, source of the second "B" in "B. B. W."

This essay will take that second "B" as an occasion to weigh the relative importance of the Breckinridges and the Princetonians for Warfield's identity as a theologian, scholar, and polemicist. Other Breckinridge kin will play supporting roles, but the primary emphasis will rest on the parallels and contrasts between Warfield and his grandfather. I will argue that Warfield ultimately chose to follow the example of Charles Hodge more than that of his own grandfather, admonished by the history of Breckinridge-Princeton relations and of Breckinridge battles elsewhere. At the same time, Warfield sought to emulate the incisiveness and the bravery of his vociferous grandfather—to carry on as a skillful warrior, but of a more scholarly and even-tempered kind. He thus sought to incorporate the best aspects of both Hodge and Breckinridge.

The Warrior from the West

Robert Jefferson Breckinridge (1800–1871) impressed the early Princeton theologians as a man of exceptional talent and promise. The son of Thomas Jefferson's attorney general (hence the middle name), Breckinridge inherited great political gifts: a prodigious memory, an ardent spirit, masterful use of oratory to move his hearers, and a keen ability to cut to the heart of a contested issue. Everyone who met him, friend or foe—and he had plenty of foes—admitted this. His father shared the deistic ideas of President Jefferson, but his mother was an earnest Christian who eventually saw three of her sons become leading ministers in the Presbyterian church. Breckinridge's biographer, Edgar Mayse, notes the irony that a Jeffersonian deist who backed the Unitarians in the Breckinridges' home town of Lexington, Kentucky, should sire three staunch Calvinist ministers. Indeed, Mayse credits Princeton College with the "recovery of orthodoxy" in the Breckinridge family, since Cabell and John came to faith in college

16

revivals there.[7] The Breckinridge brothers, especially Cabell, were in the vanguard of conversions among the gentry and lawyers of Kentucky.[8]

Robert, too, went to Princeton, but his college experience proved far less elevating. A hot-blooded youth who at age six lost his father, he got into trouble at college. He spent money extravagantly ($1,205 in one year) and in March 1818 got into a violent fight with a senior from Texas named Furman Morford. According to a summary of the college records (presumably the Faculty Minutes, which are replete with student discipline issues), Breckinridge started the fight, rekindled it after friends broke it up, and then "reviled [his opponent] exceedingly and made use of language in a high degree profane, insulting and abusive." Morford then used a stick to knock Breckinridge senseless, giving him "a considerable contusion over the eye." Breckinridge's grandsons recalled the story differently, however: as they understood it (perhaps from his telling), it was the Texan who was knocked unconscious when Breckinridge smashed a chair over *his* head. In any case, both men were expelled.[9] Though restored to his class after a decent interval, Robert was so soured toward Princeton that he requested honorable dismissal. He studied briefly at Yale and then at Union College, from which he graduated in 1819. Mayse suggests that this early disciplinary action marked the beginnings of Breckinridge's lifelong distaste for Princeton.[10]

7. Edgar Caldwell Mayse, "Robert Jefferson Breckinridge: American Presbyterian Controversialist" (Th.D. diss., Union Theological Seminary, Richmond, Va., 1974), 65–66 (hereafter "RJB" for this Mayse title, RJB for correspondence). Mayse's work gives exceedingly close treatment to Robert Jefferson Breckinridge's myriad writings and controversies, and this essay owes a great deal to his tilling of a very extensive field. Mayse notes that the rich and cultivated members of Lexington society were distinctly out of sympathy with the evangelical revivals. On the Transylvania University battle, see George M. Marsden, *The Soul of the American University: From Protestant Establishment to Established Nonbelief* (New York: Oxford University Press, 1994), 72. For a general cultural-history take on the conversion of Southern and Western elites, see Christine Leigh Heyrman, *Southern Cross: The Beginnings of the Bible Belt* (New York: Knopf, 1997).

8. Robert H. Bishop, *An Outline of the History of the Church in the State of Kentucky* (Lexington: Thomas T. Skillman, 1824), 400, cited in Mayse, "RJB," 67 n. 87.

9. Mayse, "RJB," 51. Mayse cites for the first account Edmund A. Moore, "The Earlier Life of Robert J. Breckinridge, 1800–1845" (Ph.D. diss., University of Chicago, 1932), 6; and for the second account Ethelbert D. Warfield, untitled article in the *Princeton Alumni Weekly*, January 17, 1930.

10. Ibid., 52–53. Robert's oldest brother and guardian, Cabell, was himself suspended from Princeton College for participating in a student uprising. Klotter, *Breckinridges of Kentucky*, 95;

The college fight was far from the first manifestation of Breckinridge's hot temper. All of the Breckinridge brothers, in fact, had a reputation for bellicosity. Their spirited mother had admonished her fatherless boys "never to allow themselves to be whipt."[11] When the Mexican War came, and the Civil War after that, the brothers' sons made ardent and colorful officers. A story printed years later illustrates the point: in 1849, when Robert was running for representative to the new state constitutional convention and his nephew John C. Breckinridge was running for Congress, the two "met on 'the stump' somewhere."

> The Doctor indulged in a little pleasantry at the expense of the Major, as he then ranked. "His nephew, Major B., was a distinguished warrior; when the Mexican authorities heard that he had entered the field, they at once sued for peace." Whereupon John C., without rising from his seat, cried out, "If uncle Robert had been there, they would be fighting yet."[12]

Some years after Robert came to faith, his mother heard "that some persons doubted whether her son Robert had any true religion. Said she, 'I haven't the slightest doubt of his being a converted man. You ought to have known him before he got religion.'" And when she learned that her son John was taking on Archbishop Hughes of Baltimore in a newspaper debate on Catholicism versus Presbyterianism, she said, "'John had better let Robert manage that fight; for he has been a man of war from his youth.'"[13]

The Breckinridges prided themselves on their reputation as fighting men—but violence of temper has, of course, its down side. Once young Robert poured salt into a blind cousin's coffee, and when his brother John beat him for it, Robert drew a butcher knife. John, not to be outdone, gave Robert a thorough thrashing—"beat him, and stamped

---

for further particulars, see Lowell H. Harrison, "A Young Kentuckian at Princeton, 1806–1810: Joseph Cabell Breckinridge," *Filson Club Historical Quarterly* 38 (1964).

11. John Breckinridge to RJB, October 10, 1833 (Breckinridge Papers, Library of Congress [hereafter LC]), quoted in Mayse, "RJB," 738.

12. L. G. Barbour, "The Breckinridges," undated article clipped from the *Presbyterian Monthly*, ca. 1880s (Warfield Papers, PTS), 428.

13. Ibid., 426.

him and kicked him." On attaining his sixteenth birthday, Robert gave a whipping to his mother's old black carriage driver, as he had planned for some time to do, just to demonstrate his manhood.[14]

Conversion to Christ did not change the Breckinridge temperament, but it did channel it into churchly service. John became an ardent advocate of missions and engaged in lengthy polemics against Catholicism.[15] William, the least turbulent of the brothers, took part in several battles within the General Assembly. But it was Robert, the last brother to come to faith,[16] whose gifts and bravery wowed the Presbyterian leadership. When he joined the church in 1829, he found a cause of causes worth fighting for, and an institution that—perhaps too soon—rewarded his brilliance and leadership with significant responsibility. He was quickly ordained as an elder and within a year was attending the meetings of the Synod of Kentucky, where he strongly advocated the use of camp meetings for the conversion of the world. A lawyer friend complimented him, "You must have had a double portion of grace given you [at Synod] or you could not have kept your fiery temper in order—so as to meet fully the approbation of the fathers of the church."[17]

The next year, 1831—only two years after conversion—Robert served as a delegate to the General Assembly in Philadelphia. He had begun reading theology on his own, and this, together with his natural self-confidence, emboldened him to take a prominent part in the Assembly's work. He gave a speech at the conclusion of the trial of Albert Barnes, filed a lengthy complaint on a point of ecclesiastical order, and worked on a committee concerned with the relations of the

14. His mother was right about the pre-conversion Robert! Klotter, *Breckinridges of Kentucky*, 42; Barbour, "The Breckinridges," 426.

15. John Breckinridge and John Hughes, *A Discussion: Is the Roman Catholic Religion Inimical to Civil or Religious Liberty? Is the Presbyterian Religion Inimical to Civil or Religious Liberty?* (1836; repr., New York: Da Capo Reprints, 1970). The debates stretched over five months in 1833, appearing as articles alternating in the Philadelphia *Presbyterian* and the *Catholic Herald*. See also Mayse, "RJB," 285–88.

16. Robert's conversion is described in Klotter, *Breckinridges of Kentucky*, 49, and at greater length in Mayse, "RJB," 65–76. John, the brother who thrashed Robert so soundly in the story above, played an important role in repeatedly exhorting the wayward Robert to turn to Christ. See also "A Chapter from the Journal of the Rev. R. J. Breckinridge," unidentified newspaper clipping (ca. 1880) in B. B. Warfield's Scrapbooks 2 (Warfield Papers, PTS).

17. John Green to RJB, October 29, 1830 (Breckinridge Papers, LC), quoted in Mayse, "RJB," 81.

church's mission board and the powerful American Home Missionary Society—all this as an elder, not a clergyman. These issues and others would eventuate in the Old School/New School split of 1837. From this, his first General Assembly, Breckinridge "was in the vanguard of that militant group whose efforts were forcing the church toward division."[18]

Princeton looked upon Breckinridge's rise to church prominence, initially, with rejoicing. According to his lifelong friend and admirer, Andrew B. Cross, Breckinridge arose at the Assembly of 1831 like a David to champion the flagging cause of conservative Presbyterianism against the inroads of the New Divinity. The New School men had at that time a giant of a debater in Dr. Nathan S. S. Beman, who "had so roughly handled the fathers that spoke and the Old side generally"— including Princeton Seminary professor Samuel Miller and the school's founder and director Ashbel Green—"that they were paralyzed, and conferring with one another on abandoning the contest."

> There was a pause, a silence, a despair on the part of the Fathers. A young, delicate man arose, it was the first time he had ever seen an Assembly, he was so feeble during the session that at times he could not attend, and the prayers of the Assembly were offered for him. It was considered the height of imprudence, and as he began to speak the great body thought it a rash act, for so feeble a man to venture in the face of the Goliath of the New School party, . . . who supposed he had slain all the strong men in the opposition.[19]

The sickly young man was Robert Jefferson Breckinridge, who protested against the "moral attainder" nearly accomplished,

> where the two parties for peace, propose or are agreeing to smother and suppress the truth of God, and abandon the principles of our system. Many of my fathers and brethren think it will be better for

18. Mayse, "RJB," 83–84.

19. Andrew B. Cross, "The Calumny of Dr. C. S. Robinson . . . on the Late Rev. Dr. R. J. Breckinridge," *Baltimore Presbyterian*, February 3, 1881. Clipping in Scrapbook 3 (Warfield Papers, PTS, box 41), 61–62. Cross did not exaggerate Beman's prowess: his New School colleagues called him "that prince of debaters." Jonathan F. Stearns, in *Presbyterian Reunion Memorial Volume, 1837–1871* (New York: De Witt C. Lent & Co., 1870), 68.

us to give it up and peaceably retire. I cannot be one to that act. It is a matter of little moment what becomes of us but we must stand for the truth, and stand in the church, not out of it.

Cross commented,

His speech on that day showed a moral courage and power, a vigor of mind, and capacity and aptness for debate, that surprised [*sic*] all, and that gave encouragement and strength to the Old side, and such a scathing of Dr. Beman for his assaults upon such old men as Drs. Green, Miller, Fisk, Blythe, Mathews, &c.,[—]and they were men in those days—that it startled the whole Assembly. The daily papers spoke of it with wonder, and commended him for his manly defence of those fathers from the assaults of Dr. Beman. We had no telegraph in those days, nor railroads nor locomotives, but somehow the report of that speech did fly over the Church, and the orthodox men awoke to their position and took courage.

Breckinridge had made his reputation in the church. When next he addressed the Assembly,

. . . you could see the lobby running in till there was not standing room, and would have heard a pin fall. He was known as the elder from the west. Dr. Beman tried to silence him in many ways, but the vigor and manliness, with the home thrusts that he gave Dr. B. who was admitted to be the most skillful and adroit debater in the house, made many think of John Knox.[20]

The following year, Cross visited Princeton and called on Archibald Alexander. The professor asked about delegates to the impending General Assembly. When Cross named Robert Breckinridge among them, Alexander was thrilled. "His eyes brightened as all who knew him will recall when interested, and lifting both his arms, clapping his hands together, he exclaimed: 'He is a host! He is a host!'"[21]

What Alexander so admired in Breckinridge was not the sophist's skill at winning an argument by clever maneuvering, but the

20. Cross, "Calumny," 62.
21. Archibald Alexander, quoted in ibid.

orator's ability to "make a subject so plain that you could not help understanding it." Contemporaries marveled at Breckinridge's amazing memory for details, his ability to extemporize, his complete lack of hesitation when seeing his duty, and above all his incisiveness. "He not only saw quickly the real issue," wrote Cross, "but was as prompt and ready, ably to present it and defend or expose it and was not afraid to do it."[22]

A fine example of Breckinridge's rhetorical skill is recounted in Charles Hodge's review of the General Assembly of 1862. In that second year of the Civil War, Breckinridge submitted for the Assembly's adoption a paper on "The State of the Country," declaring it the duty of every Christian to support the federal union. In the course of the debate over his paper, Breckinridge said:

> Some say they are sorry for me, that I should have been so unfortunate as to introduce this paper here! Now, I will agree to do this—I will even "compromise" with them; and I make them this proposition—that I will take unto and upon myself all the blame that may attach on this account before men, if, when we have all gone up above, they will not claim the glory there! (Laughter.) Every speech giving utterances from a disloyal bosom seems to signify that it would be no harm, by silence, to disgrace the church; and yet deem any plain and unequivocal allusion to the difficulty as exceedingly harmful. One very hot day, a West India lady directed her servant to take some ice, and some *liquor*, and some water, and some lemon, and mix them for her to drink. "And, if you please, mistress," said the servant, "shall I put in a little nutmeg?" "Begone, you beast!" screamed the mistress; "*do you think I would drink punch!*" (A laugh.) So, now, when I would put in the "nutmeg," and make the question unequivocal, the brethren manifest abhorrence of the whole matter. (Continued merriment.)[23]

This excerpt demonstrates several of Breckinridge's leading qualities. He thought quickly on his feet, finding a metaphor that was not only apt but entertaining. He had wit both in the sense of intelligence

22. Cross, "Calumny," 62.
23. Robert Jefferson Breckinridge, in Charles Hodge, "The General Assembly," *Biblical Repertory and Princeton Review* 34 (1862): 512.

and humor—and combined the two winningly. However, he was also prone to personalize his battles. Just before this utterance he remarked, "I have observed that every speech on this subject, even to that of my friend Dr. Backus, involved either a direct or covert attack upon me."[24]

In the summer and fall of 1832, like his brothers before him, Robert went to Princeton Seminary for a theological education. A married man and father with an already established reputation in the church, Breckinridge received special treatment at Princeton. His course amounted to a guided study directed by his brother's father-in-law, professor Samuel Miller. After five intensive months, Breckinridge took up the pastorate of a significant urban congregation: the Second Presbyterian Church of Baltimore.[25]

Princeton admired Breckinridge's skill with the rhetorical sword, his stand on principle, his bravery, his penetration. But along with these gifts came an ego easily bruised and a radical's assurance that the clarity of his perception demanded immediate and decisive action—and demanded as well that his doctrinal comrades follow his tactical leadership. When Princeton hesitated at Breckinridge's church-political moves, the great David felt betrayed—and he nursed that sense of betrayal for decades.

Princeton versus Breckinridge: The Old School/ New School Controversy

The very brashness that made Robert Breckinridge a valuable ally also made him something of a problem for the genteel scholars of Princeton. To their minds he was too prone to rush to judgment; he lacked experience and needed tempering. His early revivalism is a good example. Impressed with the prospect of bringing large numbers quickly to Christ, Breckinridge held a "great woods-meeting" on his

24. Ibid. Breckinridge engaged in extremely bitter personal battles in the course of his colorful and distinguished career, which both he and his antagonists published abroad in pamphlets and letters to newspaper editors. Battles with former Lexington friend Robert Wickliffe and Danville colleague Stuart Robinson were especially nasty. See Klotter, *Breckinridges of Kentucky*, and Mayse, "RJB."
25. Mayse, "RJB," 90.

own estate, Braedalbane, north of Lexington, in the fall of 1831, which was attended by upward of forty thousand people. It was through this camp meeting that he felt confirmation of his call to the gospel ministry.[26] Two years later, as a pastor in Baltimore, Breckinridge led a highly successful urban revival. More than 1,500 people came, and more than 130 of them made professions of faith. Samuel Miller wrote to caution his former student against revivalist methods such as anxious seats and the granting of immediate church membership to new converts, for such means tended "to fill the church with premature, superficial, half-converted professors, who will be led in a multitude of cases, to mistake temporary excitement and transient animal sympathy for true religion."[27] Similarly, when Breckinridge expressed himself unguardedly in opposition to the doctrine of limited atonement, orthodox men in the church were careful to correct him.[28] The corrections were effective: Breckinridge soon became thoroughly Old School in both doctrine and practice—but so much so that the professors of Princeton again found themselves balking at his moves.

The rift came in the course of the Old School/New School controversy of the mid-1830s, when, as Breckinridge saw it, the valiant Kentuckian stepped out on the field of battle only to find his rear exposed as the Princeton gentlemen remained comfortably aloof, enjoying the luxury of theoretical discussion when decisive action was desperately needed. As Princeton saw it, the brilliant but unsubtle Breckinridge had overstepped the bounds of proper church procedure, arrogated to himself the role of theological leadership, and inflamed the church at just the time when calm judgment was most needed. The falling out of Princeton and Breckinridge in the 1830s—and the resultant polarized sets of virtues personified in Charles Hodge and Robert J. Breckinridge—would years later present to Benjamin Breckinridge Warfield two conflicting models of leadership in the church.

Breckinridge's mentor, Samuel Miller, warned him in 1834 that "your constitutional ardor and decision (that common accompaniment

26. "Breckinridge, Robert Jefferson," in *Encyclopaedia of the Presbyterian Church in the United States of America, Including the Northern and Southern Assemblies*, ed. Alfred Nevin (Philadelphia: Presbyterian Encyclopaedia Publ. Co., 1884), 95–96; Mayse, "RJB," 85.

27. Samuel Miller to RJB, February 5, 1834 (Breckinridge Papers, LC), quoted in Mayse, "RJB," 97 n. 152.

28. Mayse, "RJB," 98–106.

of strong minds) may betray you into unguarded movements—movements which are most of all to be dreaded and avoided in *ecclesiastical matters . . . ."* This indeed proved to be the case. In the Old School/New School conflict Breckinridge became, in the words of his daughter (Warfield's mother), "the fighting man – of His Church."[29]

It is easy to multiply attestations to Breckinridge's storminess, and tempting to write off his vehemence in church politics as the product solely of his temperament. An admirer (not a detractor!) wrote, "The Rev. Dr. Robt. J. probably never had peace on any subject, with any person, at any place, during a long and tempestuous life." Yet at the outset of his church-political career he appeared more *moderate* than the "ultra" Old School party, and more *liberal* than the Princetonians. To Joshua Wilson, whose fieriness out-flared Breckinridge's on many an occasion, Breckinridge wrote: "It is one thing to be a sound Presbyterian, in this land and age; . . . another to be fierce over against those who are essentially with us . . . ."—a statement that could have come from the pen of Charles Hodge. But in his advocacy of camp meetings and "new measures" for revivals, and his denial of limited atonement, Breckinridge shared significant ground with the New School. Joshua Wilson, his own brother John, and Samuel Miller soon set him straight, so that Breckinridge's zeal for doctrinal orthodoxy was the zeal of a convert, and a corrected convert at that—but a zeal that Princeton had a hand in producing.[30]

In the event, Wilson and other Old School "ultras" pushed the spirited Kentuckian well beyond Princeton's moderation in ecclesiastical matters, planting in him a suspicion that Princeton's peacemaking efforts were, in effect, traitorous to the cause of church purity. Wilson warned Breckinridge that Miller's *Letters to Presbyterians*

29. Samuel Miller to RJB, February 17, 1834 (Breckinridge Papers, LC), quoted in Mayse, "RJB," 105; Mary Cabell Warfield to BBW, February 11, 1881 (Warfield Papers, PTS, box 13).

30. A. A. Thomas, *Anti-Slavery Correspondence*, quoted in Lewis G. Vander Velde, *The Presbyterian Churches and the Federal Union, 1861–1869* (Cambridge, Mass.: Harvard University Press, 1932), 147–48; RJB to Joshua Wilson, January 9, 1834 (Durrett Collection, Joshua L. Wilson Papers, University of Chicago), quoted in Mayse, "RJB," 101. Mayse credits Wilson with pushing Breckinridge to the extreme Old School position. The *Presbyterian Encyclopaedia*, putting Wilson's truculence in the best possible light, states, "In or out of a deliberative body, he would have followed his convictions of duty, if they had required him to break every earthly tie or even led him to the martyr's stake" (1019).

(1833), which exposed the fact that some ministers ordained under the Plan of Union did not uphold the Westminster Standards despite their subscription to the Confession, "captivates and misleads at the same time," for Miller shows these men to be "ecclesiastically base as swindlers, counterfeiters and perjured persons and yet takes them by the hand and cries *peace, peace!*" It was only after admonitions such as this that Breckinridge joined the ultras of the Old School, aligning himself in semi-opposition to Princeton.[31]

The issues that brought the Presbyterian church to the power struggles of the 1830s were, according to Old School interpreters as well as recent historian George M. Marsden, at heart theological. Since the Plan of Union of 1801, which set up such a level of cooperation between Presbyterians and Congregationalists in the churching of frontier areas that their ministers were virtually interchangeable, Presbyterians of the "Old School" had feared the loss of distinctive Presbyterian church government and, even more importantly, of sound Calvinism. They believed the New England theology had reached the point of semi-Pelagianism in the work of Nathaniel W. Taylor, and now threatened to poison the doctrine of the Presbyterian church. Several related issues entwined themselves with these core theological concerns: confessional allegiance and confessional subscription, presbyterial versus congregational polity, the proper role of voluntary societies vis-à-vis church boards, revivalistic methods, and antislavery.[32] On most if not all of these, Breckinridge and Princeton were in substantial agreement. Their differences erupted over tactical considerations, or what Charles Hodge at the time called "matters of expediency." In the heat of battle and the stress of desperation, both sides would hurt each other deeply.

Stress levels ran high in 1834 for those who, like Breckinridge and the Princetonians, feared that the "Yankeeizing of the Church in the North and West"[33] would compromise proper church government and the doctrines of grace. Synods organized under the Plan

31. Mayse, "RJB," 100–106.
32. George M. Marsden, *The Evangelical Mind and the New School Presbyterian Experience: A Case Study of Thought and Theology in Nineteenth-Century America* (New Haven, Conn.: Yale University Press, 1970), 66–67.
33. Vander Velde, *The Presbyterian Churches and the Federal Union*, 13.

of Union in New York State and Ohio were growing at such a rate that their New School representatives had enjoyed a majority in the General Assemblies since 1831. Joshua Wilson had submitted through his presbytery a "Western Memorial," protesting "the prevalence of unsoundness in doctrine and laxity in discipline" and calling for an end to the Plan of Union; but it failed to gain support in the Assembly of 1834.[34] At that point Breckinridge decided that the New School party—which to his mind did not belong in the Presbyterian church at all, being largely a Congregational faction brought in under the Plan of Union—had achieved such control of the Assembly that unusual measures were now necessary. At the end of the Assembly of 1834 he penned an "Act and Testimony" which exceeded even the forceful-ness of the Western Memorial. It listed the errors of the New School, called for the restoration of the church to "our ancient purity," called concerned churchmen to a convention to meet in Pittsburgh before the General Assembly of 1835 in order to strategize for a successful reformation at that Assembly, and urged ministers to subscribe to the list of concerns and to require such subscription of all new ministerial candidates.[35] The Act and Testimony stirred up the church as never before. Writes J. H. Patton:

> At no previous time was there so much discussion within the Church as from the adjournment of the assembly of 1834 to the meeting of that of 1835. The agitation penetrated individual churches, dividing the eldership, and even threw a shadow over friendships among the private members themselves. The religious papers engaged in all the absorbing controversy, while some of the secular press took a hand in the fray.[36]

34. Quoted in Marsden, *Evangelical Mind*, 60; cf. Mayse, "RJB," 129.

35. Mayse, "RJB," 129–30; Marsden, *Evangelical Mind*, 60–61; Jacob Harris Patton, *A Popular History of the Presbyterian Church in the United States of America* (New York: D. Appleton and Co., 1903), 420–23; Archibald Alexander Hodge, *The Life of Charles Hodge* (London: T. Nelson and Sons, 1881), 293. The text of the Act and Testimony may be found in the General Assembly Minutes for 1834. For a recent interpretation of the schism of 1837, admirably detailed and set in transdenominational and transatlantic context, see Peter J. Wallace, "'The Bond of Union': The Old-School Presbyterian Church and the American Nation, 1837–1861" (Ph.D. diss., University of Notre Dame, 2004), chap. 1.

36. Patton, *Popular History*, 423.

Patton, sympathizing with the liberalizing element in the church's history, emphasizes the divisive impact of Breckinridge's move. But divisive it was, and Breckinridge exulted in the controversy he had stirred up. Some 374 pastors signed the document by May 1835, as did nearly 1,800 elders. But the venerable fathers of Princeton were conspicuously absent from the ranks of signers.[37]

Charles Hodge devoted two lengthy articles in the *Biblical Repertory* to a criticism of the Act and Testimony. He prefaced his critique with an expression of his solidarity with the Old School "in doctrine," his sympathy "in their disapprobation and distrust of the spirit and conduct of the leaders of the opposite party," and his harmony with them "in all the great leading principles of ecclesiastical policy." Nevertheless, he went on to denounce the Act and Testimony for three important reasons. First, it amounted to a new test of orthodoxy, supplementing the Confession itself. Second, it overestimated the prevalence of error in the church, inflaming the situation unnecessarily. Third, and following from the first two points, it aimed at division rather than reform and reconciliation.[38] "It is an act of gross injustice to multitudes of our soundest and best men," Hodge complained; "it is the effectual means of splitting the church into fragments, and of alienating from each other men, who agree in doctrine, in views of order and discipline, and who differ in nothing, perhaps, but in opinion as to the wisdom of introducing this new League and Covenant."[39] In Hodge's judgment, the crisis simply was not as acute as Breckinridge made it out to be. Until the church arrived at full-blown apostasy, not merely potential apostasy, such an irregular measure as the Act and Testimony, stepping clearly outside established church order, was inexcusable.[40]

When the New School party labeled Breckinridge "the Robespierre of the Presbyterian Church," he could take it; but when Hodge and Princeton concurred in the judgment, calling the Act and Testimony "essentially a revolutionary proceeding," Breckinridge felt stung and

---

37. Mayse, "RJB," 130; David B. Calhoun, *Princeton Seminary*, vol. 1, *Faith and Learning, 1812–1868* (Edinburgh: Banner of Truth, 1994), 243–44.

38. Charles Hodge, quoted in A. A. Hodge, *Life of Charles Hodge*, 292; Calhoun, *Princeton Seminary*, 1:246.

39. Charles Hodge, quoted in Calhoun, *Princeton Seminary*, 1:246.

40. Mayse, "RJB," 154. Hodge in effect disavowed the "slippery slope" argument.

betrayed.[41] To justify himself and register his ill-treatment at the hands of Princeton Seminary, Breckinridge issued a "Plain Statement" in the Philadelphia *Presbyterian* of April 16, 1835, alleging that "Dr. Hodge dictated, with the aid of the manuscript put into his hands by me, and drawn in part from Dr. Miller's letters, then recently published, the very words and letters now found under the head of 'Errors' in the Act and Testimony."[42] The Princetonians had helped him draw up the document; how could they disavow it now? It seems that Breckinridge had visited Hodge during the Philadelphia General Assembly back in May 1834 and asked for help in preparing a document to enumerate the errors of the New School party. Hodge had complied, not knowing that Breckinridge would use the list as anything other than an expression of doctrinal concerns. When the list appeared in the Act and Testimony, Hodge was chagrined to discover that Breckinridge had used it not just as a declaration of principles, but as "an invidious Test Act" that attempted "to number the people" (shades of David's sin in 2 Samuel 24:2!) to identify who stood on which side. "What right have I to publish a declaration of truth and order to the churches, and call upon everyone to sign it on pain of being denounced as a heretic or revolutionist?" Hodge asked. Surely this was a violation of the very church order the Old School ultras claimed to be defending.[43]

To Breckinridge's mind, Hodge had given him every expectation of support for the Act and Testimony in May, only to turn around in October and denounce the thing before the whole church readership. And when Breckinridge protested in his "Plain Statement" that Princeton had turned tail after initially aiding his efforts, the Princetonians published swift denials. John Maclean, professor in Princeton College, whom Breckinridge named as a witness to the meeting with Hodge in

41. Charles Hodge, "Act and Testimony," *Biblical Repertory and Theological Review* 6 (1834): 517. Hodge compared Breckinridge's attempt to the Nullification Crisis of a few years before—something more fitting than perhaps he knew, for Breckinridge's father had been involved in the drafting of the Kentucky and Virginia Resolves of 1798, to which South Carolina appealed for precedent.

42. Robert Jefferson Breckinridge, quoted in A. A. Hodge, *Life of Charles Hodge*, 311.

43. Charles Hodge, "The Act and Testimony," 506. Cf. A. A. Hodge, *Life of Charles Hodge*, 292–95, 311–14. Samuel Miller did not consider Breckinridge's transgression quite so grave. See his *Life of Samuel Miller* (Philadelphia: Claxton, Remsen and Haffelfinger, 1869), 1:251.

Philadelphia, avowed that Hodge had made it clear at that meeting that he did not "give his countenance to the measures proposed," but had only helped Breckinridge to clarify and consolidate his list of errors, as a favor to a friend. Two weeks later Hodge himself published another account of the meeting, confirming Maclean's story. College professor Albert B. Dod, to whom Hodge had confided about the meeting immediately afterward, added a piece of his own. The denials were polite, but firm: Breckinridge had misconstrued Hodge's help; Hodge's criticisms in the *Biblical Repertory* were consistent with his actions at the interview in Philadelphia; Breckinridge had unfortunately misunderstood him.[44]

Breckinridge never got over the feeling of betrayal, and the story lived on in family memory. Nearly half a century later, Breckinridge's daughter would admonish her son, B. B. Warfield, concerning a rehashed allegation against her father: "Do'nt you begin to see why I dred to see you my darling – thrown forward as the fighting man of the church? Princeton always stood behind walls – and Pa & men of his stamp did the hard fighting."[45] Family friend Andrew B. Cross, writing at the same post-Civil War moment, explained it in fittingly Breckinridgean style, by the use of an apt metaphor:

> The man who stands behind strong fortifications with heavy guns and ammunition in abundance, and who can carefully survey the ground, and see the point at which he can do the most execution, and calmly take aim, is in a very different position from the man or men who are out in the field of conflict, and where the enemy is charging upon your cannon to take your position, as on Cemetery Hill at Gettysburg, and drive you from the field. This last requires the hand-to-hand conflict, and that the commander shall be able to wield his sword according to the position of the enemy. This was the condition of the Act and Testimony men, and if they had not stood their ground manfully, where would Princeton have been?[46]

44. The letters published in the *Presbyterian* in April 1835—Breckinridge's, Maclean's, Hodge's, and Dod's—are excerpted in A. A. Hodge, *Life of Charles Hodge*, 311–14.
45. Mary Cabell Warfield to BBW, February 20, 1881 (Warfield Papers, PTS, box 13). Misspellings and oddities of punctuation characterize all the letters of the witty Mrs. Warfield.
46. Cross, "Calumny," 66.

Breckinridge and his supporters believed they were rescuing the church, and with it Princeton Seminary, from invasion by New England. If the Act of Union were permitted to stand, and the New School to continue to increase in power, then the church would be New England-ized—and when the time came to replace the aging fathers of Princeton (Archibald Alexander, 63, and Samuel Miller, 65), their powerful chairs would be filled by New School men. Charles Hodge, too, feared for the future of Princeton: Breckinridge's Act and Testimony, by its extreme and extra-constitutional measures, might divide the conservative Calvinists and precipitate an Old School secession. In that case, Hodge warned, the church, and with it the seminary, would fall into solidly New School hands. Far from rescuing Princeton *from* ruin, in Hodge's view Breckinridge and his party were bringing Princeton *to* ruin.[47] The sickening fear and feelings of betrayal, then, were mutual.

But Breckinridge did something more to sour Princeton on him. Hurt by Hodge's criticisms in the *Biblical Repertory*, Breckinridge retaliated swiftly at the Synod of Philadelphia by moving that it adopt the Act and Testimony and appoint a committee to consider shifting its support away from Princeton Seminary—either to Western (Allegheny, Pennsylvania) and Union (Virginia), or to a new seminary to be founded under ultra-orthodox leadership. Both motions passed. In the pages of the *Presbyterian* and in pamphlet form, Breckinridge published abroad the threatening words, "the General Assembly must be reformed, or the orthodox must have a school not subject to its control." Writes Edgar Mayse, "The controversy between the militants and the moderates now began in earnest. If Princeton would not support the efforts of the ultras to cleanse the church of heresy, Princeton would have to suffer the consequences."[48]

47. Calhoun, *Princeton Seminary*, 1:246. Hodge wrote to his brother, "The Act and Testimony is doing what was from the first apprehended—splitting the Old School portion of the church. . . . If they succeed we shall be ruined for the next ten or twenty years. That is if by their ultraism a portion of the Old School party is broken off, it will leave the remainder completely in the power of the New School men and give them the command of our Seminaries, Boards of Education and Missions." Charles Hodge to Hugh Lenox Hodge, November 21, 1834, printed in full in A. A. Hodge, *Life of Charles Hodge*, 305–06.

48. Mayse, "RJB," 154–57; Robert Jefferson Breckinridge, "General Defence of the Act and Testimony," *Presbyterian*, November 4, 1834, quoted in Mayse, 157. Writing to his brother on November 21, 1834, Hodge reported that his criticism of the Act and Testimony in the October *Biblical Repertory* "has given prodigious offence to the Philadelphia men. The Synod

Now it was Hodge's turn to take personal affront and let his feelings show—but unlike Breckinridge, he did so in private. In a letter dated November 13, 1834, Hodge arraigned Breckinridge for ingratitude to his Princeton mentors, Drs. Alexander and Miller, since Breckinridge had portrayed them as unfit to be trusted in matters ecclesiastical. Hodge threw Breckinridge's youth and inexperience in his face, pointing out that the action of the Synod of Philadelphia was guided "in a great measure by young men, a year or two in the ministry, after a few months, or years of study as the case may be—men, who I am sure could not now tell what orthodoxy is, according to their own standards, unless Dr. Alexander should tell them." There was a world of difference between the seasoned judgment of Princeton and the brash activism of Breckinridge, Hodge explained with obvious bitterness. "That a man accustomed all his life to the rough and tumble warfare of western politicians as you have been should not sometimes know whether he is on his head or heels is not a matter of surprise to me or anyone else."[49]

On the same date, so that their letters must have crossed in the mail, Breckinridge wrote Hodge a private letter as well. His tone there was considerably more respectful and pleading: "You have driven us to the wall." On receiving Breckinridge's letter, Hodge was somewhat mollified by Breckinridge's expression of fear that a New School–dominated General Assembly would destroy Princeton as a bastion of orthodoxy. Hodge now felt that the move to withdraw synodical support from Princeton was an expression of distrust in the Assembly, not in the seminary, and said so to Breckinridge in a second letter. "But the damage to the Breckinridge ego had been made," writes Mayse. The Kentuckian administered to Hodge "a full dose of the famous Breckinridge invective."

> I fully claim the right to support just what school I please, and just
> for what reasons I please . . . and I smile at all attempts to over-
> come me with great names, or overwhelm me with accusations, of

---

passed a vote which amounts to a formal declaration of want of confidence in the Seminary. They propose transferring their patronage to Pittsburgh, or to found a new institution." In A. A. Hodge, *Life of Charles Hodge*, 306.

49. Hodge to RJB, November 13, 1834 (Breckinridge Papers, LC), quoted in Mayse, "RJB," 157–58.

ignorance, incapacity and folly . . . . Your only hope to retain the orthodox (and if we don't know unless we are told, we will try to guess what is orthodoxy) is to let the Assembly and therefore the Church be reformed.[50]

Even with this note of sarcasm, Breckinridge was sincerely trying to persuade Princeton to abandon its policy of moderation and join the "orthodox." Similarly, Hodge was trying to persuade the orthodox to abandon their policy of precipitating schism and join the moderates. The conflict between the two men amounted to a contest for leadership of the conservative wing of the church, and in Breckinridge's view it had to do not just with tactical considerations, urgent though they were, but with the principle of representative leadership enshrined in presbyterial polity. "I smile at all attempts to overcome me with great names," he wrote—positing a fundamental contest between elitism and republicanism in church government. This theme would recur in later conflicts.

In view of these developments, family friend Andrew Cross seems to have overstated Breckinridge's loyalty and service to Princeton.

No man in the Church fought more bravely and effectively and heartily, for Princeton than did Dr. B., as I have said, at Princeton, especially to Dr. H. No man fought as hard for you as Dr. B., yet some of you did as much as you could to weaken his hands, and I know while he had unbounded personal esteem for you all, he always felt it.[51]

Cross's take echoes Mrs. Warfield's: "Princeton always stood behind walls – and Pa & men of his stamp did the hard fighting." Clearly this was the family line on the unfortunate falling-out between Breckinridge and Princeton in the 1830s. But the Princetonians, of course, felt something, too—they felt imperiled by their valiant, rash, and sometimes spiteful in-law from Kentucky.[52]

50. Mayse, "RJB," 158–59; RJB to Charles Hodge, November 22, 1834 (Breckinridge Papers, LC), quoted in Mayse, 159.

51. Cross, "Calumny," 66.

52. It should be noted that Breckinridge was not the only close connection of Princeton's "association of gentlemen" to trouble them with his "ultra" views and policies. Ashbel Green,

Further Breckinridge-Princeton Relations

Happily for both Breckinridge and Princeton, the Old School/ New School controversy ended well enough. Thanks in large part to Breckinridge's machinations, the Old School gained a majority in the Assemblies of 1835 and 1837, abrogated the Plan of Union and made that action retroactive, exscinded the synods that had been organized under the Plan of Union, and so "reformed" the church. The New Schoolers were out; Princeton, the moderates, and the militants remained. Robert's brother John, who had been in an uncomfortable position as a Breckinridge in a professorship at Princeton Seminary, breathed a sigh of relief in the "happy union, once and forever," of the Princeton party and the militants of the Old School.[53]

But the battle was not yet over: the New School synods took the Old School to court and, in a decision that was later reversed, were awarded full rights to the name and property of the Presbyterian church. For a brief but terrifying moment, the Princetonians envisioned themselves turned out of the very seminary they had founded and elevated to uncontested leadership in the church. This of course did not ingratiate Breckinridge, the manager of the split, to them. In 1839 a higher court overturned the decision, and Princeton was finally safe.[54]

Nor did the final result usher in the "happy union, once and forever" for which John Breckinridge so fervently hoped. When Robert Breckinridge was elected Moderator of the General Assembly in 1841—the highest honor in the Presbyterian church—he wrote to his wife, "The Princeton and Philadelphia brethren and the extreme South went in a body against me: the *Church* elected me."[55] In the next decade Breckinridge and Princeton would disagree publicly over

former president of Princeton College and one of the three leaders in the founding of Princeton Seminary, was the leader of the pack of "Philadelphia men"—a large component of the ultra party that included Breckinridge and Wilson as well. It was Green who in 1831 labeled the parties "Old School" and "New School." Calhoun, *Princeton Seminary*, 1:242.

53. John Breckinridge to RJB, June 8, 1837 (Breckinridge Papers, LC), quoted in Mayse, "RJB," 181. Mayse observes, "As long as John Breckinridge lived there was someone to stand between the radicals and their attacks upon Princeton. Following his death in 1841, Robert and William felt little loyalty to their theological alma mater" (423 n. 150).

54. A. A. Hodge, *Life of Charles Hodge*, 314–16.

55. RJB to Sophonisba Preston Breckinridge, May 21, 1841 (Breckinridge Papers, LC), quoted in Mayse, "RJB," 402 n. 98.

the office and rights of ruling elders, the evangelical assessment of Roman Catholicism, and the proper method for theological education. Breckinridge had great confidence in his power to persuade the church to his side, whether or not the Princetonians agreed.

Ruling Elders

Samuel Miller taught Breckinridge the parallel between Presbyterian polity and American government: namely, the shared use of the representative principle and the system of checks and balances. Miller called it "Presbyterian republicanism." Ruling elders functioned as a check against clerical power, on the one hand, and against lay arrogation of clerical functions, on the other. The office of ruling elder thus steered Presbyterians between the dangers of prelacy (as in the Episcopal and Catholic churches) and democracy (as in lay preaching in frontier areas, and lay leadership of voluntary associations). Goaded on by his ultra-orthodox comrades in the years leading up to the Disruption, however, Robert Breckinridge went beyond Miller to embrace the *jure divino* theory of church government: the belief that the New Testament laid down an explicit constitution for the government of Christ's church, and that any departure from that law was as serious an error as doctrinal heresy.[56] This belief fueled much of his party's fervor in the Old School/New School battles. In the years after 1837, having delivered the church from New School errors, Breckinridge turned to constructive action: he wanted to see *jure divino* Presbyterianism put into full practice in his church. To that end he focused his ecclesiastical energies on establishing the full dignity and prerogatives of the office of ruling elder—the office in which he himself had risen to prominence.

The "elder question" brought Princeton and Breckinridge to another public disagreement—and once again it was Breckinridge who opened the issue by conducting a pre-Assembly campaign. In *The Spirit of the Nineteenth Century*, one of two concurrent newspapers he

---

56. Calhoun, *Princeton Seminary*, 1:299; cf. Mayse, "RJB," 113: "In the thought of Robert Breckinridge, ecclesiastical order was on a par with doctrinal purity." For a full account of *jure divino* Presbyterianism, see Ernest Trice Thompson, *Presbyterians in the South, Volume One: 1607–1861* (Richmond: John Knox Press, 1963), chap. 33.

founded in his busy Baltimore years, Breckinridge published a series of "Letters to the Ruling Elders," hoping to rouse a complacent church to recognition of the importance of his *jure divino* principles.[57] His old mentor, Samuel Miller, rose to counter Breckinridge's position, and was soon joined by Charles Hodge and Albert Dod.

Writing under the pseudonym "Calvin" (note the connotations of longstanding orthodoxy), Miller called Breckinridge's view of elders an innovation virtually unknown in Presbyterian history, and charged it with disturbing the proper system of checks and balances, since elders as laymen ought to represent the people. Breckinridge replied under the name "Presbyter," and the exchange of letters lasted two months. Hodge reviewed the exchange in the *Biblical Repertory and Princeton Review*, explicitly rejecting the *jure divino* notion and averring that the church was free to govern itself along the lines of general principles revealed in the Bible. Princeton had contradicted Breckinridge publicly again, and Breckinridge was not pleased. He complained that Hodge had taken an axe to the "root of our whole doctrine of Church order, which might well enough have been expected from an Erastian, a Prelatist, or a New Schoolman—but surely not from Princeton."[58]

At the Assembly of 1843 Princeton men successfully defeated Breckinridge's hopes. Samuel Miller preached a sermon on the eldership, and John Maclean led the forces that downed a proposal that would have required the presence of ruling elders at pastoral ordinations and presbyterial meetings. Not willing to let the matter rest there, Breckinridge gave a two-hour address on the subject at the Synod of Philadelphia meeting that fall in his own church in Baltimore. The synod voted him down, but Breckinridge was tenacious: a few days later he fought for six hours to regain the floor, spoke for two hours after gaining it, and finally at midnight lost again. His powers of persuasion seemed to be failing him; the church repeatedly decided against him—but still he pressed on. He then printed the address for distribution as a pamphlet, "Presbyterian Government Not a Hier-

57. A detailed exposition of Breckinridge's letters is found in Mayse, "RJB," 404–10.

58. Calhoun, *Princeton Seminary*, 1:300–301; Mayse, "RJB," 410–15. The quotation comes from the *Spirit of the Nineteenth Century*, Short Notices for May 1843, quoted in both Calhoun and Mayse.

archy, But a Commonwealth," taking his cause, fittingly enough in his mind, to the people.[59]

More and more Breckinridge was identifying the gentlemen of Princeton with an elitist view of church leadership, and himself with "the church"—even when the church courts did not go along with him. In April 1844 Albert Dod published a scathing and dismissive review in the *Biblical Repertory and Princeton Review*. Dod's opening words set the tone: "It is truly mortifying that the Presbyterian Church, at this period in her history, instead of 'leaving the first principles of the doctrine of Christ and going on unto perfection,' should be employed in the juvenile task of laying again the foundation of the 'doctrine of laying on of hands.'" Pointing out that Breckinridge was pressing the issue after decisive defeats at two Assemblies (1842 and 1843)—"the deliberate judgment of the church expressed through its highest court"—Dod scorned Breckinridge's claim that "'the principle here involved is practically the question between an aristocratical hierarchy, and a free Christian commonwealth.' That Dr. Breckinridge should believe this is not perhaps surprising," Dod went on, "for nothing is more common than for men who find themselves out of sympathy with the community to which they belong, to manifest a certain extravagant tendency of opinion as well as of feeling."

> That Dr. Breckinridge's convictions and feelings should run out into great exaggeration, that matters of small import should be magnified into vital principles, and things that are totally dissimilar be confounded as identical, was nothing more than was to be expected from any uninspired man occupying the position in which he feels himself to stand.[60]

It is hard to imagine a more condescending answer to Breckinridge's ardor. It shows that the feeling of enmity was very far from one-sided. Dod and Hodge were fast friends, and Hodge must have shared enough of his friend's view to print such biting words. Breckinridge, of course, was incensed. He fired off a letter to the editors of

59. Mayse, "RJB," 423–30.
60. Albert B. Dod, "The Elder Question," *Biblical Repertory and Princeton Review* 17 (1844): 277, 279, 282–83.

the *Review*, branding Dod "an Evangelist who teaches Mathematics and lectures on Architecture in Nassau Hall"[61]—a colorful way of drawing attention to the fact that Dod was a minister without charge, the personification of the evil divide between churchmen and theological leadership that Breckinridge's position on ruling elders sought to address. After suffering a third defeat at the General Assembly of 1844, he complained to his wife, "The bitterness against me and my opinions, so far as the whole influence of the Princeton and Philadelphia people goes, is beyond what you can believe," and alleged, "Our church is at the feet of the organized powers that control it: Princeton, Philadelphia, the Boards, the Seminaries, the newspapers—the church is lost and swallowed up in this bottomless gulf of patronage and organized influence."[62]

Anti-Catholicism

Writing to James Henley Thornwell, his comrade-in-arms on the elder question, Breckinridge confided, "I seriously believe that the germ of High Churchism and Popery is to be found in the ultimate principles, which lead our ministers to the cast of opinion which prevails around us. . . . The germ of all seems to me to be a notion of their own exaltation."[63] As Edgar Mayse observes, Breckinridge connected the Princetonian position on elders (and more basically on their role in the church) with popery and prelacy.[64] In the 1830s and 1840s, when anti-Catholicism was at high tide, it was not uncommon to oppose American republican principles to Catholic ones. Breckinridge figured among the most prominent and vitriolic anti-Catholics of the day, and in alleging that the Princetonians were in principle sliding

61. Robert Jefferson Breckinridge, quoted in Calhoun, *Princeton Seminary*, 1:301.

62. RJB to Sophonisba Preston Breckinridge, May 17, 1844, and June 4, 1844 (Breckinridge Papers, LC), quoted in Mayse, "RJB," 435–36. His complaint against the newspapers refers to the decision of the Philadelphia *Presbyterian* to refuse to print any more letters from him on the elder question. "I had rather have had you on our side, than every man, woman, child in Princeton put together," Breckinridge lamented to the editor. RJB to William Engles, n.d. (Breckinridge Papers, LC), quoted in Mayse, 432. Mayse covers the whole agitation over the elder question in luxuriant detail (399–439). Cf. several other sources listed in Calhoun, *Princeton Seminary*, 1:477 n. 22.

63. RJB to James Henley Thornwell, July 13, 1843 (Breckinridge Papers, LC), quoted in Mayse, "RJB," 419–20.

64. Mayse, "RJB," 420 n. 140.

toward Catholicism he was calling them one of the worst names he knew. But he sincerely believed that his treatment at the hands of a Princeton-led church revealed an ominous tendency away from that genius of Presbyterian polity, the representative principle, toward the elitism that manifested itself in rule by bishops and popes.

On the issue of Catholicism itself we again find the Breckinridges and Princeton at odds. In Philadelphia in 1834–35, John Breckinridge engaged in a series of debates with Fr. John Hughes that appeared in two newspapers and were later published as a fat book. In Baltimore, "the seat of the Beast" in America, Robert Breckinridge found the city's newspapers resistant to anti-Catholic controversial pieces and so launched a monthly newspaper of his own. The *Baltimore Literary and Religious Magazine* ran from 1835 to 1843, printing scores of rabidly anti-Catholic articles.[65] During the same period Hodge's *Biblical Repertory and Princeton Review* expressed many an anti-Catholic sentiment, too, yet the contrast between Hodge and the Breckinridges was stark. Once again the Breckinridges stepped out on the field of battle and felt themselves exposed to real danger, while the Princetonians, safe in their village retreat, counseled the church to moderation.

Robert took a page from his brother's playbook when in 1835 he issued in the *Baltimore Magazine* a challenge to the archbishop and priests of the city. He declared his readiness to prove

> that the Roman Church is not the church of Jesus Christ; that she is the anti-Christ of the Scriptures; that she is an enemy to the Bible; to human liberty and to republicanism and that the conscientious adherence to and practice of her doctrines, is not only dangerous, but is destructive of all purity of life, all peace of conscience, all present freedom, and all future hope.[66]

The Catholic officials of Baltimore wisely steered clear of Breckinridge's taunts and accusations over the entire lifetime of his newspaper, as he printed articles with such suggestive titles as "The Number of the

65. Ibid., 285–92.
66. Robert Jefferson Breckinridge, "Address of the Protestant Association of Baltimore," *Baltimore Religious and Literary Magazine* 1 (December 1835): 380, quoted in Mayse, "RJB," 294–95.

Beast is 666," "The Antiquity of the Protestant Faith," "Trial of the Anti-Christ," "Can Protestants, with a Safe Conscience, Be Present at the Popish Mass?" and "Papal Doctrine and Policy for the Extirpation of Protestants." In his fervor Breckinridge came honestly to believe that the nuns of Baltimore were held captive against their will, that secret tunnels and torture chambers lay hidden somewhere within St. Mary's Cathedral (he even took an exploratory trip there to find them), and that he might well be captured and killed for his efforts to expose the ways of Antichrist.[67] Finally, in 1840, the state of Maryland brought suit against Breckinridge for libelous statements he had made against a Catholic superintendent of the county poorhouse. During the trial Breckinridge lectured on "Papism" eleven times in the space of two weeks, drawing large crowds to his church each evening. The readership of his *Baltimore Magazine* soared. Letters of congratulation flooded in, including one from Samuel Miller.[68]

On this issue the General Assembly sided with Breckinridge against Charles Hodge. In 1835 it declared the Roman Church "essentially apostatized from the religion of our Lord and Savior Jesus Christ" and therefore not "a Christian Church," and in 1840 it provided for an annual sermon to the Assembly on "the evils of popery," the inaugural sermon to be delivered by—who else?—Robert Jefferson Breckinridge.[69] The Presbyterian Board of Missions even appointed him a missionary to France, to bring "the true light into the dark regions of popery."[70] In 1845 the Assembly addressed the question of whether Roman Catholic baptism was valid Christian baptism, deciding in the negative by an overwhelming majority of 173 to 8. Hodge bemoaned the decision in his annual review of the Assembly, maintaining that despite its many errors, the Roman Church still held the essentials of the Christian faith—including sound doctrines of the Trinity, atonement, forgiveness of sins, resurrection of the body, eternal life, and judgment. Rome taught "enough truth to save the soul." These words stirred

67. These articles and more are discussed in Mayse, "RJB," 300–309. On Breckinridge's conspiracy theories on Catholicism, see ibid., 318, 335–45.

68. Ibid., 346–49. Mayse suggests that Breckinridge lost his nerve after the libel trial, for he dropped entirely the "charges of Catholic licentiousness, priestly sensuality, and escapes from the unclean cages of nunnery" (350).

69. Calhoun, *Princeton Seminary*, 1:304.

70. Mayse, "RJB," 333.

up considerable opposition, but a year later Hodge still argued that "the great body of people constituting the Roman Catholic Church do profess the essentials of the true Christian religion, whereby many of them bear the image of Christ, and are participants of His salvation."[71] But Breckinridge and the nativist spirit generally carried the day.

Theological Education

Breckinridge made good on his threat to transfer allegiance to a seminary other than Princeton when, in 1853, after the considerable behind-the-scenes ecclesiastical machinations that had become his trademark, he became the founding president of Danville Theological Seminary in his home state of Kentucky.[72] With many others, he had long hoped to establish a bastion of orthodoxy in the West to counter the influence of the New School's seminary (Lane) in Cincinnati. Danville enjoyed rather stunning early success, both in finances (it had an endowment of $130,000 and was debt-free by 1860) and in the reputation of its president. Writes Edgar Mayse, "Breckinridge was convinced that he had established a great seminary in the West which would correct the church's myopic attraction for Princeton and the East."[73]

Two aspects of Breckinridge's foray into theological education deserve attention in a consideration of his relationship to Princeton, especially in light of the later career of his grandson. First, he set out to reinvent ministerial training, to loosen its ties to the ivory tower of scholarship and tighten its ties to the life of the church. Second, he undertook the creation of a grand theological system that would preserve forever the crystalline purity of divine truth.

As early as 1835 Breckinridge stated publicly in his plain-spoken *Baltimore Magazine* that "of all good things in the Presbyterian Church, theological schools are amongst the most questionable"—this in an article titled "Humbug—Theological and Literary." Expanding on this

71. Charles Hodge, "The General Assembly," *Biblical Repertory and Princeton Review* 18 (1845): 441–71, and "Is the Church of Rome a Part of the Visible Church?" *Biblical Repertory and Princeton Review* 19 (1846): 321–45, both quoted in Calhoun, *Princeton Seminary*, 1:304–5. See also A. A. Hodge, *Life of Charles Hodge*, 340–43.

72. Mayse, "RJB," details the process on pp. 497–500.

73. Ibid., 506–7.

idea five years later, he faulted the American system of seminaries for giving "theological instruction, as if it were to youth, and not as if it were to men, as if it were an education and not a profession"—teaching men "to recite, rather than turning them out full of knowledge, thought and force." It was a charge with a familiar ring even today: seminaries did not train ministerial students for the actual work of parish ministry, nor to address live issues of the surrounding culture. He capped these public criticisms of the seminaries with the publication of a book, *The Christian Pastor*, in 1844.[74] With an eye probably to the apprenticeship-style training he had received when "reading at law" prior to his conversion to church work, Breckinridge recommended that seminary professors be active churchmen with pastoral experience themselves—"an obvious slap," Mayse notes, "at Charles Hodge."[75] At Danville, Breckinridge launched his experiment in professionalized ministerial education. Its main features included the collection of all students into one class (rather than division into the usual three classes: junior, middler, senior); the requirement that professors bring at least five years of pastoral experience and serve as pastors to the students; and the limitation of readings to a short list of basic texts.[76] While this system had the advantage of treating students as adults and providing pastoral supervision to the whole man, it also presupposed a rather simplistic, if not anti-intellectual, concept of theological truth. And it stood in stark contrast to the arrangement of "ministers without charge" teaching at Princeton.

Also at Danville, Breckinridge ventured into the systematization of biblical knowledge, revealing more clearly an almost positivistic notion of the science of theology. The Princeton theologians have of course been faulted for so conceiving of the theological task, but Breckinridge's static objectivism far surpassed theirs. Mayse comments, "Theology was for him a series of exclamation points, but no question marks."[77] Divine truth is unchangeable, reasoned Breckinridge, and so

74. Robert Jefferson Breckinridge, "Humbug—Theological and Literary" and "Theological Seminaries," *Baltimore Literary and Religious Magazine* 1 (February 1835): 55; and *BLRM* 6 (September 1840): 399, both quoted in Mayse, "RJB," 485–87; Calhoun, *Princeton Seminary*, 1:374.

75. Mayse, "RJB," 487 n. 106.

76. Ibid., 502–3.

77. Ibid., 509.

theology "ought to remain," from generation to generation, "the most uniformly settled—and the least liable to change" of all departments of knowledge. Charles Hodge famously likened theological science to natural science; Breckinridge likened it to geometry.[78] The contrast is instructive: Hodge chose for his analogy a young and yet changing department of knowledge, acknowledging the progressive character of theological work; Breckinridge chose the area of knowledge whose unique characteristics are inescapable demonstration and permanent structure. Hodge's analogy left room for the interpretive step; Breckinridge's did not. Accordingly when Breckinridge brought out the first volume of his projected three-volume theology, *The Knowledge of God, Objectively Considered* (1857), he claimed no originality at all save that of an arranger, a representative mind of the age who put the great accumulated truth of past epochs into systematic form according to the light of his century.[79]

The apex of Breckinridge's objectivism came in a proposal he twice brought before the General Assembly: that the church include in its celebration of the bicentennial of the Westminster Assembly the production of a Presbyterian commentary on the Bible, "according to the system embodied in our standards." The proposal stunned Charles Hodge, who minced no words in the *Princeton Review*:

> If the mere suggestion of such an idea does not strike a man dumb with awe, he must be impervious to all argument. It is a fearful thing to give church authority even to articles of faith gathered from the general sense of Scripture. . . . This is more than all the popes, who ever lived, merged in one, would dare to propose. It is a thousand fold more than Rome, when most drunk with pride, ever ventured to attempt. Where is there such a thing? Who has ever heard of such a thing as a Church Commentary? . . . There is no such thing as the sense of the Westminster Confession as to the true interpretation of thousands of passages of Scripture. . . . To assume to act as the

78. Robert Jefferson Breckinridge, "Some Thoughts on the Developments in the Presbyterian Church," *Southern Presbyterian Review* 3 (1848): 327, quoted in Mayse, "RJB," 509; Charles Hodge, *Systematic Theology*, 3 vols. (New York: Charles Scribner & Sons, 1872), 1:10–12; RJB to John B. Adger, January 21, 1857 (Breckinridge Papers, LC), quoted in Mayse, 512.

79. Mayse, "RJB," 513.

mouthpiece of the church in this matter is a task which none but an idiot or an angel would dare to undertake.[80]

This is about as strong language as Hodge ever penned—and the reference to the popes was surely calculated to sting. Breckinridge-Princeton relations were severely strained by 1858.

What restored the relationship was, ironically, the dissolution of the nation. As the country fell apart over slavery and states' rights, Breckinridge and Princeton moved closer together. The first move came in 1849, when Breckinridge, campaigning for a delegate's seat at the convention to draw up a new Kentucky state constitution, published a pamphlet strongly urging the state to adopt a plan of gradual emancipation tempered by compensation to slaveholders and colonization of the freedpeople in Liberia. Hodge wrote a glowing review of what he considered Breckinridge's eminently sane, reasonable, and judicious position.[81] When secession came, both Hodge and Breckinridge took strong Union stands. Breckinridge's bravery and dedication to his chosen causes now shone once more, as he supported the Union in a crucial border state. He faced unflinchingly the defection of sons and nephews to the Confederacy and the loss of his closest *jure divino* comrades (John B. Adger and J. H. Thornwell) to the Southern church. Ecclesiastical politics had driven Breckinridge and Hodge apart; now national politics brought them together, even in the General Assembly, where both argued against the propriety of the church's making Union loyalty a test of communion, while standing stoutly for loyalty itself.[82]

In Lexington, Kentucky, the town house of Breckinridge's daughter Mary Warfield became a kind of headquarters for the Union branch of the family. Grandson Ben Warfield, on the cusp of his teens, watched his grandfather's shining hour in defense of country and of solidarity in the church. Two years after war's end, Breckinridge enrolled his

---

80. Charles Hodge, "The General Assembly," *Biblical Repertory and Princeton Review* 30 (1858): 561–64.

81. Charles Hodge, "Emancipation," review of "The Question of Negro Slavery and the New Constitution of Kentucky," by Robert Jefferson Breckinridge, *Biblical Repertory and Princeton Review* 21 (1849): 582–607.

82. Klotter, *The Breckinridges of Kentucky*, chap. 7; Mayse, "RJB," chap. 7; A. A. Hodge, *Life of Charles Hodge*, chap. 11.

son John (Warfield's half-uncle by Breckinridge's second marriage) at Nassau Hall—the first Breckinridge to go to Princeton College or Seminary since his own short stint in the early 1830s. The following year Ben Warfield followed suit.

Warfield and His Grandfather's Legacy

John R. Breckinridge described in detail the arrival of James McCosh as Princeton College's eleventh president in the fall of 1868—the same semester that Ben Warfield entered Princeton. Some days after the official festivities, the students were introduced one by one to the new president. As John related proudly to his father, the Scottish president newly arrived from across the ocean "asked my name, and inquired what relation I was to you. He professed to be highly delighted that your son was under him—and that I was your son,—shook my hand heartily and begged to be remembered to you."[83] John made no mention to his father of nephew Ben's reception by the new president, but there is no doubt that he, too, found that the Breckinridge name preceded him.

What was Warfield's experience of this history of strained Breckinridge-Princeton relations? He was well aware of his grandfather's heroics during the Civil War and his leadership in the permanent division of Northern and Southern Presbyterianism.[84] He wrote almost no letters to his grandfather from college—at least none that survive—though understandably enough there are dozens of letters from John to his father. But the lack of written correspondence need not imply distance of relationship. Warfield's parents were Breckinridge's closest and most loyal family members. When grandfather Breckinridge died in the winter after Ben graduated from college, it was his father, William Warfield, who sat up all night at the old man's death-bed, William Warfield whom Breckinridge appointed executor of his estate, and the Warfield home to which the pall-bearers carried the body from the church funeral service.[85]

83. John R. Breckinridge to RJB, November 1, 1868 (Breckinridge Papers, LC, box 263).
84. Thompson, *Presbyterians in the South*, chap. 8; Mayse, "RJB," chap. 8.
85. W. C. P. Breckinridge to Issa Desha Breckinridge, December 28, 1871 (Breckinridge Papers, LC, box 279); Robert Jefferson Breckinridge's will, Fayette County (Ky.) Will Book 2 (microfilm at Lexington Public Library).

Certain aspects of Breckinridge's temperament and interests lived on in his Princetonian grandson. Like his grandfather, Warfield gained a reputation in college for being a fighter. In chapel one day he drew an unflattering caricature of a fellow student, and the two came to blows when chapel was dismissed. The incident earned Warfield the honorific title of "Pugilist" at the Class Day exercises at graduation.[86] Like his grandfather, Warfield brought a somewhat lawyerly frame of mind to controversial subjects in the church, such as his reasoning that the burden of proof in the matter of biblical inerrancy rested on the shoulders of those who would deny that long-cherished belief of the church, not those who defended it.[87] Like his grandfather, Warfield had a strong taste for church history, a deep love for the Westminster Confession, and (in the Briggs case) a willingness to use the church courts—and to rally support for church decisions in preparation for the Assembly's meetings—to secure an orthodox future.[88] Warfield inherited his grandfather's incisive mind, power of decision, and prodigious memory.[89] Like his grandfather, he focused his career activities on particular issues of the day, and made full use of the press as founder and editor of more than one periodical.[90]

But Warfield studied theology under Charles Hodge, and came to revere the aged Princeton theologian. At the time of Hodge's death in 1878, Warfield had just been called to an instructorship at Western Theological Seminary, his first academic post. He wrote to another Hodge protégé, Caspar Rene Gregory:

How sad it is to us all to know that that both great & sweet old man, Dr Hodge, [is] no longer with us. To those who have the g[ood] of

86. Hugh Thomson Kerr, "Warfield: The Person Behind the Theology," ed. William O. Harris (without attribution), *Princeton Seminary Bulletin* 25 (2004): 92; Kim Riddlebarger, "The Lion of Princeton: Benjamin Breckinridge Warfield on Apologetics, Theological Method and Polemics" (Ph.D. diss., Fuller Theological Seminary, 1997), 1. Oddly, the incident escaped notice in the Faculty Minutes, where disciplinary actions are usually carefully recorded. Evidently the fight was so minor as not to require punishment.

87. A. A. Hodge and B. B. Warfield, "Inspiration," *Presbyterian Review* 2 (1881): 225–60.

88. See Warfield's correspondence 1889–93, PTS.

89. Ethelbert D. Warfield, "Biographical Sketch of Benjamin Breckinridge Warfield," in B. B. Warfield, *Revelation and Inspiration* (Grand Rapids: Baker, 1981).

90. Warfield founded and edited the *Presbyterian and Reformed Review*, co-edited the *Bible Student* with William M. McPheeters, and put in motion the *Princeton Theological Review* as successor to the *PRR* (though he did not edit the *PTR*).

the Church at heart I take it, this comes more as a desolation than a bereavement. You yourself will feel it deeply. – I also [with] you. Why not one of us babes instead of that g[i]ant? – The ways of Providence are sure past finding out. – So far as human eyes could see, the mere presence & personal influence of Dr. Hodge at Princeton, was worth more [to] the Church than all the efforts of the rest of its teachers put together: – & that if [he] had been able to do no teaching even, but could only live out his beautiful Xian life as an example to those gathered there around him. – The only thing left [to] us to do is to be followers of him even as he was of Christ.—[91]

Warfield would follow Hodge more than Breckinridge in several notable ways. He became an academic theologian par excellence— never holding a pastorate himself, serving only briefly as stated supply in Baltimore (a Breckinridge connection there) and Dayton. Like Hodge, Warfield began his theological career as a New Testament scholar and moved later to the chair of systematics. He believed wholeheartedly in the Princeton system of seminary education: a hothouse period of intense academic study that left the gaining of practical experience to the post-seminary years. In 1909, a student revolt against Princeton's academic focus left him unmoved, as did faculty support for a less intellectually rigorous program in the following in the decade.[92] Most of all, like Hodge he pulled no punches in doctrinal polemics, yet fought with gloves on, treating opponents with unfailing fairness and cool penetration. He made careful theological distinctions, playing always to reason rather than playing on emotions. In this, especially, he departed markedly—and consciously—from his illustrious grandfather.

This last point recalls Francis Landey Patton's eulogy: "He lacked the clarion tones of impassioned oratory, but oratory of this kind was not natural to him. He kept the calm level of deliberate speech, and his

91. BBW to Caspar Rene Gregory, June 28, 1878 (Gregory Papers, Harvard; photocopy in Warfield Papers, PTS, box 40). The photocopy is imperfect along one edge—hence the brackets.

92. Ned B. Stonehouse, *J. Gresham Machen: A Biographical Memoir*, 3rd ed. (Edinburgh: Banner of Truth, 1987), 149–52; David B. Calhoun, *Princeton Seminary*, vol. 2, *The Majestic Testimony, 1869–1929* (Edinburgh: Banner of Truth, 1996), 266–69. See also Faculty Minutes and Faculty Reports, Princeton Theological Seminary.

words proceeded out of his mouth as if they walked on velvet."[93] To accomplish this smooth, cushioned texture, Warfield made a deliberate effort to rise above his grandfather's violent temper. Such conscious decision on Warfield's part may be seen in an incident that arose in 1881 concerning his grandfather's reputation.

In 1881 the American Bible Society was considering adopting the new Revised Version of the scriptures. A Rev. C. S. Robinson, writing in *Scribner's Magazine* in support of the Revised Version, indulged in the disparagement of past worthies who had opposed the revision—Robert Breckinridge, now nine years in his grave, among them. Robinson revived allegations from the 1850s that Breckinridge had plagiarized from J. F. Stapfer's *Institutiones Theologiae Polemicae* (1743), a book Breckinridge assigned to all theology students at Danville, in a long section of the second volume of his theology. Breckinridge had in fact relied exclusively on Stapfer for chapters 18 and 19 of his book.[94] Stapfer had written in Latin; Breckinridge translated the passage but did not cite Stapfer as his source. Breckinridge's theology as a whole lacked footnotes or references, but he freely acknowledged in the preface that his work amounted to a rearrangement of the work of others. Still, the oversight occasioned grave criticism in 1858, and the revival of this "calumny," as the family called it, summoned surviving sons, sons-in-law, and friends to Breckinridge's defense.[95]

First into the fray was Warfield's Confederate uncle, William Campbell Preston Breckinridge, whose defection from the Union had caused Robert Breckinridge considerable pain. Uncle Willie, a lawyer and politician like his father, had ample psychological reason to want to make up for the distress he had caused his father in life. He fired off a "card" to several newspapers, briefly presenting evidence to counter the allegations, then quoting his father's words from the time

93. Francis Landey Patton, "Benjamin Breckinridge Warfield: A Memorial Address" (pamphlet reprinted from the *Princeton Theological Review*, July 1921), 2.

94. Robert Jefferson Breckinridge, *The Knowledge of God, Subjectively Considered* (New York: Robert Carter and Brothers, 1859).

95. Charles S. Robinson, "The Bible Society and the New Revision," *Scribner's Magazine*, January 1881; William C. P. Breckinridge, "A Card," *Presbyterian*, February 12, 1881, clipping in Warfield's Scrapbook 3 (Warfield Papers, PTS). The charge of plagiarism is fully discussed in Mayse, "RJB," 523–32.

of the original accusation: "'. . . the whole attack was a conspiracy for definite and wicked ends—ferocious in its manner, infamous in its conception—and . . . I could treat it no otherwise than I would treat a brutal attempt at personal assassination.'" In an air of righteous indignation, Breckinridge's prodigal son now added,

> And now that he is dead, I, his son, in the presence of that God, whom he loved and served, and of all brave and upright men, of whom he was a lofty type, do denounce this revival of that slander as "false and malicious," "infamous in its conception," and dishonoring and contemptible in its execution; and this I submit to the judgment of all good men.[96]

Uncle Willie wrote to his nephew Ben, urging him to join in the fight. "You are a scholar & man of brains, as well as the grandson of this dead man. You are competent to make the fight & I trust you feel called to do it." He asked Warfield "to show (1) exactly how much Pa was indebted to Stapfer; (2) how much of this Stapfer had taken from others, showing that it was the common property of the church; (3) how what was apparently taken from Stapfer had been changed by passing thro' the alembic of Pa's hand."[97]

Mary Warfield, whose relationship to Willie had remained strained since the war, counseled her son differently. "I don't want you mixed up in this fight," she wrote, urging him instead to insert "a very – delicate gentle card – of the shortest in Scribner itself."

> I do not think – I have or can make – clear to you – what is on my mind about you and controversies – but I will make one more effort – Your [sic] are by nature controversial – argumentative – and also most emotional and sensitive – this in a frail body – and overworked nerves – after [a] while – if God is good, in spairing your life – when your position is thoroughly established – (to the whole church, instead of the brains of the church) your age of weight – it may be – God will use you, as he did – my poor father, as the fighting man – of His Church – meantime, I want you to – keep out of fights and side issues –[98]

96. William C. P. Breckinridge, "A Card."
97. William C. P. Breckinridge to BBW, February 18, 1881 (Warfield Papers, PTS, box 13).
98. Mary Cabell Warfield to BBW, February 11, 1881 (Warfield Papers, PTS, box 13).

In the eyes of his mother, Warfield had indeed inherited his grand-father's temperament, including an argumentative nature, emotional sensitivity, and "overworked nerves." This was not the first time she had counseled him to avoid controversy and thereby the fate of her "poor father." And several days later she added:

All this admonishes me however – of the necessity – for a thorough compileing – of the former publications – in this matter – by you – for the future use or defense – No period of time – will make my fathers character safe – from attacks; – and you now are the only person fit to do the necessary work – You and Ethelbert – alone – will feel like or be able, to protect your Grandfathers good name – You stand alone – at one with him, theologically and politically – Do'nt you begin to see why I dred to see you my darling – thrown forward as the fighting man of the church? Princeton always stood behind walls – and Pa & men of his stamp did the hard fighting – I do'nt doubt – it will be you after-while – but I want that day defered – till your age is greater – and the necessity also greater – Oh well – I just am a woman – and can not endure the idear of haveing my son bully-riged – I expect this is it – Yes God reigns – and He forces His own – just where He needs them –[99]

But though he and his brother, alone among the Breckinridge clan, "stood at one with him, theologically and politically," Warfield was not about to siphon off his energies to the endless task of compiling his grandfather's papers against any future attacks. When family members urged him to write his grandfather's biography, Warfield demurred—as did his brother Ethelbert, an avid genealogist and published historian, whom one might expect to relish the task. The brothers were not eager to take up their grandfather's cause. Impressed by his heroics during the war, they seem to have been admonished too by his many public outbursts and confrontations.

And so Warfield wrote Uncle Willie a direct and very revealing reply. "I am sick at heart over the whole matter," he confided. Whereas Willie wanted to publish a lengthy rebuttal to Robinson in the news-papers, Warfield counseled that a brief answer in *Scribner's*—where

99. Mary Cabell Warfield to BBW, February 20, 1881 (Warfield Papers, PTS, box 13). Idiosyncrasies of spelling and punctuation are all hers.

the charge had first appeared—was the one thing needful. That answer must be "calm" and "temperate"; "we want a few words so temperately spoken that they carry conviction with them & the feeling that the writer is standing on such secure ground that he need not be angry over *any* charge." And as to the charge itself,

> The resurrection of old strifes is always disagreeable: & it does no man's character good to be always defending it. I, for one, could be deeply grieved to have parallel columns of Stapfer & Grandpa printed in Scribner. Grandpa did borrow from Stapfer. The adequate defense is that the amount of borrowing is fully covered by the acknowledgement of his preface.[100]

Willie's "card" had so angered Dr. Holland, the editor of *Scribner's*, that Holland threatened not to allow any further word on the matter to appear in the magazine. Warfield wrote a very diplomatic letter to Holland that mollified the editor enough to gain a place in the April issue. Warfield suavely expressed regret at the appearance of "what I must esteem the very unfortunate paper" that appeared in the January number. Warfield did not even give Robinson's name a noticeable place in his opening words. "That paper, in needlessly reviving old and worn-out controversies, and worse than that, in reviving with them the long well-forgotten bitterness which grew out of them, cannot help bringing pain to all right thinking minds." In this tone Warfield proceeded: "I would hesitate greatly to impute any unworthy motives to Dr. Robinson, the author of this statement. He is not only a minister of God's word, but has a reputation for a kindly heart. But the statement itself cannot but leave a very false impression . . . ." Warfield briefly countered a few of Robinson's misstatements and closed his argument with the only quotation he would make from Breckinridge's book: the disclaimer in the preface that "the details which have been wrought out by learned, godly, and able men in all ages, of many creeds and in many tongues, have been freely wrought into the staple of this work, when they suited the place and the purpose, and turned precisely to my thought." He

---

100. BBW to William C. P. Breckinridge, draft, February 22, 1881 (Warfield Papers, PTS, box 13).

closed with an admonition to lay to rest "that charge—manifestly the child of the time of spite—in these cooler days, when the heat of conflict is over . . . ."[101]

Warfield had heeded his mother's urgings and succeeded in getting a calm, temperate answer into the magazine that had printed the calumny in the first place. To Uncle Willie he explained as follows. (Words he struck from the sent version are indicated in brackets.)

> Forgive me, if I seem to you to be unfeeling or even [presuming] presumptuous. I do not mean it so. [But I schooled myself when I wrote first to Scribner to expect & receive in silence anything personal, or contained in private letters: so only I could thereby gain my first object: – viz. get a reply into Scribner. And I cannot help regretting most sincerely that you did not find it in your heart, just to let Dr. J's first letter lie unanswered. What could that do of harm to anyone?—]
>
> My grandfather's memory is sacred to me. [You may be sure that I shall always be ready to defend it to the best of my ability: – but always as briefly & calmly as possible. I revere it too highly to wish to raise a contest about it. – that is *all*.][102]

Here in his draft letter we see evidence of Warfield "schooling himself" to subdue personal feeling, restraining himself even in his admonition to Uncle Willie. Even in private, he considered the effect his words might have on his uncle, and decided to leave them unsaid. And in public, he would honor his grandfather's name by taking care not to repeat his grandfather's errors of rashness, public posturing, and displays of emotion. This deliberate restraint, this reigning in of a sensitive and argumentative nature, would characterize Warfield's career as Princeton's lead man in the chair of the Hodges. He would indeed serve as a kind of "fighting man of the church," but in a more Hodgean vein—choosing his battles with some care, treating his opponents with scrupulous fairness, yet taking a clear stand and—in a distinct echo of his grandfather's gifts—penetrating to the heart

101. B. B. Warfield, "'The Bible Society and the New Revision.' In Defense of Dr. Breckinridge," *Scribner's Monthly*, April 1881, reprinted in the *Kentucky Gazette*, a clipping of which is in Warfield's Scrapbook 3 (Warfield Papers, PTS, box 41).

102. BBW to William C. P. Breckinridge, draft, February 22, 1881.

of an issue with an apt metaphor and well-turned phrase. Benjamin Breckinridge Warfield would graft onto the Breckinridge spunk and brilliance the mild manner of Charles Hodge and the calm assurance of Princeton Seminary.

❧ 2 ❧

A "Rather Bald" Rationalist?
The Appeal to "Right Reason"

PAUL KJOSS HELSETH

Princeton Seminary was founded in 1812 in order to defend bibli-cal Christianity against the perceived crisis of "modern infidelity."[1] Its founders took their stand between the extremes of deism, on the one hand, and "mysticism" (or "enthusiasm"), on the other, and resolved "to fit clergymen to meet the cultural crisis, to roll back what they perceived as tides of irreligion sweeping the country, and to provide a learned defense of Christianity generally and the Bible specifically."[2] Throughout the nineteenth and into the twentieth centuries, theo-logians from Princeton Seminary proved to be the most articulate defenders of Reformed orthodoxy in America. Their apologetical efforts have come under intense critical scrutiny, however, because critics are convinced that these efforts were based on accommoda-tion to the anthropological and epistemological assumptions of "the modern scientific revolution,"[3] not on faithfulness to the doctrinal

1. Mark Noll, "The Founding of Princeton Seminary," *Westminster Theological Journal* 42 (1979): 85.
2. Mark Noll, "The Princeton Theology," *The Princeton Theology*, Reformed Theology in America, no. 1, ed. David Wells (1985; repr., Grand Rapids: Baker, 1989), 24.
3. George Marsden, "The Collapse of American Evangelical Academia," in *Faith and Rationality: Reason and Belief in God*, ed. Alvin Plantinga and Nicholas Wolterstorff (Notre Dame, Ind.: University of Notre Dame Press, 1983), 241.

standards of Reformed orthodoxy. In fact, critics contend, the driving forces behind Old Princeton's defense of the faith were Scottish common sense realism and Baconian inductivism, despite the fact that these forces often were tempered by the Princetonians' personal piety. Critics would have us believe, therefore, that the theologians at Old Princeton Seminary were not the champions of Reformed orthodoxy that they claimed to be. They were, rather, the purveyors of a theology that was bastardized by an "alien philosophy."[4]

What, then, are we to make of this conclusion? Were the Princeton theologians in fact "nineteenth-century positivists who did not reject theology"?[5] In other words, did they really accommodate their theology to anthropological and epistemological assumptions that are diametrically opposed to those of the Reformed tradition?

I have argued elsewhere that such a conclusion cannot be justified, simply because it misses the moral rather than the merely rational nature of the Princetonians' thought.[6] When Old Princeton's

4. This is the general theme of John Vander Stelt's *Philosophy and Scripture: A Study of Old Princeton and Westminster Theology* (Marlton, N.J.: Mack Publishing, 1978). The Dutch and neoorthodox branches of the Reformed camp generally agree with this assessment of Old Princeton, as do more progressive thinkers who characterize themselves as postconservative evangelicals. See, for example, Stanley J. Grenz, *Revisioning Evangelical Theology: A Fresh Agenda for the Twenty-first Century* (Downers Grove, Ill.: InterVarsity Press, 1993). Contemporary interpreters who endorse this assessment are indebted in one way or another to Sydney Ahlstrom, "The Scottish Philosophy and American Theology," *Church History* 24 (1955): 257–72. See, for example, Ernest Sandeen, "The Princeton Theology: One Source of Biblical Literalism in American Protestantism," *Church History* 31 (1962): 307–21; Samuel Pearson, "Enlightenment Influence on Protestant Thought in Early National America," *Encounter* 38 (Summer 1977): 193–212; and George Marsden, "The Collapse of American Evangelical Academia," 219–64. Older studies that are critical of the "intellectualism" of Old Princeton include Ralph Danhof, *Charles Hodge as Dogmatician* (Goes, The Netherlands: Oosterbaan and le Cointre, 1929); John O. Nelson, "The Rise of the Princeton Theology: A Generic History of American Presbyterianism Until 1850" (Ph.D. diss., Yale University, 1935); William Livingstone, "The Princeton Apologetic as Exemplified by the Work of Benjamin B. Warfield and J. Gresham Machen: A Study of American Theology, 1880–1930" (Ph.D. diss., Yale University, 1948).

5. George Marsden, "Scotland and Philadelphia: Common Sense Philosophy from Jefferson to Westminster," *Reformed Theological Journal* 29 (March 1979): 11.

6. Please see my articles on Old Princeton: Paul Kjoss Helseth, "Are Postconservative Evangelicals Fundamentalists? Postconservative Evangelicalism, Old Princeton, and the Rise of Neo-Fundamentalism," in *Reclaiming the Center: Confronting Evangelical Accommodation in Postmodern Times*, ed. Millard J. Erickson, Paul Kjoss Helseth, Justin Taylor (Wheaton, Ill.: Crossway, 2004), 223–50; idem, "B. B. Warfield on the Apologetic Nature of Christian Scholarship: An Analysis of His Solution to the Problem of the Relationship between Christianity and Culture," *Westminster Theological Journal* 62 (2000): 89–111; idem, "'Right Reason' and the Princeton Mind: The Moral Context," *The Journal of Presbyterian History* 77, 1 (Spring 1999):

"intellectualism" is interpreted within a context that recognizes the soul as a single unit that acts in all of its functions—its thinking, its feeling, and its willing—as a single substance, it becomes clear that the Princeton theologians were not cold, calculating rationalists whose confidence in the mind led them to ignore the import of the subjective and the centrality of experience in religious epistemology.[7] They were, rather, Reformed scholars who acknowledged more often than not that subjective and experiential concerns are of critical importance in any consideration of religious epistemology.[8] Indeed, they recognized that the operation of the intellect involves the "whole soul"—mind, will, and emotions—rather than the rational faculty alone, and as a consequence they insisted that the ability to reason "rightly"—that is, the ability to see revealed truth for what it objectively is, namely, glorious—presupposes the regenerating activity of the Holy Spirit on the "whole soul" of a moral agent. In short, Old Princeton's "intellectualism" was grounded in an endorsement of the classical Reformed distinction between a merely speculative and a spiritual understanding of revealed truth rather than in accommodation to the assumptions of Enlightenment philosophy.[9]

13–28; idem, "B. B. Warfield's Apologetical Appeal to 'Right Reason': Evidence of a 'Rather Bald Rationalism'?" *Scottish Bulletin of Evangelical Theology* 16 (Autumn 1998): 156–77; idem, "The Apologetical Tradition of the OPC: A Reconsideration," *Westminster Theological Journal* 60 (1998): 109–29.

7. The word "rationalism" and its cognates are used in this chapter to refer to a confidence in the mind that originates in indifference to the noetic effects of sin, indifference that itself is grounded in accommodation to the assumptions of Enlightenment philosophy. This chapter argues that Warfield was not a rationalist if "rationalism" is used in this sense, the sense that leads to a kind of naïve realism. For confirmation that Warfield was not a naïve realist, see his endorsement of the distinction between archetypal and ectypal science in B. B. Warfield, "Introduction to Francis R. Beattie's *Apologetics*," in Benjamin B. Warfield, *Selected Shorter Writings*, 2 vols., ed. John E. Meeter (Nutley, N.J.: Presbyterian and Reformed, 1970, 1973), 2:99–105 (hereafter *SSW*); B. B. Warfield, "A Review of *De Zekerheid des Geloofs*," in *SSW*, 2:117–23.

8. I say "more often than not" to acknowledge the presence of apparent inconsistencies in their exposition of the relationship between the head and the heart. See, for example, Mark A. Noll, "Charles Hodge as an Expositor of the Spiritual Life," in *Charles Hodge Revisited: A Critical Appraisal of His Life and Work*, ed. John W. Stewart and James H. Moorhead (Grand Rapids: Eerdmans, 2002), 181–216. It is my contention that these apparent inconsistencies are more or less resolved when we recognize that the Princetonians conceived of the soul as a single thinking-feeling-willing whole.

9. The Princeton theologians endorsed an understanding of the soul that is grounded in a bipartite, heart-centered psychology. According to this understanding, the soul is a single unit that always acts as a single substance, and the activity of the "whole soul" is determined by the

The question arises, however, as to how the assumptions of the Reformed tradition are related to the Princeton apologetic in general and the apologetic of Benjamin B. Warfield (1851–1921) in particular. Is not Warfield's insistence that the Christian religion has been placed in the world "to *reason* its way to its dominion"[10] a particularly egregious example of Old Princeton's "rather bald rationalism"?[11] In other words, is not Warfield's apologetical appeal to "right reason" in fact evidence of accommodation to the assumptions of an essentially humanistic philosophy?[12]

This chapter argues that it is not, simply because the moral considerations that rule in the realm of epistemology also rule in the realm of apologetics. Whereas Warfield certainly affirmed that the primary mission of the Christian apologist "is no less than to *reason* the world into acceptance of the 'truth,'"[13] he nonetheless recognized that the "rightness" of the apprehension that leads to the advancement of the kingdom is produced by the *testimonium internum Spiritus Sancti*, that is, by the internal testimony of the Holy Spirit. He acknowledged, therefore, that the labors of the apologist would be of little or no consequence without the sovereign workings of the Spirit of God, for he recognized that regenerated sinners alone have the moral capacity to see revealed truth as it should be seen. That this is the case, and that a reconsideration of how we should think about the appeal to "right reason" is long overdue, will be clear after an examination of the relationship between the objective and subjective components of Warfield's religious epistemology.

---

underlying character or disposition of the agent's "heart." The soul comprises two rather than three faculties or "powers": the understanding, which takes precedence in all rational activity, and the will, which is defined broadly to include the emotions and volitions. Note that the will in this view of the soul is not a self-determining power, but a power that is determined by the motives of the acting agent. For an excellent analysis of the doctrine of free agency that flows from this psychology, see Paul Ramsey's introductory essay to Jonathan Edwards, *The Freedom of the Will* (New Haven, Conn.: Yale University Press, 1957), esp. 38–40. For an excellent statement of the distinction between a merely speculative and a spiritual understanding of the gospel, see Jonathan Edwards, "Christian Knowledge," in *The Works of Jonathan Edwards*, 2 vols. (Edinburgh: Banner of Truth, 1992), 2:157–63.

10. Warfield, "Introduction to Francis R. Beattie's *Apologetics*," in *SSW*, 2:98–99.

11. Livingstone, "The Princeton Apologetic," 186.

12. For this appeal, see Warfield, "Introduction to Francis R. Beattie's *Apologetics*," in *SSW*, 2:99–100, and Warfield, "A Review of *De Zekerheid des Geloofs*," in *SSW*, 2:120–21.

13. B. B. Warfield, "Christianity the Truth," in *SSW*, 2:213.

The Knowledge of God and Religious Faith: Conditioned by the "Ethical State" of the Soul

Warfield maintained that the proper context for understanding the relationship between the objective and subjective components of religious epistemology is that provided by Augustine's ontology of "theistic Intuitionalism" and Calvin's conception of the *sensus deitatis*. Whereas Augustine argued that "innate ideas" are "the immediate product in the soul of God the Illuminator, always present with the soul as its sole and indispensable Light, in which alone it perceives truth,"[14] Calvin insisted that the knowledge of God, as a fact of self-consciousness that is quickened by the manifestations of God in nature and providence, "is given in the very same act by which we know self. For when we know self, we must know it as it is: and that means we must know it as dependent, derived, imperfect, and responsible being."[15] Though Warfield conceded that there are some "interesting" and "significant" differences between the religious epistemologies of Augustine and Calvin, he argued that their doctrines are essentially the same, simply because both acknowledge that God is not only the God of all grace and truth, but "the Light of all knowledge" as well.[16] Both acknowledge, in other words, that

man's power of attaining truth depends . . . first of all upon the fact that God has made man like Himself, Whose intellect is the home of the intelligible world, the contents of which may, therefore, be reflected in the human soul; and then, secondly, that God, having so made man, has not left him, deistically, to himself, but continually reflects into his soul the contents of His own eternal and immutable mind—which are precisely those eternal and immutable truths which constitute the intelligible world. The soul is therefore in unbroken communion with God, and in the body of intelligible truths reflected into it from God, sees God. The nerve of this view, it will be ob-

14. B. B. Warfield, "Augustine's Doctrine of Knowledge and Authority," in *Tertullian and Augustine*, vol. 4 of *The Works of Benjamin Breckinridge Warfield* (1930; repr., Grand Rapids: Baker, 1981), 143–44.
15. B. B. Warfield, "Calvin's Doctrine of the Knowledge of God," in *Calvin and Calvinism*, vol. 5 of *The Works of Benjamin Breckinridge Warfield* (1931; repr., Grand Rapids: Baker, 1981), 31. Cf. B. B. Warfield, "God and Human Religion and Morals," in *SSW*, 1:41–45.
16. Warfield, "Augustine's Doctrine of Knowledge and Authority," 143.

served, is the theistic conception of the constant dependence of the creature on God.[17]

If Warfield was persuaded that the knowledge of God that is reflected into the soul constitutes the foundational fact of human self-consciousness, he was also convinced that this knowledge is the source of religious expression as well. The justification for this contention is found in his assertion that "man is a unit, and the religious truth which impinges upon him must affect him in all of his activities, or in none."[18] Because he recognized that the soul is a single unit that acts in all of its functions as a single substance, Warfield argued that the knowledge of God that is reflected into the soul and quickened by the manifestations of God in nature and providence "can never be otiose and inert; but must produce an effect in human souls, in the way of thinking, feeling, willing."[19] In other words, it must produce an effect that manifests itself first in the conceptual formulation of perceived truth (perception "ripening" into conception), and second in the religious reaction of the will (broadly understood to include emotions and volitions) to the conceptual content of this formulated perception ("as is the perception ripening into conception, so is the religion").[20]

But if it is the knowledge of God that is reflected into the soul that underlies the religious reaction of the will, then why, we must ask, are there are so many forms of religious expression? Why, in other words, do not all rational agents react to the knowledge of God that is manifest in nature and providence in the same fashion? The answer

17. Ibid., 145–46. On the "very interesting and . . . very significant differences" between Augustine's and Calvin's ontologies of knowledge, see Warfield, "Calvin's Doctrine of the Knowledge of God," 117.

18. B. B. Warfield, "Authority, Intellect, Heart," in *SSW*, 2:668. Anyone who doubts that Warfield endorsed a bipartite, heart-centered psychology should read this short yet extremely important essay. See also Warfield, "Augustine's Doctrine of Knowledge and Authority," 150–51.

19. Warfield, "Calvin's Doctrine of the Knowledge of God," 37.

20. B. B. Warfield, review of *Foundations: A Statement of Christian Belief in Terms of Modern Thought*, by Seven Oxford Men, in *Critical Reviews*, vol. 10 of *The Works of Benjamin Breckinridge Warfield* (1932; repr., Grand Rapids: Baker, 1981), 325; cf. B. B. Warfield, "The Idea of Systematic Theology," in *Studies in Theology*, vol. 9 of *The Works of Benjamin Breckinridge Warfield* (1932; repr., Grand Rapids: Baker, 1981), 53–54; Warfield, "Calvin's Doctrine of the Knowledge of God," 37–38.

lies in Warfield's warning against supposing that "the human mind is passive in the acquisition of knowledge, or that the acquisition of knowledge is unconditioned by the nature or state of the acquiring soul."[21] While Warfield maintained that the religious reaction of the will is determined by the conceptual formulation of perceived truth, he nonetheless recognized that the conception of the mind is itself conditioned by the moral or "ethical state" of the perceiving soul.[22] It is the "ethical state" of the perceiving soul that determines the religious reaction of the will, Warfield argued, for it is the "ethical state" of the soul that conditions the purity or clarity of perception and thereby the purity or clarity of the conception that underlies religious expression. Since knowledge is a function of the "whole man" rather than of the rational faculty alone, we must conclude that there is more than one form of religious expression, simply because the knowledge that kindles the religious reaction of the will is qualified and conditioned by the "whole voluntary nature" of the agent that knows.[23]

The Relationship between the Conception of the Mind and the Religious Reaction of the Will

Having established that the "ethical state" of the soul conditions the perception as well as the conception of the mind, we must now consider how this conception is related to the religious reaction of the will. Why, in short, does "the nature of our [theological] conceptions so far from having nothing, [have] everything, to do with religion"?[24] The key to understanding the relationship between conception and religious expression is found in Warfield's assertion that "religion is not only the natural, but the necessary product of man's sense of dependence, which always abides as the innermost essence of the whole crowd of emotions which we speak of as religious, the lowest

21. Warfield, "Augustine's Doctrine of Knowledge and Authority," 149.
22. Ibid., 149 n. 37. Cf. Warfield, "Calvin's Doctrine of the Knowledge of God," 31–32, 38; B. B. Warfield, "Augustine and the Pelagian Controversy," in *Tertullian and Augustine*, 295–96, 401–4.
23. Warfield, "Augustine's Doctrine of Knowledge and Authority," 149 n. 37; cf. 149–50.
24. B. B. Warfield, *The Power of God Unto Salvation* (Philadelphia: The Presbyterian Board of Publishing and Sabbath-School Work, 1903), 243–44.

and also the highest."[25] While Warfield insisted that the knowledge that we are dependent on God is the foundational fact of human self-consciousness, he also maintained that the manifestation of this consciousness in religious expression unveils the flowering of this sense of dependence in a manner that is determined by the moral agent's conceptual formulation of perceived truth.[26] In what I am calling Warfield's key assertion, however, he links religious expression with the sense of dependence in a manner that seems to bypass the determining role of conceptual truth. Religion, in other words, is in this instance not explicitly regarded as the vital effect of the knowledge of God in the human soul, but as the necessary product of the natural sense of dependence, that is, of "the innermost essence of the whole crowd of emotions" that constitute the very core of human being. How, then, does Warfield reconcile what might appear to be a contradiction at this point? How can he maintain that religious expression is both the vital effect of the knowledge of God in the human soul and the necessary product of the natural sense of dependence without appearing to suggest that religion has its origin in more than one source (one rational and objective, the other emotional and subjective)? The solution to this apparent contradiction will be clear after a brief analysis of the mental movement called faith.

In response to the notion that responsibility attaches to faith only when the act of faith is grounded in the "free volition" of an autonomous moral agent, Warfield argued that we are responsible for our faith simply because faith—from its lowest to its highest forms—is an act of the mind the subject of which is "the man in the entirety of his being as man."[27] While Warfield acknowledged that the mental movement called faith "fulfills itself" or is specifically "formed" in that voluntary movement of the sensibility called trust, he insisted that the act of faith includes—indeed is based on—"a mental recognition of what is before the mind, as objectively true and real, and therefore depends on the evidence that a thing is true and real and is determined by this evidence; it is the response of the mind to this evidence and

25. Warfield, "God and Human Religion and Morals," in *SSW*, 1:42.
26. See B. B. Warfield, "On Faith in Its Psychological Aspects," in *Studies in Theology*, 338.
27. Ibid., 341.

61

cannot arise apart from it."[28] Since faith is a mental conviction that as such is "determined by evidence, not by volition," Warfield concluded that the act of faith is best defined as that "forced consent" in which "the movement of the sensibility in the form of trust is what is thrust forward to observation."[29]

It is important to note, however, that though Warfield insisted that the fulfillment of faith in the movement of trust is determined or "forced" by what is rationally perceived, he never suggested that the consent of the mind is "the mechanical result of the adduction of the evidence."[30] "There may stand in the way of the proper and objectively inevitable effect of the evidence," he argued, "the subjective nature or condition to which the evidence is addressed."[31] But how can this be? If faith is indeed a "forced consent," then how can "the subjective nature or condition to which the evidence is addressed" block "the objectively inevitable effect of the evidence"? In short, Warfield was convinced that "objective adequacy and subjective effect are not exactly correlated," simply because "'Faith,' 'belief' does not follow the evidence itself . . . but the judgment of the intellect on the evidence."[32] According to Warfield, the "judgment of the intellect" does not refer to an act of the rational faculty alone, but to an act of the mind in which the "complex of emotions" that reflects the "ethical state" of the soul and forms the "concrete state of mind" of the perceiving agent plays the decisive or determining role.[33] What, then, does the "complex of emotions" that forms the "concrete state of mind" of the perceiving agent do? Why, in other words, is the "judgment of the intellect" the most prominent element in the movement of assent, the "central movement in all faith"?[34] In a word, it is the most prominent element in the movement of faith because the "complex of emotions" that forms the "concrete state of mind" of the perceiving

28. Ibid., 342, 315.
29. Ibid., 317, 331.
30. Ibid., 314, 336.
31. Ibid., 314, 336.
32. Ibid., 318.
33. Ibid., 314, 331.
34. Ibid., 341. The movement of assent is the central movement in faith because it "must depend" on a prior movement of the intellect, and the movement of the sensibilities in the act of "trust" is the "product" of assent. Thus assent ties together the intellectual and the volitional aspects of faith. Cf. 341–42.

agent determines not only the "susceptibility" or "accessibility" of the mind to the objective force of the evidence in question, but also the reaction of the will to what is rationally perceived.[35] When the "judgment of the intellect" is conceived in this fashion—a fashion which recognizes that "judgment" is the act of the "whole man" that "underlies" the agent's response to perceived truth[36]—it becomes clear that the conception of the mind is related to the religious reaction of the will, simply because the "complex of emotions" that forms the "state of mind" of the perceiving agent also determines the activity of the will, broadly understood. This explains, among other things, why "the evidence to which we are accessible is irresistible if adequate, and irresistibly produces belief, faith."[37]

The "Faith" of Sinners in Their Natural State

The foregoing analysis has established that faith for Warfield is both the vital effect of the knowledge of God in the human soul and the necessary product of the natural sense of dependence, simply because it is the response of the "whole man" to the knowledge of God that is reflected into the soul and quickened by the manifestations of God in nature and providence. The question that we must now consider is what makes the faith that expresses the religious reaction of the will "saving" faith. If it is indeed true that "no man exists, or ever has existed or ever will exist, who has not 'faith,'"[38] then what for Warfield sets the faith of the elect apart from the faith of those who are perishing? The forthcoming discussion answers this question by examining the nature of faith in moral agents that are fallen and moral agents that are renewed. It suggests, in short, that the regenerate form their consciousness of dependence in a manner that renders their salvation certain because the regenerate alone have the moral ability to see revealed truth for what it objectively is, namely, glorious.

35. Ibid., 336–37; cf. B. B. Warfield, review of *The Christian Faith: A System of Dogmatics*, by Theodore Haering, in *Critical Reviews*, 412.
36. Warfield, "On Faith in Its Psychological Aspects," 314.
37. Ibid., 336.
38. Ibid., 338.

Again following Augustine and Calvin, Warfield maintained that "it is knowledge, not nescience, which belongs to human nature as such."[39] He insisted, therefore, that had human nature not been disordered by the "abnormal" condition of original sin, all moral agents—"by the very necessity of [their] nature"[40]—not only would have known God in the fullest creaturely sense of the term, but would have entrusted themselves to his care because their consciousness of dependence would have taken "the 'form' of glad and loving trust."[41] This capacity for true knowledge and loving trust was lost, however, when Adam's sin plunged his posterity into a state of spiritual death. Why, then, does spiritual death prohibit the unregenerate from responding to the consciousness of dependence in a loving and trusting fashion? The answer has to do with the "noetic as well as thelematic and ethical effects" of the fall.[42] Warfield argued that the unregenerate remain largely indifferent—indeed hostile—to revealed truth because the knowledge of God that is reflected into their souls is "dulled," "deflected," and twisted by the power of sin.[43] Whereas "unfallen man" had an intimate knowledge of God because the truth of God was reflected clearly in his heart, the unregenerate are incapable of such knowledge and love because the sinful heart "refracts and deflects the rays of truth reflected into it from the divine source, so rendering the right perception of the truth impossible."[44] While "abnormal man" thus remains conscious of his dependence on God and believes in God in an intellectual or speculative sense, he can neither "delight" in this dependence nor trust in the God on whom he knows he is dependent, simply because the truth of God is deflected by a corrupt nature "into an object of distrust, fear, and hate."[45]

39. Warfield, "Augustine's Doctrine of Knowledge and Authority," 158.
40. Warfield, "Calvin's Doctrine of the Knowledge of God," 36, 43.
41. Warfield, "Review of *De Zekerheid des Geloofs*," in *SSW*, 2:116; cf. Warfield, "On Faith in Its Psychological Aspects," 338. On the relationship between "the disease of sin" and Warfield's contention that "man as we know him is not normal man," see Warfield, "Augustine's Doctrine of Knowledge and Authority," 156–58; Warfield, "Calvin's Doctrine of the Knowledge of God," 32, 70.
42. Warfield, "Augustine's Doctrine of Knowledge and Authority," 158.
43. Warfield, "Calvin's Doctrine of the Knowledge of God," 32; cf. Warfield, "Augustine's Doctrine of Knowledge and Authority," 155–56.
44. Warfield, "Augustine's Doctrine of Knowledge and Authority," 155. On the failure of general revelation, see Warfield, "Calvin's Doctrine of the Knowledge of God," 39–45.
45. Warfield, "On Faith in Its Psychological Aspects," 338, 339; Warfield, "God and Human Religion and Morals," in *SSW*, 1:42; cf. Warfield, "Review of *De Zekerheid des Gel-*

Since the fallen sinner's consciousness of dependence is formed by fear and hate rather than by loving trust, it follows—given the intimate nature of the relationship between the conception of the mind and the religious reaction of the will—that the fallen sinner is unable to respond to the consciousness of dependence in glad and loving trust because the sinner as such is morally unable to do so. Herein lies the heart of the depravity that constitutes the fallen condition. While the fallen sinner cannot escape the knowledge that he is and always will be dependent upon God in every aspect of his existence, he is morally incapable of entrusting himself to God because "he loves sin too much,"[46] and thus cannot use his will—which in the narrower sense is "ready, like a weathercock, to be turned whithersoever the breeze that blows from the heart ('will' in the broader sense) may direct"[47]—for believing. As such, the fallen sinner neither will nor can trust in God, not because there is a physical defect in the constitution of his being, but because his sinful heart lacks the moral ability to "explicate" its sense of dependence and obligation "on right lines."[48] It lacks the moral ability to form its consciousness of dependence in loving trust, in other words, because it is blind to the true significance of what it can rationally perceive.[49]

Saving Faith: The Certain Consequence of a "Right" Knowledge of God

But does this "abnormal" state of fallenness prevent the descendents of Adam from ever delighting in the knowledge of God? In other words, does spiritual death make it impossible for fallen sinners to know God in a saving sense? According to Warfield, it does not for the elect because God removes their natural incapacities and thereby

---

oofs," in *SSW*, 2:116.

46. B. B. Warfield, "Inability and the Demand of Faith," in *SSW*, 2:725; cf. Warfield, "On Faith in Its Psychological Aspects," 339.

47. Warfield, "Augustine and the Pelagian Controversy," 403–4.

48. Warfield, "God and Human Religion and Morals," in *SSW*, 1:44.

49. For a more comprehensive discussion of the relationship between the inability to see revealed truth for what it objectively is and the "infinite variety" of "religions and moralities" that are produced by "reprobate minds." Cf. ibid., 1:42–44.

rescues them from their "intellectual imbecility"[50] by imparting a supernatural revelation that "supplements" and "completes" the truth manifest in general revelation.[51] Whereas God reveals himself in the natural constitution of the moral agent as well as in nature and providence, this general revelation "is insufficient that sinful man should know Him aright" because it is not reflected clearly in minds that are blinded by sin.[52] As the remedy for this inability to know God aright, God reveals himself to fallen sinners in a fashion that is adapted to their needs. It is this special revelation, the purpose of which is to "neutralize" the noetic effects of sin by providing a "mitigation for the symptom," that then serves as the objective foundation for the "proper assimilation" of the knowledge of God manifest in general revelation.[53] "What special revelation is, therefore—and the Scriptures as its documentation—is very precisely represented by the figure of the spectacles. It is aid to the dulled vision of sinful man, to enable it to see God."[54]

While special revelation as such is "the condition of all right knowledge of higher things for sinful man,"[55] it is clear that this revelation alone—its objective adequacy notwithstanding—will not yield a true and compelling knowledge of God if the soul to which it is addressed is morally incapable of seeing it for what it objectively is. This is due to the fact that sinners who are at enmity with God need more than external aid to see God rightly; they need "the power of sight."[56] In

50. Warfield, "Augustine's Doctrine of Knowledge and Authority," 159–60; cf. Warfield, "Calvin's Doctrine of the Knowledge of God," 47.

51. B. B. Warfield, "Christianity and Revelation," in SSW, 1:27.

52. Warfield, "Calvin's Doctrine of the Knowledge of God," 32; cf. Warfield, "Augustine's Doctrine of Knowledge and Authority," 222.

53. Warfield, "Augustine's Doctrine of Knowledge and Authority," 159, 222.

54. Warfield, "Calvin's Doctrine of the Knowledge of God," 69. Warfield suggested that general and special revelation together form an "organic whole" that includes all that God has done—in nature, history, and Scripture—to make himself known. As such, special revelation was not given to supersede general revelation, but to meet the altered circumstances occasioned by the advent of sin. Cf. Warfield, "Christianity and Revelation," in SSW, 1:28.

55. Warfield, "Augustine's Doctrine of Knowledge and Authority," 161. Note that Warfield's reference to "higher things" in this quotation ought not to be interpreted as referring merely to "spiritual" or "supernatural" kinds of things. The discussion in the preceding paragraph, as well as the discussion in the forthcoming chapter, suggests that the "right knowledge" made possible by special revelation has to do with "all things," including "scientific" or "natural" kinds of things.

56. Warfield, "Calvin's Doctrine of the Knowledge of God," 70.

other words, they need a remedy for their moral bondage to sin so that "the light of the Word itself can accredit itself to them as light."[57] Wherein, then, is this remedy found? Warfield insisted that it is found in the central component of regenerating grace, namely, the *testimonium internum Spiritus Sancti*.[58] Whereas the subjective corruption of the fallen sinner's moral nature precludes the possibility of a "hospitable reception" for the truth of God in the perceiving mind and heart,[59] the testimony of the Spirit renders the reception of the truth certain because the internal operation of the Spirit renews and inclines the powers of the soul "in the love of God," that is, in affection not only for the knowledge of God that is reflected into the soul, but for the consciousness of dependence on God as well.[60] Since regenerating grace radically alters the moral nature and thereby the certain operation of the "whole soul," it follows that the elect perceive and receive the truth of God because they have been enabled by grace to "feel, judge, and act differently from what [they] otherwise should."[61] As a consequence, "[they] recognize God where before [they] did not perceive Him; [they] trust and love Him where before [they] feared and hated Him; [and they] firmly embrace Him in His Word where before [they] turned indifferently away."[62]

Yet how, specifically, does the testimony of the Spirit render the reception of the truth certain? Why, in other words, is the witness of the Spirit effectual? Warfield maintained that the internal operation of the Spirit accomplishes its ordained end simply because it implants, or rather restores, "a spiritual sense in the soul by which God is recognized in His Word."[63] This restoration of susceptibility to spiritual truth then has two certain effects. In the first place, it enables the

57. Ibid., 32.

58. Please note that at this point Warfield is following Calvin's understanding of the remedy rather than Augustine's, which has to do with the stress he laid on the church. Cf. note 17 above.

59. Warfield, "God and Human Religion and Morals," in *SSW*, 1:43.

60. Warfield, "On Faith in Its Psychological Aspects," 339. On the relationship between regeneration and the "habits or dispositions" that govern the activity of the soul, see B. B. Warfield, "Regeneration," in *SSW*, 2:323; B. B. Warfield, "New Testament Terms Descriptive of the Great Change," in *SSW*, 1:267–77.

61. Warfield, "Calvin's Doctrine of the Knowledge of God," 111.

62. Ibid.

63. Ibid., 33.

regenerate to reason "rightly." Though Warfield acknowledged that the witness of the Spirit is not revelation in the strictest sense of the term, he insisted that it

> is just God Himself in His intimate working in the human heart, opening it to the light of the truth, that by this illumination it may see things as they really are and so recognize God in the Scriptures with the same directness and surety as men recognize sweetness in what is sweet and brightness in what is bright.[64]

Despite the fact that the testimony of the Spirit thus "presupposes the objective revelation and only prepares the heart to respond to and embrace it," nevertheless it is the source of all our "right knowledge" of God because it is the means by which the regenerate are enabled to "see" through the spectacles of Scripture, that is, to "discern" the beauty and truthfulness of God's Word.[65]

If the restoration of susceptibility to spiritual truth is the means by which the regenerate are enabled to see and know things "as they really are," it is also the less direct though no less effectual means to the rise of saving faith in the regenerated soul. The justification for this contention lies in Warfield's commitment to the unitary operation of the soul. Because he recognized that there is an intimate connection between the conception of the mind and the religious reaction of the will, Warfield insisted that a "right" apprehension of revealed truth will immediately and irresistibly manifest itself in an act of saving faith, simply because the sense that informs the perception of the mind is the same sense that determines the activity of the will, broadly understood. Since the knowledge of God that is communicated to the regenerated soul via the "conjoint divine action" of Word and Spirit is a "vital and vitalizing knowledge of God" that "takes hold of the whole man in the roots of his activities and controls all the movements of his soul,"[66] we must conclude that the testimony of the Spirit renders both true knowledge and saving faith absolutely certain because it is the implanted sense of the divine that "forces" regenerated sinners to

64. Ibid., 79, 32, 111–12.
65. Ibid., 32, 121, 70, 79.
66. Ibid., 31, 75.

see and pursue that which they perceive (rightly) to be both true and trustworthy. It follows, therefore, that

> if sinful man as such is incapable of the act of faith, because he is inhabile to the evidence on which alone such an act of confident resting on God the Saviour can repose, renewed man is equally incapable of not responding to this evidence, which is objectively compelling, by an act of sincere faith. In this its highest exercise faith thus, though in a true sense the gift of God, is in an equally true sense man's own act, and bears all the character of faith as it is exercised by unrenewed man in its lower manifestations.[67]

The Appeal to "Right Reason": An Appeal to the "Stronger and Purer Thought" of the Christian Apologist

Having established that the "keystone" of Warfield's doctrine of the knowledge of God is found in the "conjoint divine action" of Word and Spirit,[68] the question that we must finally consider has to do with how we should interpret his apologetical appeal to "right reason." Must we conclude, along with the consensus of critical opinion, that Warfield was a rationalist whose approach to apologetics presupposed an almost "Pelagian confidence"[69] in the rational competence of even unregenerate minds? Must we conclude, in other words, that Warfield's apologetic was based on accommodation to anthropological and epistemological assumptions that are diametrically opposed to those of the Reformed tradition? The remainder of this chapter argues that we must not, unless we want to seriously misrepresent Warfield's understanding of the task of apologetics.

Before unfolding this argument, however, let us articulate the conclusion to what we have learned thus far, for doing so will outline the epistemological context within which Warfield's "intellectualism" must be interpreted. To this point we have seen that objective and subjective

---

67. Warfield, "On Faith in Its Psychological Aspects," 337–38. On the essential correspondence between faith in "renewed man" and faith in "unfallen man," see 340.

68. Warfield, "Calvin's Doctrine of the Knowledge of God," 113; cf. 82–83.

69. Jack Rogers and Donald McKim, *The Authority and Interpretation of the Bible* (San Francisco: Harper & Row, 1979), 290.

factors were of critical importance in Warfield's religious epistemology, simply because he recognized that the soul is a single unit that acts in all of its functions as a single substance. We may plausibly conclude, therefore, that Warfield's "intellectualism" had its likely origin not in accommodation to the rationalistic assumptions of Enlightenment thought, but in the desire to preserve two important elements of the Reformed tradition in an increasingly subjectivistic age. The first has to do with the classical Reformed distinction between a merely speculative and a spiritual understanding of the gospel. Because he recognized that the moral or "ethical state" of the soul determines the quality of both perception and conception, Warfield maintained that there is "a shallower and a deeper sense of the word 'knowledge'—a purely intellectualistic sense, and a sense that involves the whole man and all his activities."[70] While he conceded that all moral agents are religious beings because all moral agents "know God" in at least an intellectual or speculative sense, he insisted that the regenerate alone know God in a spiritual or saving sense because it is only in their souls that there is "perfect interaction" between the objective and subjective factors that impinge upon religious epistemology and underlie religious life and practice.[71] Since Warfield was convinced that saving or "real" knowledge of God involves the "whole soul" and as such "is inseparable from movements of piety towards Him,"[72] it is clear that the charge of rationalism cannot be sustained, simply because in his thought there is more to a saving apprehension of revealed truth than the merely rational appropriation of objective evidence.

If Warfield's "intellectualism" was inspired, on the one hand, by the desire to safeguard the enduring significance of the distinction between a merely speculative and a spiritual understanding of the gospel, it was driven, on the other, by the prospect of upholding the

70. B. B. Warfield, "Theology a Science," in *SSW*, 2:210.
71. Warfield, "Authority, Intellect, Heart," in *SSW*, 2:669; cf. Warfield, "Review of *De Zekerheid des Geloofs*," in *SSW*, 2:115ff.
72. Warfield, "Calvin's Doctrine of the Knowledge of God," 37. For more on how objective and subjective factors are related in "sound religion" and "true religious thinking," and on how there is a symbiotic relationship between religion and theology because of the unitary operation of the soul, see Warfield, "Authority, Intellect, Heart," in *SSW*, 2:668–71; Warfield, "Theology a Science," in *SSW*, 2:210; Andrew Hoffecker, "Benjamin B. Warfield," in *The Princeton Theology*, ed. David Wells, 67.

foundational principle of Augustinian and Reformed piety, namely, that "it is God and God alone who saves, and that in every element of the saving process."[73] Whereas the vast majority of Warfield's contemporaries reduced the Christian religion to a natural phenomenon by bending Scripture "into some sort of conciliation" with the latest pronouncements of modern science, philosophy, and scholarship,[74] Warfield championed both the objective basis of Christian faith and the absolute sovereignty of God in salvation by grounding the gift of saving faith in the ability to reason "rightly." "Christianity is not," he argued, "a distinctive interpretation of a religious experience common to all men, much less is it an indeterminate and constantly changing interpretation of a religious experience common to men; it is a distinctive religious experience begotten in men by a distinctive body of facts known only to or rightly apprehended only by Christians."[75] Since Warfield was convinced that the act of saving faith is a "moral act and the gift of God" as well as an act with "cognizable ground in right reason,"[76] we must conclude that he was neither an overt nor a covert rationalist who undermined the sovereignty of God in salvation by emptying saving faith of its subjective and experiential components. Rather, he was a consistently Reformed scholar who recognized that because the operation of the intellect involves the "whole soul" rather than the rational faculty alone, the "taste for the divine" that informs the ability to reason "rightly" and leads to the fulfillment of faith in the movement of trust "cannot be awakened in unbelievers by the natural action of the Scriptures or any rational arguments whatever, but requires for its production the work of the Spirit of God *ab extra accidens*."[77]

Given Warfield's clear stand within the epistemological mainstream of Reformed orthodoxy, what, then, are we to make of his apologetical response to the modern era's relocation of the divine-human nexus? What are we to make, in other words, of his apologetical appeal to "right reason"? An important indication of how we should approach

---

73. B. B. Warfield, *The Plan of Salvation* (Philadelphia: Presbyterian Board of Publications, 1915), 59.
74. B. B. Warfield, "Heresy and Concession," in *SSW*, 2:675.
75. Warfield, review of *Foundations*, 325–26.
76. B. B. Warfield, "Apologetics," in *Studies in Theology*, 15.
77. Warfield, "Calvin's Doctrine of the Knowledge of God," 124 n. 99.

this question is suggested by Warfield's definition of the term "apologetics." Whereas "apologies" are defenses of Christianity "against either all assailants, actual or conceivable, or some particular form or instance of attack," "apologetics" is "a positive and constructive science" that undertakes "not the defense, not even the vindication, but the establishment . . . of that knowledge of God which Christianity professes to embody and seeks to make efficient in the world."[78] While "apologies" thus derive their value from that which is incidental to the propagation of the Christian religion, namely, the defense of Christianity against "opposing points of view," "apologetics" is of the essence of propagation because it

> finds its deepest ground . . . not in the accidents which accompany the efforts of true religion to plant, sustain, and propagate itself in this world . . . but in the fundamental needs of the human spirit. If it is incumbent on the believer to be able to give a reason for the faith that is in him, it is impossible for him to be a believer without a reason for the faith that is in him; and it is the task of apologetics to bring this reason out in his consciousness and make its validity plain.[79]

When we approach Warfield's appeal to "right reason" with the positive and constructive nature of apologetics in mind, it becomes immediately clear that whatever we make of the appeal must give due consideration to the inherently offensive orientation of the apologetical task. It is this realization, then, that brings us to a critical interpretive juncture. Is the appeal that plays a "primary" role in "the Christianizing of the world" addressed to the regenerated reason of the Christian apologist, that is, to the individual who is laboring to establish the "objective validity" of the gospel of Christ?[80] Or, is the appeal addressed to the potential targets of apologetical science, unbelievers

---

78. Warfield, "Apologetics," 3.
79. Ibid., 4, 15. The apologist must validate the truth that has been established simply because faith, though it is a moral act and the gift of God, "is yet formally conviction passing into confidence." Validation is necessary, therefore, because an intellectual conviction of the truth of the Christian religion is "the logical *prius* of self-commitment to the Founder of that religion." Warfield, "Review of *De Zekerheid des Geloofs*," in *SSW*, 2:113.
80. Warfield, "Introduction to Francis R. Beattie's *Apologetics*," in *SSW*, 2:99.

who are analyzing the grounds of faith that are being established by the Christian apologist? Whereas the consensus of critical opinion would have us believe that the appeal to "right reason" is an appeal "to the *natural man's* 'right reason' to judge of the truth of Christianity,"[81] our analysis of the relationship between the objective and subjective components of Warfield's religious epistemology suggests a different conclusion. We have seen that the ability to reason "rightly" presupposes the regenerating activity of the Holy Spirit on the "whole soul" of a moral agent, simply because the soul is a single unit that acts in all of its functions as a single substance. When we interpret the appeal to "right reason" in this light, it follows that the appeal was not an invitation to unbelieving minds to judge of the truth of Christianity. It was, rather, a call to "the men of the palingenesis" to establish the integrity of "the Christian view of the world" by urging their "'stronger and purer thought' continuously, and in all its details, upon the attention of men."[82] This interpretation not only does justice to the context of the appeal,[83] but more importantly it explains why Warfield could insist that the Christian religion will "*reason* its way to the dominion of the world"[84] without being a "rather bald rationalist."

81. Jack Rogers, "Van Til and Warfield on Scripture in the Westminster Confession," in *Jerusalem and Athens: Critical Discussions on the Philosophy and Apologetics of Cornelius Van Til*, ed. E. R. Geehan (Nutley, N.J.: Presbyterian and Reformed, 1971), 154.

82. Warfield, "Introduction to Francis R. Beattie's *Apologetics*," in *SSW*, 2:102–3, 100–102. While Warfield acknowledged that there "do exist . . . 'two kinds of men' in the world" who give us "two kinds of science," he insisted that the difference between the science of the regenerate and the science of the unregenerate is not "a difference in *kind*," but a difference in "perfection of performance." The science of the regenerate is of a higher quality than that of the unregenerate, he argued, not because it is "a different kind of science that [the regenerate] are producing," but because the entrance of regeneration produces "the better scientific outlook" and thereby "prepares men to build [the edifice of truth] better and ever more truly as the effects of regeneration increase intensively and extensively" (100–102). For a more extensive discussion of this point, please see the next chapter.

83. Just as the soldier in combat appeals to his sword as the means to advancing the objectives of the commander in chief, so too the Christian apologist appeals to his "right reason" as the means to bringing the "thinking world" into subjection to the gospel of Christ. To conceive of "right reason" as anything other than the offensive weapon of the Christian apologist—for instance, as the "self-established intellectual tool" of the autonomous natural man (Cornelius Van Til, "My Credo," in *Jerusalem and Athens*, 11)—is to fundamentally misconstrue the word picture being painted in the context of the appeal. It is to make Warfield guilty, moreover, of reducing the Christian religion to a natural phenomenon, and of endorsing what he elsewhere describes as "autosoterism." Cf. B. B. Warfield, "How to Get Rid of Christianity," in *SSW*, 1:60.

84. Warfield, "Review of *De Zekerheid des Geloofs*," in *SSW*, 2:120.

In short, Warfield was convinced that the Christian religion will bring the "thinking world"[85] into subjection to the gospel of Christ not because he had "unbounded confidence in the apologetic power of the rational appeal to people of common sense,"[86] but because he recognized that "the Christian view of the world" is true and capable of vindication "in the forum of pure reason" through the superior science of redeemed thought.[87]

> The Christian, by virtue of the palingenesis working in him, stands undoubtedly on an indefinitely higher plane of thought than that occupied by sinful man as such. And he must not decline, but use and press the advantage which God has thus given him. He must insist, and insist again, that his determinations, and not those of the unilluminated, must be built into the slowly rising fabric of human science. Thus will he serve, if not his own generation, yet truly all the generations of men.[88]

Conclusion: B. B. Warfield and the Task of Apologetics

This chapter has challenged the prevailing historiographical consensus by interpreting Warfield's "intellectualism" in a fashion that is compatible with the anthropological and epistemological assumptions of the Reformed tradition.[89] Whereas the consensus of critical opinion would have us believe that Warfield was a rationalist who accommodated the assumptions of Enlightenment philosophy, this chapter has demonstrated that no such conclusion can be justified, simply because Warfield's "intellectualism" was moral rather than merely rational. This is historically significant not only because it

85. Ibid.

86. George Marsden, *Fundamentalism and American Culture: The Shaping of Twentieth-Century Evangelicalism 1870–1925* (New York: Oxford University Press, 1980), 115.

87. Warfield, "Introduction to Francis R. Beattie's *Apologetics*," in *SSW*, 2:103.

88. Ibid. Thus, the efforts of the apologist are not directed toward arguing the unregenerate into the kingdom of God, but toward establishing the "objective validity" of "the Christian view of the world." The apologetical task, therefore, is focused primarily on the labor of the apologist, and only secondarily on the mind of the unregenerate.

89. For a substantial challenge to the historiographical consensus, see Kim Riddlebarger's outstanding dissertation, "The Lion of Princeton: Benjamin Breckinridge Warfield on Apologetics, Theological Method and Polemics" (Ph.D. diss., Fuller Theological Seminary, 1997).

neutralizes the rather tenuous claim that Warfield and his colleagues at Old Princeton gave the back of their collective hand to the subjective and experiential components of religious epistemology,[90] but also because it gives us a clear understanding of why Warfield engaged in the task of apologetics. While Warfield acknowledged that "rational arguments can of themselves produce nothing more than 'historical faith,'" he nonetheless insisted that "historical faith" is "of no little use in the world" because what the Holy Spirit does in the new birth is not to work "a ready-made faith, rooted in nothing and clinging without reason to its object," but "to give to a faith which naturally grows out of the proper grounds of faith, that peculiar quality which makes it saving faith."[91] Since the Holy Spirit "does not produce faith without grounds,"[92] it follows that Warfield engaged in apologetics not to argue the unregenerate into the kingdom of God, but to facilitate their engagement in the most basic activity of human existence, namely, reaction to the truth of God that is reflected into their souls. As Andrew Hoffecker has incisively argued, the underlying assumption of this approach to apologetics is, of course, that the Spirit—who blows where he wills—will enable the elect to see revealed truth for what it objectively is, thereby rendering certain their saving response to the truth.[93]

---

90. For example, see Daniel B. Wallace, "Who's Afraid of the Holy Spirit?" *Christianity Today* (September 12, 1994): 38; Sandeen, "The Princeton Theology," 307–19.

91. Warfield, "Review of *De Zekerheid des Geloofs*," in *SSW*, 2:115; cf. Warfield, "Calvin's Doctrine of the Knowledge of God," 124–25 n. 99; Andrew Hoffecker, *Piety and the Princeton Theologians* (Phillipsburg, N.J.: Presbyterian and Reformed / Grand Rapids: Baker, 1981), 101–3, 108–9.

92. Warfield, "Review of *De Zekerheid des Geloofs*," in *SSW*, 2:115.

93. Cf. Hoffecker, *Piety and the Princeton Theologians*, 109; Warfield, "Introduction to Francis R. Beattie's *Apologetics*," in *SSW*, 2:99.

❧ 3 ❧

Old Princeton, Westminster, and Inerrancy

Moisés Silva

Warm devotion to the Reformed faith. Noble aggressiveness in the defense of historical orthodoxy. Emphasis on the exegesis of the original languages of Scripture. Commitment to the blending of piety and intellect. Willingness to engage opposing viewpoints with scholarly courtesy and integrity. These and other qualities combined to give Princeton Theological Seminary, from its inception through the 1920s, a powerful distinctiveness in the ecclesiastical and academic worlds. It was this distinctiveness that the founders of Westminster Theological Seminary sought to preserve when the new institution was established in 1929.

We would betray the genius of this tradition if we were to identify any one issue as all-important or determinative. And yet, given the historical contexts that brought Princeton into new prominence in the late nineteenth century and that brought Westminster into existence half a century ago, one must fully acknowledge the unique role played by the doctrine of inerrancy as that doctrine has been understood by

This essay was originally a lecture delivered by the author upon his inauguration as professor of New Testament at Westminster Theological Seminary, February 19, 1985. In revised form, the lecture was published in the *Westminster Theological Journal* 50 (1988): 65–80, and it is reproduced here with some minor changes.

its best exponents, most notably B. B. Warfield. It may be an exaggeration, but only a mild one, to say that the infallibility of Scripture, with its implications, has provided Westminster's *raison d'être*. Indeed, as far as the present faculty is concerned, we would sooner pack up our books than abandon our conviction that the Scriptures are truly God's very breath.

What I would like to stress in this chapter, however, is the definition of inerrancy implied by the words in the previous paragraph: *as that doctrine has been understood by its best exponents*. The contemporary debate regarding inerrancy appears hopelessly vitiated by the failure—in both conservative and nonconservative camps—to mark how carefully nuanced were Warfield's formulations. The heat generated by today's controversies has not always been accompanied by the expected light, and for every truly helpful statement one will easily encounter ten that blur the issues. The unfortunate result is that large numbers of writers and students assume, quite incorrectly, that their ideas about inerrancy correspond with the classic conception.

One effective way to demonstrate this point would be to conduct a survey that asked people to identify selected quotations. Take the following statement on biblical inspiration:

> It is not merely in the matter of verbal expression or literary composition that the personal idiosyncrasies of each author are freely manifested . . . , but the very substance of what they write is evidently for the most part the product of their own mental and spiritual activities. . . . [Each author of Scripture] gave evidence of his own special limitations of knowledge and mental power, and of his personal defects as well as of his powers.

Here is another one:

> [The Scriptures] are written in human languages, whose words, inflections, constructions and idioms bear everywhere indelible traces of error. The record itself furnishes evidence that the writers were in large measure dependent for their knowledge upon sources and methods in themselves fallible, and that their personal knowledge and judgments were in many matters hesitating and defective, or even wrong.

77

Where do these remarks come from? A nineteenth-century liberal like Briggs? Some recent radical theologian like Bultmann? Those words, it turns out, come from what is widely regarded as the classic formulation of biblical inerrancy by the two great Princeton theologians A. A. Hodge and B. B. Warfield.[1] Most evangelicals, I am sure, would be quite surprised to hear this. Some of them might even decide that Warfield didn't really believe the Bible after all. The situation is even worse among nonevangelical writers, very few of whom would be able to understand that the quotations above are indeed consistent with a belief in inerrancy.

This widespread ignorance works to the detriment of the doctrine. For example, when modern conservative scholars seek to nuance the discussion, they are more often than not accused of putting the doctrine to death through a thousand qualifications. Indeed, these scholars are perceived as backpedaling on their commitment to inerrancy and redefining its boundaries more or less after the fact—as though they were making up the rules as they go along. Sadly, that assessment is accurate enough in certain cases, and one can fully understand (and even share) the concern expressed in some quarters.

The passages quoted above, however, should make it plain that, in its original form, the Princetonian doctrine was carefully qualified, and that contemporary scholars who do the same are not necessarily undermining inerrancy but possibly preserving it. The common conception of Warfield is that he came up with a "deductive" approach to inspiration that did not take into account the phenomena of Scripture. Such an approach would in any case have been unlikely when one considers Warfield's expertise in the fine points of textual criticism and exegesis,[2] and our two quotations leave no doubt that the common view is a grotesque misconception. Similarly, it makes little

---

1. A. A. Hodge and B. B. Warfield, *Inspiration* (1881; repr. Grand Rapids: Baker, 1979), 12–13, 28. Interestingly, the second quotation was attacked at the time of publication as reflecting a lowered view of inspiration. Cf. Warfield's responses, included as appendices 1 and 2 in *Inspiration*, 73–82.

2. Warfield became a member of the Society of Biblical Literature and Exegesis as early as 1882 and contributed a number of technical articles to the *Journal of Biblical Literature* and other periodicals. One interesting example is "Notes on the *Didache*," *JBL* (June 1886): 86–98. For other material, see John E. Meeter and Roger Nicole, *A Bibliography of Benjamin Breckinridge Warfield 1851–1921* (Nutley, N.J.: Presbyterian and Reformed, 1974).

sense to accuse modern evangelical scholars of (a) being insensitive to the text if they happen to believe in inerrancy, or (b) being untrue to inerrancy if they take fully into account the human qualities of Scripture.

Before proceeding any further, however, it is crucial to point out that the two passages quoted above cannot be taken, by themselves, as an adequate representation of the Hodge/Warfield view. The whole thesis of their famous work is that the Bible, whose primary author is God, teaches no errors. That thesis is the broad context necessary to understand their qualifications. One can easily imagine how some contemporaries who wish to preserve their identity as evangelicals while abandoning the doctrine of inerrancy might gleefully inscribe those two quotations on their personal banners and announce to the world their solidarity with Warfield.

But that is hardly fair to the Old Princeton theology. Indeed, it would constitute one more example of the kind of shoddy use of sources that got us into our present confusion to begin with. Writers (liberals and conservatives) who like to quote Warfield's strongest expressions of inerrancy without paying attention to the nuances that accompany them are no worse than individuals who look for the qualifications alone and ignore the very thesis that is being qualified.

Without seeking to exegete those two quotations, we should at least identify the basic qualification that the authors have in view, namely, the need to distinguish between official teaching and personal opinion. Elsewhere Warfield stated that such a distinction

> seems, in general, a reasonable one. No one is likely to assert infallibility for the apostles in aught else than in their official teaching. And whatever they may be shown to have held apart from their official teaching, may readily be looked upon with only that respect which we certainly must accord to the opinions of men of such exceptional intellectual and spiritual insight. . . . A presumption may be held to lie also that [Paul] shared the ordinary opinions of his day in certain matters lying outside the scope of his teachings, as, for example, with reference to the form of the earth, or its relation to the sun; and it is not inconceivable that the form of his language, when incidentally

adverting to such matters, might occasionally play into the hands of such a presumption.[3]

Warfield did not mean, of course, that every chapter of the Bible may well contain erroneous personal opinions and that we are left to our subjective judgment regarding the authoritative character of each proposition. Such an interpretation of Warfield's words would be a complete travesty. What he surely had in view was the occasional occurrence of certain forms of expression, such as conventional phrases, that *reflect* commonly held views regarding history, nature, and so on.

Inspiration does not convey omniscience, and since the personal limitations of any one biblical writer are not all miraculously suspended by virtue of his being inspired, we may expect to see here and there some evidences that he was indeed a limited human being. The marvel of inspiration resides precisely in this fact, that the divine origin of Scripture ensures the preservation of both the divine truth being communicated and the unique personality of each writer. The Holy Spirit, in other words, prevents the authors from teaching falsehood or error without overriding their personal traits.

Warfield's distinction between the "official teaching" of Paul and those "matters lying outside the scope of his teachings" is exceedingly important for our concerns. In effect, it forces us to consider the thorny issue of authorial purpose or intention.[4] And this issue in turn reminds us of the crucial role that exegesis must play in our discussion. Not everything found in the Scriptures is actually affirmed or taught by the biblical authors (e.g., "There is no God," Ps. 14:1). The text must therefore be studied so that we can determine what it teaches. Such is the task in view when we say that we must identify the author's intent. To put it simply, we must figure out what the writer wishes to communicate. Unfortunately, the words *intention* and *pur-*

3. B. B. Warfield, *The Inspiration and Authority of the Bible* (Philadelphia: Presbyterian and Reformed, 1948), 196–97. The passage comes from an article, "The Real Problem of Inspiration," originally published in the *Presbyterian and Reformed Review* 4 (1893): 177–221.

4. One issue that cannot detain us here, however, is the distinction among such factors as divine meaning, author's meaning, audience meaning, and so on. I must assume that the readers of this essay recognize the primary importance of ascertaining the original historical meaning of a document (whatever credence they may or may not give to the possibility of additional meanings intended by God or read into the text by later readers).

pose have become veritable shibboleths in the contemporary debate. Some writers, in fact, argue that the appeal to intention undermines biblical authority.[5]

Their concern is understandable, since these terms are a little vague. A theologian, for instance, may have in mind the broad purpose of Scripture and argue that, while the Bible could be full of errors, yet it is infallible in its explicit teachings about salvation. Again, another writer may suggest that the intention of the biblical author is a psychological element behind the text and to be distinguished from the text—a position reminiscent of the old argument that it is the thoughts, not the words, of Scripture that are inspired and infallible. These and comparable formulations are indeed destructive of biblical authority and must be rejected.[6]

It would be a grave mistake, however, if we allowed these abuses to force us into the indefensible position of denying the crucial exegetical role played by an author's intention, for this is the fundamental element of the principle of *sensus literalis*. Grammatico-historical exegesis is simply the attempt to figure out what the biblical writer, under divine guidance, was saying. The basic question is then, What did the author mean? The only evidence we have to answer that question is the text

5. Nelson Kloosterman, for example, speaks pejoratively of those who "hold to a Bible whose authority is limited by the human author's intentions, intentions which can presumably be exposed and defended by a certain kind of theological scholarship." Nelson Kloosterman, "Why You Need Mid-America Theological Seminary," *The Outlook* 31, no. 12 (December 1981): 3. Similarly, Harold Lindsell, in *The Battle for the Bible* (Grand Rapids: Zondervan, 1976), makes the same point repeatedly. Even Lindsell, of course, finds it necessary to appeal to the concept of intention, as in his discussion of the parable of the mustard seed: "The *American Commentary* says of this passage that it was popular language, and it was the intention of the speaker to communicate the fact that the mustard seed was 'the smallest that his hearers were accustomed to sow.' And indeed this may well be the case. In that event there was no error" (169).

6. Norman L. Geisler has rightly attempted to discredit these approaches in "The Relation of Purpose and Meaning in Interpreting Scripture," *Grace Theological Journal* 5 (1984): 229–45. Unfortunately, Geisler draws too sharp a distinction between meaning and purpose. Determining the purpose of a text is one of the elements necessary to identify the context of the document. On p. 231 Geisler attacks interpreters of Gen. 1–2 who believe that those chapters intend merely to draw men to worship God. Geisler seems unaware that his own understanding of those chapters (with which I concur) also assumes a certain purpose, namely, the intent to state certain historical facts. Cf. these comments by Hodge and Warfield: "No objection [to inspiration] is valid . . . which overlooks the prime question: What was the professed or implied purpose of the writer in making this statement? . . . Exegesis must be historical as well as grammatical, and must always seek the meaning *intended*, not any meaning that can be tortured out of a passage." *Inspiration*, 42, 43; italics in the original.

itself. In other words, we dare not speak about the Bible's infallibility in such a way that it legitimizes random and arbitrary interpretations of the text.

Our best theologians made it clear all along that inerrancy was being claimed for the Bible on the assumption that the Bible would be interpreted responsibly, and such a proper interpretation consists in determining what the original author meant, what he intended. As Hodge and Warfield stated it: the Bible gives us "a correct statement of facts or principles intended to be affirmed. . . . Every statement accurately corresponds to truth just as far forth as affirmed."[7]

It may be useful to illustrate our problem by referring to 1 Corinthians 10:8, where Paul makes mention of 23,000 Israelites who died because of their immorality, in apparent conflict with Numbers 25:9, where the number given is 24,000. Notice the following attempt to solve the problem: "It is not unheard of, *when there is no intention* of making an exact count of individuals, to give an approximate number. . . . Moses gives the upper limits, Paul the lower."

The next quotation, though longer, seems to make the same point:

> Neither of the writers *intended to state* the exact number, this being of no consequence to their object. . . . It was not at all necessary, in order to maintain their character as men of veracity, that they should, when writing *for such a purpose*, mention the exact number. The particularity and length of the [exact] expression would have been inconvenient, and might have made a less desirable impression of the evil of sin, and the justice of God, than expressing it more briefly in a round number; as we often say, with a view merely to make a strong impression, that in such a battle ten thousand, or fifty thousand, or half a million were slain, no one supposing that we mean to state the number with arithmetical exactness, as *our object does not require this*. And who can doubt, that the divine Spirit might lead the sacred penman to make use of this principle of rhetoric, and to speak of those who were slain, according to the common practice in such a case, in round numbers?

7. Hodge and Warfield, *Inspiration*, 28–29. It is very important to note that Warfield emphasized this particular qualification when he responded to criticisms of the article (cf. 79–80).

Here is another author who takes a similar approach:

> Are there errors in the Bible? Certainly not, so long as we are talking in terms *of the purpose of its authors* and the acceptable standards of precision of that day. . . . *For the purpose* that Paul had in mind [the variation] made no difference. His concern was to warn against immorality, not to give a flawless performance in statistics.

All three of these writers seem concerned to deny that the apostle is guilty of an error, yet none of them attempts some artificial harmonization (for example, the view that Paul is speaking about those who fell "in one day," while Numbers includes the additional 1,000 who died later). Moreover, all three of them assume that inerrancy does not necessarily demand mathematical exactness. Finally, all of them appeal to Paul's intention or purpose to use a round number. I am unable to see any substantive difference among these three explanations.

The three authors quoted above happen to be John Calvin, the nineteenth-century American theologian Leonard Wood (one of the most forceful defenders of biblical inerrancy prior to B. B. Warfield), and our contemporary Robert H. Mounce.[8] My reason for bringing these three quotations together is to point out that Harold Lindsell quotes the third of those statements as evidence that Mounce does not believe in inerrancy, yet a few pages later he presents the quote from Calvin as giving an acceptable treatment of the problem![9] It may be that the tone of Mounce's brief article (it sounds as though the author is apologizing for the evangelical view) led Lindsell to believe that Mounce had indeed rejected the doctrine of inerrancy. It is impossible, however, to prove that point from the quotation above—or, for that matter, from the other statements by Mounce to which Lindsell refers.

In any case, we can see clearly how easy it is to misconstrue qualifying statements, even when the qualification in view is very much a

---

8. John Calvin, *The First Epistle of Paul the Apostle to the Corinthians* (Grand Rapids: Eerdmans, 1961), 208–9; Leonard Wood, *The Works of Leonard Wood, D.D.*, 5 vols. (Boston: Congregational Board of Publications, 1854), 1:173; Robert H. Mounce, "Clues to Understanding Biblical Accuracy," *Eternity* 17, 6 (June 1966): 18. (The italics are mine, except for the phrase *for such a purpose* in the second quotation.) In connection with Wood, note the very helpful discussion of pre-Warfield inerrantists by Randall H. Balmer, "The Princetonians and Scripture: A Reconsideration," *Westminster Theological Journal* 44 (1982): 352–65.

9. Lindsell, *Battle for the Bible*, 168.

part of the evangelical tradition. In short, the appeal to the author's intent, if properly understood, is an integral element in the classical affirmations of biblical inerrancy. And the reason is, if I may repeat myself, that we cannot claim to know what the Scripture infallibly teaches unless we have done our exegetical homework.

Our discussion so far has made it apparent that one can hardly speak of inerrancy without getting involved in hermeneutics. And yet, an exceedingly important caveat is necessary here, for while the two concepts are closely related or even inseparable, they are also distinct. For inerrancy to function properly in our use of Scripture, an adequate hermeneutics is a prerequisite. But that is a far cry from suggesting that the doctrine of inerrancy automatically provides us with the correct hermeneutics, except in the rather general sense that it precludes any interpretation that makes out God to lie or to err.

A few examples will clarify the issue. As recently as two decades ago it was not unusual to come across devout Christians who were persuaded that, when interpreting prophecy, a premillennialist eschatology was the only approach consistent with the doctrine of infallibility. For many of these brethren—of whom a few remain, I am sure—a so-called literal interpretation of prophetic passages was taken as evidence, maybe even as the most important piece of evidence, that an individual believed the Bible; and it was taken for granted that amillennialists, therefore, were "liberals." But such an equation is baseless, since the doctrine of inerrancy does not determine that any one prophecy (or set of prophecies) must be interpreted "literally." That can be determined only by an exegesis of the passage(s) in question.

Let's take a more disturbing example: the historicity of Genesis 1–3. All inerrantists, so far as I know, believe in the factual character of that material. This state of affairs creates a certain presumption that inerrancy *by itself* demands such an interpretation. But the presumption is false; indeed, it is an equivocation. The doctrine of biblical infallibility no more requires that narratives be interpreted "literally" than it requires that prophetic passages be interpreted "literally." That decision must be arrived at by textual evidence and exegetical argument.

Now I happen to believe that the essential historicity of Genesis 1–3 is a fundamental article of Christian orthodoxy. It would surely require hermeneutical prestidigitation to argue that the original writer meant those chapters to be taken as "less historical" than the later patriarchal narratives (and could the original audience have discovered any such distinction between the early and the later chapters of the book?). For that reason and others, such as Paul's argumentation in Romans 5 and 1 Corinthians 15, I would want to argue very strongly that the proper interpretation of the Genesis material is one that does justice to its historical claim.

And yet I would want to argue just as strongly that such an interpretation is independent of my commitment to inerrancy. These are two distinct questions. Of course, once we have established exegetically that the first three chapters of Genesis teach historical facts, then our belief in infallibility requires us to accept those chapters as factual. But infallibility, apart from exegesis, does not by itself determine historicity. Otherwise we would be obligated to accept as historical Nathan's story in 2 Samuel 12:1–4 or even the parable of the trees in Judges 9:7–15.

I have deliberately chosen my two examples from polar opposites. Relatively few evangelicals would argue that inerrancy entails premillennialism, but many seem ready to argue that it does require a historical interpretation of Genesis 1–3. Between these two extremes are countless interpretations that have traditionally been held by conservatives and that are viewed as necessary consequences of accepting biblical infallibility. It may therefore prove worthwhile pointing out that the Princeton/Westminster tradition, though it has stood forcefully and unequivocally for biblical inerrancy, has never degenerated into the practice of assuming, apart from exegetical demonstration, that this doctrine requires the adoption of particular interpretations.

My first example comes from the area of the relationship between the Bible and science. Students familiar with Warfield's writings are well aware of his positive attitude toward modern scientific theories regarding origins. Though it is a little difficult to determine specifically Warfield's position, it appears that his view came relatively close to what we call theistic evolution (without compromising, to be sure, the direct creation of man).[10] J. Gresham Machen, in sharp contrast

10. Cf. Mark A. Noll, *The Princeton Theology, 1812–1921: Scripture, Science and Theological Method from Archibald Alexander to Benjamin Breckinridge Warfield* (Grand Rapids: Baker, 1983), 289, 293–94.

with the fundamentalism of his day, refused to become involved in the evolution controversy.[11] More recently, Meredith G. Kline proposed an interpretation of Genesis 1 that parted company with traditional views. Kline's colleague on the Westminster faculty, E. J. Young, took issue with that interpretation, but at no point in his argument did he accuse Kline of abandoning the doctrine of infallibility. Nor did Young simply assume that such a doctrine entailed the traditional view of Genesis but rather sought to refute Kline through careful exegetical argumentation.[12]

A second example has to do with higher criticism. This is one area, it must be admitted, where a belief in inerrancy appears to have a direct bearing on interpretation. If the author of a New Testament epistle, for example, claims to be the apostle Paul, we would be questioning the moral integrity of the author if we were to argue that the letter was not in fact written by Paul. Yet this set of questions too has to be decided on exegetical grounds, and not on the assumption that inerrancy entails a traditional view of authorship, date, and so forth. It is no secret that E. J. Young, who was uncompromisingly conservative on virtually every higher-critical issue, came to the conclusion that the book of Ecclesiastes was not composed by Solomon, even though that appears to be the claim of the book itself.[13] Professor Young was among the most conservative in the long line of biblical scholars at Old Princeton and Westminster. It is doubly significant, therefore, that he did not apparently see a necessary connection between a belief in inerrancy and the traditional view of Solomonic authorship for Ecclesiastes.

A third and particularly instructive example is the way different writers approach the difficult problem of gospel harmonization. Take the story of the rich young ruler. According to Mark 10:17–18 and Luke 18:18–19, this ruler addressed Jesus as "Good Teacher" and asked what he could do to inherit eternal life; Jesus replied, "Why do

11. See Ned B. Stonehouse, *J. Gresham Machen: A Biographical Memoir* (Grand Rapids: Eerdmans, 1954) 401–2.

12. E. J. Young, *Studies in Genesis One* (Philadelphia: Presbyterian and Reformed, 1964) 58–64.

13. E. J. Young, *An Introduction to the Old Testament* (Grand Rapids: Eerdmans, 1949), 340. The revised 1964 edition omits the strongest paragraph, but it is clear that his position had not changed (even though not a few feathers had been ruffled by it).

you call me good?" In Matthew 19:16–17, however, the word "good" is transferred to the man's actual question ("Teacher, what good thing shall I do. . . ?") and so Jesus' rebuke takes a different form: "Why do you ask me about the good?" Our first quotation seeks to solve the problem by incorporating both versions into one account:

> In all probability, the full question was, "Good teacher, what good thing shall I do that I may possess eternal life?" To this the complete answer of the Lord may have been, "Why callest thou Me good and why askest thou Me concerning that which is good?" . . . No one of the evangelists, however, has seen fit to give the complete question or the complete answer.

The second quotation reflects quite a different approach:

> One must allow for the possibility that Matthew in his formulation of 19:16, 17 has *not only been selective* as regards subject matter but also that he used some freedom in the precise language which he employed. The singular use of the adjective "good" might then be a particularly clear example of his use of that freedom. . . . One tendency [in the history of the harmonization of the Gospels], that is both conservative and simple, has been to join divergent features and to seek to weave them together into a harmonious whole. Where, however, the divergent elements are exceedingly difficult to combine in that way, it is insisted that the narratives must be regarded as reporting different events or different sayings. . . . There is, in my judgment, a sounder attitude to most problems of harmonization than that which was characterized above as conservative and simple.

Neither of these writers is against harmonization in principle, but they differ rather substantially in what they consider necessary to defend the integrity of the narrative. One could certainly argue that the second writer is directly reacting against the viewpoint espoused by the first. Remarkably, these two passages were written by contemporaries on the Westminster faculty. The first one comes from E. J. Young's famous work on inerrancy, published in the late 1950s, while the second statement was written just a few years later by Ned B. Stonehouse.[14] One is intrigued by the question of whether Stonehouse remembered Young's discussion; if so, was he deliberately distancing himself from that approach? In any case, the differences are most instructive.

What shall we infer from these examples?[15] Should evangelical scholars be insulated from criticism if they appear to be bucking historic Christian tenets without clear biblical support? Far from it. The Princeton/Westminster tradition has consistently deepened the evangelical conception of biblical authority within the framework of Reformed orthodoxy. No doubt, some may wish to appeal to the disagreements described above and argue that, therefore, "anything goes"—that the increasingly positive attitude toward higher criticism by a number of contemporary evangelical scholars is quite consistent with the doctrine of inerrancy. Such a move would hardly be honest, however, especially when one considers that the Princetonian formulations of inerrancy were meant precisely to counteract the growing popularity of nineteenth-century critical theories. What then can we learn from the history we have briefly surveyed?

The hermeneutical flexibility that has characterized our tradition would probably come as a surprise to many observers who view Westminster as excessively rigid. Ironically, our confessional documents, the Westminster Confession and Catechisms, are far more extensive and detailed than those found in most evangelical institutions. Our theological parameters are indeed very clearly defined, and yet those parameters themselves have made possible a diversity of viewpoints that would not have been tolerated in some other institutions.

14. E. J. Young, *Thy Word Is Truth: Some Thoughts on the Biblical Doctrine of Inspiration* (Grand Rapids: Eerdmans, 1957), 131; Ned B. Stonehouse, *Origins of the Synoptic Gospels: Some Basic Questions* (Grand Rapids: Eerdmans, 1963), 108–9, my emphasis. Warfield's own approach, which seems close to Young's, may be found in B. B. Warfield, *The Person and Work of Christ* (Philadelphia: Presbyterian and Reformed, 1950), 160: "It lies in the nature of the case that the two accounts of a conversation which agree as to the substance of what was said, but differ slightly in the details reported, are reporting different fragments of the conversation, selected according to the judgment of each writer as the best vehicles of its substance."

15. Other intriguing examples of diversity could be mentioned. Particularly important (because of its relation to the field of ethics) is the case of Paul Woolley, professor of church history, who took a rather "liberal" position on a wide variety of social and political issues. On many questions of this sort Professor Woolley stood alone or nearly alone within the Westminster faculty, but to the best of my knowledge his devotion and commitment to biblical authority was never called into question.

It can even be argued, I think, that there is a direct connection between such a diversity and the fact that the Princeton/Westminster tradition has provided consistent leadership to the evangelical world in the area of biblical authority. Why is this so? The doctrine of infallibility assures us that we can have total confidence in God's revelation to us. It does not mean, however, that we may have total confidence in our particular interpretations of the Bible.

For many believers, unfortunately, assurance that the Bible is true appears to be inseparable from assurance about traditional interpretive positions, so that if we question the latter we seem to be doubting the former. George E. Ladd is absolutely right when he states:

> "Thus saith the Lord" means that God has spoken His sure, infallible Word. A corollary of this in the minds of many Christians is that we must have absolute, infallible answers to every question raised in the historical study of the Bible. . . . This conclusion, as logical and persuasive as it may seem, does not square with the facts of God's Word; . . . the authority of the Word of God is not dependent upon infallible certainty in all matters of history and criticism.[16]

I do not know to what extent Ladd agrees or disagrees with Warfield's position, but this quotation is perfectly consistent with it; more to the point, Ladd's qualification belongs to the very essence of the classical doctrine of inerrancy. Yet—inexplicably—Lindsell quotes those words as evidence that Ladd has abandoned biblical infallibility.[17]

Uncertainty is not a pleasant thing, and our instinct to avoid it can lead us into trouble. Concerned not to leave the door open to excesses, we are tempted to raise artificial barriers. But this medicine can be worse than the disease. I mention these things because there is a strong current of opinion in evangelical circles that says we need to tie inerrancy down to certain hermeneutical boundary lines. But to speak in this way is once again to increase the conceptual confusion. It is of course true that a commitment to inerrancy entails that we

---

16. George E. Ladd, *The New Testament and Criticism* (Grand Rapids: Eerdmans, 1967), 16–17.

17. Lindsell, *Battle for the Bible*, 114. In fairness to Lindsell, I should point out that Ladd's language (in the larger section from which the quotation is taken) does not seem designed to inspire confidence in biblical infallibility.

will believe such interpretations as are clearly demonstrable from the scriptural text, but inerrancy does not automatically settle interpretive debates, such as the mode of baptism, the doctrine of unconditional election, the practice of charismatic gifts, and so on.

Many evangelicals have awakened to the fact that belief in inerrancy does not ensure acceptance of traditional positions, and several recent writers have emphasized the wide and significant disagreements that exist within the evangelical community. Some infer, not surprisingly, that the doctrine of inerrancy is of little value for Christian living and should therefore be given up. Conservatives then tend to overreact and argue that we need to define inerrancy in such a way as to guarantee that evangelicals will agree on important issues.[18]

Nothing could be more wrong-headed. Forced hermeneutical unanimity is meaningless; worse, it would be destructive of biblical authority. To say that the doctrine of inerrancy demands acceptance of a particular interpretation is to raise human opinion to the level of divine infallibility; in such a case, said interpretation cannot be questioned and need not be defended. On the other hand, to acknowledge a measure of interpretive ambiguity, rattling though that may be, indicates our conviction that the Bible, and the Bible alone, is inerrant. To be sure, the Christian church may and must condemn hermeneutical approaches as well as specific interpretations that contradict the teaching of Scripture. But the point is this: the church cannot simply appeal to the infallibility of the Bible. The church is obligated to show persuasively that these interpretations are wrong. In short, we must exegete that infallible Bible and demonstrate that we have understood its teachings.

Perhaps it is now clear why, in my opinion, the hermeneutical flexibility that has found expression on the faculties of Old Princeton and Westminster has actually contributed to (instead of undermining) the influence these institutions have exerted with regard to the doctrine of biblical authority. Precisely because they accepted the reality of hermeneutical uncertainty, they worked especially hard to remove that uncertainty through careful exegesis.

18. I have treated this matter more extensively in Moisés Silva, *Has the Church Misread the Bible? The History of Interpretation in the Light of Current Issues* (Grand Rapids: Zondervan, 1987).

It is no accident that Old Princeton and Westminster have been so obnoxious in requiring students to learn Greek and Hebrew. It was not some methodological misconception that led John Murray to teach courses in systematic theology that looked more like courses in exegesis. It was no blunder that made a Warfield or a Machen or a Stonehouse pay an enormous amount of attention to the work of liberal and radical scholars. These and other "oddities" are direct consequences of a commitment not to leave any stones unturned to find out what the Bible really says. Our whole ministry is, in its own way, a response to our Lord's penetrating criticism, "You err because you do not know the Scriptures." With Warfield we devote ourselves to the task of knowing the unerring Scriptures so that we will not err.

❧ 4 ❧

Warfield and the
Doctrine of Scripture

Raymond D. Cannata

The Church, then, has held from the beginning that the Bible is the Word of God in such a sense that its words, though written by men and bearing indelibly impressed upon them the marks of their human origin, were written, nevertheless, under such an influence of the Holy Ghost as to be also the words of God, the adequate expression of His mind and will. It is always recognized that this conception of co-authorship implies that the Spirit's superintendence extends to the choice of the words by the human authors (verbal inspiration) and preserves its product from everything inconsistent with a divine authorship—thus securing, among other things, that entire truthfulness which is everywhere presupposed in and asserted for the Scriptures by the Biblical writers (inerrancy).

—B. B. Warfield[1]

Parts of this essay were originally delivered as a lecture before the Charles Hodge Society in Princeton in 1995, and a version appeared in Dembski and Richards, eds., *Unapologetic Apologetics* (Downers Grove, Ill.: InterVarsity Press, 2001). The present essay is substantially revised and updated.

1. B. B. Warfield, *Revelation and Inspiration*, vol. 1 of *The Works of Benjamin Breckinridge Warfield* (1927; repr., Grand Rapids: Baker, 1981), 173.

On September 14, 1889, Charles Augustus Briggs, Davenport Professor of Hebrew and Cognate Languages at Union Theological Seminary in New York, caused a major stir in the church and in the academy with the publication of a new book. Simply titled *Whither?* the book was in fact a "withering" attack on Princeton Seminary and particularly the school's teaching on the doctrine of Scripture. Briggs was not one to spare anyone's feelings, but he did recognize the need to explain the seeming severity and brutality of the tone of his critique.[2] In the preface he makes clear that the stakes are so high that all means are justified. He believed that the church might be on the brink of entering a great religious Promised Land, where, in Briggs's words, "the barriers between the Protestant denominations may be removed and an organic union formed. An Alliance may be made between Protestantism and Romanism and all other branches of Christendom."[3]

Briggs felt that there was chiefly one speed bump on the straight highway leading to utopia, and this was precisely where the road cut through Princeton, New Jersey. If it had been up to him, he would have had the road built to avoid Princeton, but it was too late for that now. Briggs explains, "The theology of the elder and younger Hodge that has in fact usurped the place of the Westminster theology in the minds of a large proportion of the ministry of the Presbyterian Churches, now stands in the way of progress . . . and there is no other way of advancing truth except by removing the errors that obstruct our path."[4] Apparently the Princeton divines were somehow single-handedly responsible for delaying the coming of the millennial kingdom on earth through their poisonous influence on their followers. This being the case, they must be refuted and discredited by whatever means necessary.

Briggs was not bluffing. In the next three hundred pages he goes to such great pains that he embarrassed even his most sympathetic progressive supporters. Dripping with heavy sarcasm, he attempts to

2. Lefferts Loetscher, though clearly sympathetic with Briggs's perspective, acknowledges that in this book Briggs's "tone was so far from objective that many, including some of Briggs' friends, regretted it." Lefferts A. Loetscher, *The Broadening Church* (Philadelphia: University of Pennsylvania Press, 1964), 48.

3. Charles A. Briggs, *Whither? A Theological Question for the Times* (New York: Charles Scribner's Sons, 1889), xi.

4. Ibid., x.

lay bare every conceivable potential weakness in the Princeton doctrine of Scripture. For starters, he charges that the Princeton doctrine of full divine inspiration of Scripture left no room for the human element in its authorship. Further, its claim of the errorlessness of the Bible was being rendered progressively more absurd with each new finding of higher criticism. To evade the plain truth that our text undeniably contains errors, the Princeton divines had invented a novel theory that inspiration was guaranteed only for the original (conveniently vanished) autographs. This is a cop-out, a calculated dodge, Briggs charges. It was also ahistorical and at odds with what the saints through the ages had always taught. Most of all, such a formulation was utterly foreign to what the Bible teaches about itself. The theory does violence to the very texts it hoped to validate. Princeton had somehow "narrowed" the Westminster Confession, Briggs contends, and twisted it into a very un-Reformed caricature. He labels the Princetonians "muddy scholastics," "rationalists," "betrayers," and, ultimately, "failures." Their doctrine of infallibility had wagered the whole authority of Scripture on one proved error, and their retreat to the nonexistent "original autographs" renders our English translations of tainted copies utterly unreliable.

James McCosh, Presbyterian divine, world-renowned metaphysician, and president of Princeton College,[5] swiftly penned a firm rebuttal to Briggs's book, which he titled *Whither? O Whither? Tell Me Where.* As appreciated as this was, no doubt, the seminary did not greatly need McCosh's aid at the time. For one thing, there was no one in the English-speaking world who could surpass the massive learning, lucid pen, and sheer intellectual powers of the seminary's own B. B. Warfield.[6] And the church as a whole, including its Presbyterian variety, seemed to enjoy a fairly clear consensus on the issue. When all sides had had their say, Briggs was rebutted by the 1892 General Assembly, which passed its famous Portland Deliverance, requesting that all who denied the inerrancy of Scripture withdraw from the ministry. When Briggs went a step further in a highly inflammatory one-hundred-minute address in 1893, formal heresy charges were filed against him, soon resulting in his departure, along with Union

5. Princeton was known as the College of New Jersey prior to 1896.
6. Interestingly, Warfield co-edited *The Presbyterian Review* with Briggs for twelve years (1890 to 1902).

Seminary, from the Presbyterian church. The 1892 Assembly's pronouncements were reaffirmed each year they were reintroduced, and inerrancy was declared an "essential and necessary" article of faith at the 1910, 1917, and 1923 assemblies.

In a sense, however, Briggs has been vindicated by history. Today, sadly, the mainline Presbyterian church has overwhelmingly accepted his position on this matter. And those in the present-day church who wish to challenge the full inspiration of Scripture generally find it necessary to level basically the same charges that Briggs first outlined unsuccessfully more than a century ago.

Presbyterian scholars Donald McKim and Jack Rogers have echoed a very similar line of criticism in their book-length works on Scripture, dwelling largely on what they find deficient with Old Princeton.[7] Contemporary Princetonian Daniel Migliore contends that the teaching of scriptural infallibility can be attributed directly to a reactionary response to the "rising tide of modernity." He argues that Warfield's teachings are a Protestant version of Vatican I-style papal infallibility and became more "defensive" and "strident" over time.[8] Historian Winthrop Hudson charges that Old Princeton "attempted to keep Presbyterianism in a theological straight-jacket."[9]

Some of the most severe critics have been certain evangelicals who have embraced Princeton's intellectual rigor, its warm-hearted piety, and its academic achievements, and often even much of its Reformed dogmatics, while rejecting out of hand the doctrine of Scripture which undergirds all of these. For example, the evangelical George Marsden, while highly appreciative of nearly all other aspects of Old Princeton, contends that the Princetonians' beliefs on Scripture were "in fact built

7. See especially Jack Rogers and Donald McKim, *Authority and Interpretation of the Bible* (New York: Harper & Row, 1979), and Donald McKim, *What Christians Believe About the Bible* (Nashville: Thomas Nelson, 1985).

8. Daniel Migliore, *Faith Seeking Understanding* (Grand Rapids: Eerdmans, 1991), 44. Dr. Migliore is currently Arthur M. Adams Professor of Systematic Theology at Princeton Theological Seminary. See also Princeton's own James Barr, *Fundamentalism* (London: SCM Press, 1977), or Loetscher, *Broadening Church*.

9. Winthrop Hudson, *Religion in America* (New York: Scribner's, 1981), 167. John Oliver Nelson, formerly a trustee of Princeton Seminary, contended that the Old Princeton doctrine of Scripture leads to a "legalistic" and "impersonal" theology. See Winthrop Hudson, "Charles Hodge: Nestor of Orthodoxy," in *The Lives of Eighteen from Princeton*, ed. Willard Thorp (Princeton: Princeton University Press, 1946), 209.

on a foundation of superficial accommodation to the modern scientific revolution."[10] They were "so committed in principle to a scientifically based culture even while the scientifically based culture of the 20th century was undermining belief in the very truths of the Bible they held most dear. . . . To them, however, it might not have been obvious how hopeless their position was."[11]

Evangelicals anxious to jettison the strictures of inerrancy continue to blame Warfield for the church's woes. It has been two decades since John Woodbridge and others handily refuted Rogers and McKim's exotic thesis that Warfield essentially transformed the historic doctrine of Scripture into the theory of inerrancy.[12] But recently voices of the evangelical left such as Stanley Grenz have developed a new angle to this Rogers/McKim thesis.[13] In *Renewing the Center* (2000), Grenz admits that the Princetonians may not have altered the historic doctrine of Scripture, but charges that they exalted it from one *article* of faith into the *foundation* of the faith.[14] Grenz reflects the consensus view of the evangelical left: "We can no longer construct our doctrine of Scripture in the classical manner. The assertion of the inspiration of Scripture cannot function as the theological premise from which bibliology emerges, nor as the focal point of our understanding of the relation between Spirit and Scripture."[15] Evangelicals and liberals would seem to agree: Warfield's doctrine of Scripture is a relic best

10. George Marsden, "Collapse of American Evangelical Academia," in *Faith and Rationality*, ed. Alvin Plantinga and Nicholas Wolterstorff (Notre Dame, Ind.: University of Notre Dame Press, 1983), 241.

11. George Marsden, "Evangelicals and the Scientific Culture," in *Religion and Twentieth Century American Intellectual Life*, ed. Michael Lacey (Cambridge: Cambridge University Press, 1989), 26.

12. See D. A. Carson and John D. Woodbridge, eds., *Scripture and Truth* (Grand Rapids: Zondervan, 1983). Even anti-inerrantists such as Clark Pinnock have generally come to acknowledge that the Rogers/McKim thesis is historically inaccurate. See Pinnock, *The Scripture Principle* (San Francisco: Harper & Row, 1984), xii.

13. For a balanced critique of Grenz and the evangelical left from a mainstream evangelical perspective, see Millard J. Erickson, *The Evangelical Left: Encountering Postconservative Evangelical Theology* (Grand Rapids: Baker, 1997), or my review of this book in *Perspectives in Religious Studies* 26, 1 (Spring 1999): 79–82.

14. Stanley Grenz, *Renewing the Center: Evangelical Theology in a Post-Theological Era* (Grand Rapids: Baker, 2000), for example, 17. See D. A. Carson's critique of this book on the ModernReformation.org Web site.

15. Stanley Grenz, *Revisioning Evangelical Theology: A Fresh Agenda for the 21ˢᵗ Century* (Downers Grove, Ill.: InterVarsity Press, 1993), 116.

forgotten. So the next obvious question is, Then why in the world are we even bothering to examine this subject at all?

In preparing this essay I have learned two things by reading the secondary literature on B. B. Warfield: (1) all the critics agree that understanding Warfield on Scripture is utterly essential to understanding the contemporary debates on its authority; and (2) very few of these critics seem to have actually read much of what Warfield wrote. Contemporary Princetonian George Hunsinger has written of Karl Barth as having "achieved the dubious distinction of being habitually honored but not much read."[16] Warfield has achieved the more dubious distinction of being habitually *dis*honored and not much read. Work through contemporary textbooks of church history and of theology and practically every one will contain a page or two on Old Princeton's doctrine of Scripture, usually focusing on Warfield. Moreover, these textbooks virtually all quote the exact same clipped sound bites. Warfield penned at least two full bookshelves' worth of material, and yet it would appear from what his critics quote that all he had to say on Scripture was contained in a few sentences. A reader quickly gets the strong sense that the modern historians and theologians are not reading Warfield; they are reading what *each other* has written about Warfield.

Nonetheless, a small number of very able and gifted scholars have stepped forward in the last few years to argue forcefully that Warfield's formulations are about the most thoughtful, faithful, and relevant yet articulated by the church.[17] In fact, the remainder of this essay is simply a summary of the fine insights shared by these scholars.

Let us, then, take a closer look and judge for ourselves.

16. George Hunsinger, *How to Read Karl Barth: The Shape of His Theology* (New York: Oxford University Press, 1991), 27.

17. James M. Boice, David Calhoun, D. A. Carson, Bryan Chapell, John Frame, John Gerstner, W. Robert Godfrey, Douglas Groothius, Wayne Grudem, Carl F. H. Henry, Andrew Hoffecker, Michael Horton, Walter Kaiser, Douglas Moo, Roger Nicole, Mark Noll, Moisés Silva, James I. Packer, Richard Pratt, R. C. Sproul, John Stott, David Wells, and John Woodbridge are among contemporary churchmen who have endorsed the Old Princeton view of Scripture. The International Conference on Biblical Inerrancy's (ICBI) nineteen-article "Chicago Statement" of 1978 is basically a modern reaffirmation of the Old Princeton view as articulated by Warfield.

Warfield's Understanding of Scripture

In the definitive modern essay on Old Princeton hermeneutics, Dr. Moisés Silva cites the following statement by a prominent late-nineteenth-century biblical critic:

> It is not merely in the matter of verbal expression or literary composition that the personal idiosyncrasies of each [biblical] author are freely manifested . . . , but the very substance of what they write is evidently for the most part the product of their own mental and spiritual activities. . . . [Each author of Scripture] gave evidence of his own special limitations of knowledge and mental power, and of his personal defects.[18]

Now another:

> [The Scriptures] are written in human languages, whose words, inflections, constructions and idioms bear everywhere indelible traces of error. The record itself furnishes evidence that the writers were in large measure dependent for their knowledge upon sources and methods in themselves fallible, and that their personal knowledge and judgments were in many matters hesitating and defective, or even wrong.

Are these the words of, perhaps, Charles Briggs? Some other nineteenth-century progressive like David Swing? Harry Emerson Fosdick? No, these two passages come from the famous 1881 article titled "Inspiration" by none other than B. B. Warfield and A. A. Hodge.[19]

What the critics often miss is that Warfield's doctrine of biblical inspiration contains several subtle but key qualifications. The passages above illustrate the first one.

---

18. I was guided to this quote and several of those that follow by Moisés Silva's excellent essay titled "Old Princeton, Westminster, and Inerrancy," in *Inerrancy and Hermeneutic*, ed. Harvie M. Conn (Grand Rapids: Baker, 1988), 67–80. (This essay appears in a slightly different form as chap. 3 of the present volume.) Silva's work is by far the most helpful I found on the topic, and much of the latter portion of this essay is simply a restatement of his major themes.

19. A. A. Hodge and B. B. Warfield, "Inspiration," *Presbyterian Review* 2 (April 1881): 225–60. The largest collection of Warfield's voluminous work on the doctrine of biblical inspiration can be found in the anthology of his essays titled *The Inspiration and Authority of the Bible* (Philadelphia: Presbyterian and Reformed, 1948), which currently remains in print.

Fully Human/*Fully Divine*

Warfield consistently taught that somehow taking full account of the human qualities of Scripture does not diminish its divine qualities. Like the Word of God Incarnate (Jesus Christ), the Word of God written is fully divine and at the same time fully human, yet perfect.[20]

So what does it mean for Warfield to take the "full humanity" of the text seriously? For one thing, it means that one needs to distinguish between the official teachings of Scripture and the personal opinions of its writers. Warfield states:

> [Paul] shared the ordinary opinions of his day in certain matters laying outside the scope of his teachings, as, for example, with reference to the form of the earth, or its relation to the sun; and it is not inconceivable that the form of his language, when incidentally adverting to such matters, might occasionally play into the hands of such a presumption.[21]

Biblical passages will always reflect the historical and scientific conceptions of the human cultures in which they were written. As Silva reminds us, "Inspiration does not convey omniscience."[22] But while a passage may reflect culturally bound errors, no doubt believed incidentally by its human author, the Holy Spirit has prevented Scripture from teaching these errors, yet without doing violence to the personality of the author. Warfield is careful to separate the teaching of Paul and those "matters lying outside the scope of his teachings." This is where careful exegesis comes in. Each text must be studied for what it is actually teaching.

So, for example, if the biblical author incidentally states that in the midst of a course of events the sun was "rising over the horizon," he

20. This point is presented by J. I. Packer in *"Fundamentalism" and the Word of God* (Grand Rapids: Eerdmans, 1958). When, in the mid-1990s, I once related Scripture to Christ in this way, my systematics professor at Princeton labeled this "bibliolatry" or setting up a "fourth" person of the Trinity. But Scripture's perfection and authority is derived fully from God and is not independent of him.

21. Warfield, *The Inspiration and Authority of the Bible*, 196–97. Originally from an article titled "The Real Problem of Inspiration," *Presbyterian and Reformed Review* 4 (1893): 177–221. This is also quoted by Silva in his fine essay, "Old Princeton, Westminster, and Inerrancy."

22. Silva, "Old Princeton, Westminster, and Inerrancy," 71.

may have believed, falsely, that the earth was flat and that the sun was literally moving across the dome that encased the earth. His figure of speech may reflect that falsehood, yet it is not taught by the text. In reporting this the human author is speaking phenomenologically (as our modern weather forecasters still do), expressing the time of day, not the science of astronomy. And as one modern exponent of the Warfieldian approach states, "what Moses or the prophets . . . understood by the words they wrote down under inspiration is quite secondary to the question of what God Himself meant by those words."[23]

Likewise, when we read an account of Saul's death in 1 Samuel 31 that seems to clearly contradict the one found in 2 Samuel 1, the doctrine of inspiration is not challenged for Warfield. First Samuel 31:3–4 informs us that a Philistine arrow fatally wounded Saul. In 2 Samuel 1 we read that Saul's bodyguard, who survived the battle, tells David that Saul ordered the bodyguard to end his (Saul's) misery by his own sword.

This is not difficult to see, but how about applying the principle to a thornier text, such as the book of Jonah? Warfield most likely believed in a historic Jonah who literally survived inside the stomach of a large fish. But if he did, it was not a necessary conclusion of his view of inspiration. Warfield's doctrine of biblical inspiration does not require that all narratives be read literally. That decision must be arrived at by exegetical evidence, understandings of genre distinctions, the context, and so forth. If the author intended for the text to be read literally, then Jonah was surely historical. But if it can be demonstrated that Jonah was intended to be a parable, then a Warfieldian inerrantist could view Jonah as ahistorical without sacrificing the veracity of Scripture.[24]

There are many narratives that Warfield would clearly not read as historical, such as the events described in Jesus' parables. A Warfieldian can safely argue that in the twelfth chapter of Mark's Gospel, Jesus was not teaching about an actual vineyard owner who rented his land to

23. Gleason Archer, "Alleged Errors and Discrepancies in the Original Manuscripts of the Bible," in *Inerrancy*, ed. Norman L. Geisler (Grand Rapids: Zondervan, 1980), 67.

24. Leslie Allen, for example, reads Jonah as a parable in his 1976 contribution to the mainstream evangelical *New International Commentary on the Old Testament*. But for an Old Princetonian defense of Jonah's historicity on exegetical (not dogmatic) grounds, see *Princeton Theological Review*, new series vol. 25 (1927): 636.

wicked tenants. This conclusion, however, would be a matter of exegesis. A commitment to this understanding of biblical inspiration does not necessarily tether one to any particular interpretations of those texts.

Likewise, on the issue of authorship, Warfield arrived at fairly traditional positions, but this was not necessary to his doctrine of inspiration. If a book of the Bible unambiguously claims to be written by Paul, then Warfield's view of divine inspiration holds that the book must have been written by Paul. But this is a decision of exegesis. So, in theory, one holding to Warfield's view of inspiration could conceivably believe that David did not write some of the psalms that bear his name, if it could be shown somehow that such designations in the psalmic genre were not intended to teach that he did.

Inspiration of the Autographs

Another qualification, or nuance, of Warfield's teaching is that the Holy Spirit's unfailing guidance applies only to the creation of the *original autographs* of the biblical texts. Just as our current interpretation of the Bible is not guaranteed, neither is the honesty or the penmanship of those who over time copied its texts. Our current Bible is not, strictly speaking, completely free of error.[25]

Many have viewed this clause as a calculated dodge. When faced with an unavoidable falsehood in Scripture, Warfield can attribute this to copyist error, and appeal to the unrecoverable original text, the so-called "lost Princeton Bible."[26] But Warfield did *not*, in fact, use this idea as a "free pass" from the hard work of answering biblical critics' concerns. Even when confronted with the toughest biblical difficulties, Warfield can never be accused of appealing to the "lost" autographs.[27] In fact, Warfield began his academic career as a textual critic and believed that the modern copies of biblical texts were

25. See B. B. Warfield, "The Inerrancy of the Original Autographs," in Benjamin B. Warfield, *Selected Shorter Writings*, 2 vols., ed. John E. Meeter (Nutley, N.J.: Presbyterian and Reformed, 1970, 1973), 2:585.

26. See the charges of Briggs and those of modern critics cited by Greg Bahnsen, "The Inerrancy of the Autographa," in *Inerrancy*, ed. Geisler, 158. For Jack Rogers's criticism, see "Church Doctrine of Biblical Inspiration," in *Biblical Authority*, ed. J. Rogers (Waco, Tex.: Word, 1977), 39.

27. I have not discovered a single instance in which Warfield has ascribed an apparent difficulty in the text to a yet-undiscovered scribal error.

actually quite good and well attested.[28] He was confident that we were getting ever closer to the original words with each new linguistic and archaeological breakthrough, and that the gulf between our text and the autographs was small and rapidly diminishing. He would, no doubt, be encouraged by the progress made since his death 85 years ago. Nonetheless, the text we possess is not identical to what was originally written.

Not *by Dictation*

Another point sometimes missed by critics is that Warfield did not conceive of divine inspiration as a form of dictation, as had some of the medieval paintings that depicted the Holy Spirit whispering in Moses' ear.[29] Warfield taught that divine inspiration came by a variety of modes, some supernatural and some quite mundane. Sometimes the biblical writers, such as Matthew or John, simply reported what they remembered under the invisible guidance of the Holy Spirit. Other writers, such as the prophets, received dramatic visions or angelic visits. In either case the result, by God's will, was the same—and, again, without doing violence to the styles, cultural contexts, or personalities of the individual authors. If you had been acquainted with Paul and read the original draft of his epistle to the Philippians, you would likely recognize that the letter "sounded like" your friend Paul. The human authors were used by God "in accordance with their natures."[30]

Necessity of the Spirit's Illumination

Still another often forgotten but critically important element of Warfield's conception of Scripture was the central role of the

28. The first book Warfield wrote was the widely used *An Introduction to the Textual Criticism of the New Testament* (Toronto: S. R. Briggs, 1887), which Bruce Metzger, dean of mainline textual critics and modern Princeton professor, once told this author was the finest work of its kind of that generation.

29. See Warfield's clear rejection of a mechanical dictation theory in Warfield, *Inspiration and Authority of the Bible*, 173n.

30. Warfield, *Inspiration and Authority of the Bible*, 93; see also his inaugural address of 1880, "Inspiration and Criticism," in *Inspiration and Authority of the Bible*, 421, 437; B. B. Warfield, *The Westminster Assembly and Its Work*, vol. 6 of *The Works of Benjamin Breckinridge Warfield* (1931; repr., Grand Rapids: Baker, 1981), 262ff.

Holy Spirit in confirming its authority in our hearts. Ernest Sandeen expresses the misguided sentiment of many of the critics when he charges: "The witness of the Spirit, though not overlooked, cannot be said to play any important role in the Princeton thought. It is with the external not the internal, the objective not the subjective, that they deal."[31] This is a favorite charge of critics, who have been alarmed by the supposed rationalistic foundations of Warfield's epistemology. The Warfield sound bite, quoted out of context in so many of the history of doctrine texts, is: "It is the distinction of Christianity that it has come into the world clothed with the mission to *reason* its way to dominion."[32]

Because Warfield, a classic common sense realist, held to certain universal features of rationality shared by all humans, he believed that evidences were a useful and legitimate preparation for the special grace of the gift of faith.[33] But he was also a solid "high" Calvinist, so for him this never meant that one could *rationally compel* anyone to faith or *prove* that the Bible is the Word of God. But he did believe that evidences could and should be mustered as secondary causes, under God's sovereign supervision, to illustrate that the Bible is trustworthy, and thus prepare the way for the gracious miracle of saving faith. Despite misunderstandings of Old Princeton, these theologians were not un-Reformed or bare rationalists in this area. They always emphasized that, ultimately, commitment to biblical authority came only by the special work of the sovereign Holy Spirit. Evidence can show that the Bible is trustworthy, but evidence alone can never be sufficient to bring conviction to our souls that it is the Word of God or bring submission to its authority. Only the testimony of the Holy

31. Ernest R. Sandeen, *The Roots of Fundamentalism: British and American Millenarianism, 1800–1930* (Chicago: University of Chicago Press, 1970), 118.

32. B. B. Warfield, "Introduction to Francis R. Beattie's *Apologetics*," in *Selected Shorter Writings*, 2:99. In its context, Warfield does not mean a bare rationalism, however, but suggests that Christianity does not need to coerce as other religions do, but can reason peaceably. See more on the context in relation to Warfield's views on Kuyper in W. Andrew Hoffecker, "Benjamin B. Warfield," in *Reformed Theology in America: A History of its Modern Development*, ed. David F. Wells (Grand Rapids: Baker, 1997), 85.

33. For a modern restatement of this Reformed evidential perspective, see R. C. Sproul, John H. Gerstner, and Arthur Lindsley, *Classical Apologetics* (Grand Rapids: Zondervan, 1984). A most helpful critique of this from a modified presuppositional perspective is John Frame, *Cornelius Van Til: An Analysis of His Thought* (Phillipsburg, N.J.: P&R, 1995), esp. 401ff.

Spirit can accomplish this.[34] One can accept the presuppositionalist critiques of Warfield's epistemology without dismissing his view of Scripture as simply bound to Enlightenment rationalism.

The Historical Basis of Warfield's Understanding of Scripture

We have sketched a very basic outline of what Warfield's doctrine of biblical inspiration taught and did not teach, but a whole other line of criticism remains to be addressed: the charge that this enterprise is really a novelty, outside the mainstream of historic Christianity. Warfield's critics tell us that this formula for scriptural interpretation was the result of a reaction to late-nineteenth-century modernist theological and biblical-critical threats. Not until the late 1870s did Warfield supposedly abstract and exaggerate tendencies of the narrow school of seventeenth-century Reformed "Scholastics" (i.e., Francis Turretin)[35] to come up with a creative, but unwarranted, invention. While these critics acknowledge that the church has always taught the authority of the Word of God mediated through the biblical text, they hold that inerrancy has not always been self-consciously attributed to every statement made in the Bible, such as its natural and historical claims. It is argued that whatever the church has believed about Scripture was never systematized, or placed in a tidy, rationalistic formula like Warfield's.[36]

This is a serious charge. But there is no need to answer it comprehensively here, as John Woodbridge and others decisively demonstrated its absurdity a generation ago.[37]

34. See Andrew Hoffecker's excellent *Piety and the Princeton Theologians* (Phillipsburg, N.J.: Presbyterian and Reformed / Grand Rapids: Baker, 1981); Warfield's essays on this topic are collected in *The Person and Work of the Holy Spirit* (Amityville, N.Y.: Calvary Press, 1997).

35. Francis Turretin, seventeenth-century Genevan theologian, authored a two-thousand-page Latin work, the English title of which is *The Institutes of Elenctic Theology*. This was the basic systematics text at Princeton Seminary for nearly fifty years. The English translation is in three volumes (Phillipsburg, N.J.: P&R, 1992–97).

36. See Sandeen, *Roots of Fundamentalism*, 106, or, again, Rogers and McKim, *Authority and Interpretation of the Bible*.

37. See Carson and Woodbridge, eds., *Scripture and Truth*.

It is beyond dispute that all the elements of Warfield's formulations on inerrancy are present in the early church fathers,[38] including Augustine.[39] Luther famously contends, "One letter, even a single tittle, of Scripture means more to us than heaven and earth. Therefore we cannot permit even the most minute change."[40] Calvin's view of Scripture is identical.[41]

The normative Presbyterian creed, the Westminster Confession of Faith (1646), of course, teaches the view of scriptural inspiration that Warfield articulated.[42] And Warfield liberally quotes long passages from the writings of Richard Baxter, John Ball, John Lightfoot, Bishop Ussher, and other standard Puritan figures to support his position.

Sandeen, McKim, and Rogers, among others, charge that what has become known as the "Old Princeton position on Scripture" was a reaction to higher critical attacks on Scripture beginning in the 1870s. This position allegedly did not crystallize until the 1881 article by A. A. Hodge and Warfield. Prior to that, critics allege, the church assumed the Bible's trustworthiness because there existed no challenges to it, but these notions were not yet systematized into the supposedly

38. Geoffrey Bromiley, "The Church Fathers and Holy Scripture," in ibid., 195–220. See also the essay in defense of the Old Princeton position written by Robert D. Preus, president of Concordia Seminary (Lutheran), "The View of the Bible Held by the Church: The Early Church through Luther," in *Inerrancy*, ed. Geisler, 355–82.

39. Augustine, *De Cons. Ev. Lib*. II, c.12. See also A. D. R. Polman, *Word of God According to St. Augustine* (Grand Rapids: Eerdmans, 1961), 56, 66; B. B. Warfield, *Calvin and Augustine* (Philadelphia: Presbyterian and Reformed, 1956), 461–62.

40. Cited by A. Sevington Wood, *Captive to the Word* (Grand Rapids: Eerdmans, 1969), 145; see also M. Reu, *Luther and the Scriptures* (Columbus, Ohio: Wartburg, 1943); W. Robert Godfrey, "Biblical Authority in the Sixteenth and Seventeenth Centuries: A Question of Transition," in Carson and Woodbridge, eds., *Scripture and Truth*, 227.

41. See Godfrey, "Biblical Authority in the Sixteenth and Seventeenth Centuries," 225–34; J. I. Packer, "Calvin's View of Scripture," in *God's Inerrant Word*, ed. J. W. Montgomery (Minneapolis: Bethany, 1974), 95–114; John Murray, *Calvin on Scripture and Divine Sovereignty* (Grand Rapids: Baker, 1960); Kenneth Kantzer, "Calvin and the Holy Scriptures," in *Inspiration and Interpretation*, ed. John F. Walvoord (Grand Rapids: Eerdmans, 1957); John H. Gerstner, "The View of the Bible: Calvin and the Westminster Divines," in *Inerrancy*, ed. Geisler, 383–410. Even Karl Barth believed that Calvin had (incorrectly, in his opinion) held to the full inspiration and inerrancy of Scripture. Karl Barth, *Church Dogmatics: Doctrine of the Word of God*, part 2 (Edinburgh: T & T Clark, 1975), 520ff. A similar sentiment is found in Emil Brunner, *The Christian Doctrine of God*, trans. Olive Wyon (Philadelphia: Westminster Press, 1959), 111.

42. See especially its first chapter.

rigid, scholastic system that Warfield devised. This Rogers/McKim thesis has been adopted uncritically in many circles despite the overwhelming evidence against it. The thesis is just so handy for those who do not like Princeton's theology. It even allows one to lay the blame for fundamentalism at Princeton's door.[43]

Some of the problems with this account are obvious. First, the notion that there were no challenges to Scripture's trustworthiness prior to Julius Wellhausen and Robertson Smith is absurd. From the beginning of the Enlightenment, at least, doubts about the Scripture's accuracy were lodged openly and often. Many an eighteenth-century rationalist enchanted large audiences with charges that the biblical narratives were myths rather than history. Doubts about the authenticity of the miracle accounts, including the resurrection, were common, if unpopular. Long before Darwin or Wellhausen, Voltaire was a household name. Thomas Paine, who sold one and a half million copies of his 1791 work *The Rights of Man*, boasted in his even more popular *Age of Reason*, "I have gone through the Bible as a man would go through a wood with an ax and felled trees. Here they lie and the priest may replant them, but they will never grow."[44] To act as if there were no challenges to biblical trustworthiness prior to the rise of modern German higher criticism is frankly bizarre.

Warfield and Hodge clearly did not perceive that their article was in any way revolutionary or novel; nor, if one reads reviews of it, did their contemporaries. Certainly one could charge that for its first 1,900 years the church was wrong about scriptural inspiration, but no one can reasonably argue that the Old Princeton view is not historic or catholic. The uniqueness of the Princeton view is not found in what it said, but in the clarity and power with which it was articulated. It has become a target these days largely because of its immense success.

43. Roger Olson, *The Story of Christian Theology* (Downers Grove, Ill.: InterVarsity Press, 1999), 557, 560. Though it is a magisterial work of almost 700 pages, this book's treatment of Warfield and Old Princeton might be characterized as the sort of superficial "sound bite" approach discussed in the introduction to this essay.

44. Cited in Iain Murray, *Revival and Revivalism* (Edinburgh and Carlisle, Pa.: Banner of Truth, 1994), 113.

Conclusions

We now have a sketch of the way Scripture was understood by Warfield. The obvious question that follows is this: So what? What can be learned from all this, besides the fact that some long-departed scholar has been badly misrepresented? This exploration was not intended to be merely an exercise in antiquarianism or nostalgia. Warfield has some profound words to speak to us today, words that need to be heard even more now than in the time when they were written.

All orthodox Christians over the centuries have believed that the Word of God written was central to a living, faithful relationship to our Lord. Understanding the nature of God's self-disclosure to his people can seem like grappling with a greased pig, especially to the modern believer set amidst a swirling galaxy of contradictory theories about the Bible. If we are indeed called to submit ourselves to the authority of this book, there are immensely complicated issues that must be resolved in the process. Few, if any, of these difficulties were not addressed in an extremely sophisticated and thoughtful, yet warm-hearted, manner by Warfield. And he is rarely unclear. I believe his work offers an excellent place to discover clues to escape the modern epistemological maze. If nothing else, one who has engaged Warfield will find that his focus is continually on the God of grace, whose precious Word will never pass away.

❦ *5* ❦

Warfield on the Life of the Mind and the Apologetic Nature of Christian Scholarship

PAUL KJOSS HELSETH

In *The Outrageous Idea of Christian Scholarship*, the sequel to his highly acclaimed *The Soul of the American University: From Protestant Establishment to Established Nonbelief*,[1] George Marsden proposes that "mainstream American higher education should be more open to explicit discussion of the relationship of religious faith to learning."[2] There is no compelling reason to relegate religious perspectives to the periphery of academic life, he argues, because the postmodern critique of Enlightenment standards of objectivity has neutralized the intellectual rationale for suppressing perspectives that are considered by many to be "unscientific."[3] Since the contemporary academy "*on its own terms*" has no consistent grounds for rejecting perspectives that "are ultimately grounded in some faith or another," Marsden submits that there ought to be room at the academic table for explicitly religious points of view "so long as their proponents are willing

1. George Marsden, *The Soul of the American University: From Protestant Establishment to Established Nonbelief* (New York: Oxford University Press, 1994).
2. George Marsden, *The Outrageous Idea of Christian Scholarship* (New York: Oxford University Press, 1997), 3.
3. Ibid., 30.

to support the rules necessary for constructive exchange of ideas in a pluralistic setting."[4] In such a setting—one in which the *modus operandi* is informed by strict adherence to the ideals of the liberal pragmatic academy—the idea of self-consciously Christian scholarship will be anything but outrageous, simply because the rules that govern the life of the academy will be applied "equally to religious and nonreligious views" alike.[5]

While Marsden's proposal is commendable because it urges believing academics to take part in the life of the academy and to transform university life by working to improve those rules that marginalize the Christian perspective, nevertheless it may be critiqued for encouraging Christian scholars to accommodate their scholarly activity to rules of academic comportment that relegate the teaching of the Bible to the status of a mere "background belief."[6] Christians can reflect on the implications of special revelation within the bounds of the mainstream academy, Marsden contends, but they can do so only "by talking about them conditionally."[7] They cannot "argue on the basis of their special or private revelations," in other words, for such revelations are "ultimately mysterious, rather than scientific," and as such they are inaccessible to those who do not share the Christian worldview.[8]

Though such accommodation would certainly afford the Christian scholar a hearing in the postmodern academy, I would suggest that it might do so at the cost of equating—albeit unintentionally—the authority of Scripture with the authority of classic texts from other religious traditions. For many believing academics, such an approach would leave something to be desired not only because it seems to offer little of substance to prevent academic give and take from degenerating into mere "dialogue" (which Marsden rejects),[9] but more importantly because it could leave its practitioners open to the charge that they are

4. Ibid., 30, 45.
5. Ibid., 57.
6. Ibid., 48–51. Obviously, this is not the only way that Marsden's proposal may be critiqued. For an interesting critique from a Reformed perspective that is significantly different from the assessment I am offering here, see D. G. Hart, "Christian Scholars, Secular Universities, and the Problem with the Antithesis," *Christian Scholar's Review* 30, no 1 (Summer 2001): 383–402.
7. Marsden, *The Outrageous Idea of Christian Scholarship*, 52.
8. Ibid., 48, 50.
9. Cf. ibid., 45, 57–58.

covert, if not overt, "perspectivalists." According to Bruce Kuklick, "perspectivalism" is an essentially postmodern form of analysis that is unbecoming in the Christian scholar because believing academics do not begin "from the conceptually dubious starting point of the perspectivalist."[10] Whereas committed perspectivalists take part in the life of the academy because they suppose, as outspoken defenders of the modern distinction between religious truth and scientific truth, that there is "no rational way" of adjudicating between the competing "truth" claims of various ways of seeing the world,[11] the Christian takes part because he is convinced that the Christian perspective and the authority on which it is based are "true," as J. Gresham Machen would say, "in the plain man's sense of the word 'truth.'"[12]

How, then, should Christians who are reluctant to relegate the authority of Scripture to the status of a "control belief" go about integrating faith and learning?[13] What posture should Christians who do not want to empty Scripture of its objective significance assume, in other words, when interacting with scholarship that is neither exclu-

10. Bruce Kuklick, "On Critical History," in *Religious Advocacy and American History*, ed. Bruce Kuklick and D. G. Hart (Grand Rapids: Eerdmans, 1997), 59–61.

11. Ibid., 59.

12. J. Gresham Machen, "The Creeds and Doctrinal Advance," in *God Transcendent*, ed. Ned Stonehouse (1949; repr., Edinburgh: Banner of Truth, 1982), 165. The word "perspectivalism" can be used in both benign and pernicious senses. In the benign sense, it refers to that view of epistemology that simply acknowledges that all truth claims are grounded in metaphysical perspectives or "worldviews." In the pernicious sense—the sense in which I am using the word above—it refers to that far more foundational view of epistemology that denies even the possibility of absolute truth by reducing the worldviews that inform truth claims to the level of subjective preference. Such perspectivalism is the kiss of death to Christian scholarship, I contend, not only because it has its genesis in a naturalistic understanding of knowledge, but more importantly because it eradicates the basis for claiming that the Christian worldview is superior—both objectively and subjectively—to all others. Let me make clear at this point that I am in no way suggesting that Marsden is a perspectivalist in this sense of the term. I not only recognize that he explicitly rejects this understanding of perspectivalism, but more importantly applaud and admire his unambiguous stand for Christian truth in the postmodern academy. At the level of method, though, I wonder if his opposition to "tendentious" scholarship lends itself to asking Christians to act *as if* they are perspectivalists in this sense of the term. Given the non-subjectivistic nature of the Christian faith commitment, how do Christians in the postmodern academy go about affirming the objective truthfulness of the Christian worldview when doing so necessarily involves engaging in "tendentious" scholarship, which Marsden insists has no place in the academy? While I am not proposing an answer to this question, it is difficult for me to see what strategic benefit there is in playing by rules that deem claims to absolute truth out of bounds from the start. See Marsden's discussion of "Christian schizophrenia" in *The Outrageous Idea of Christian Scholarship*, chap. 3.

13. Ibid., 50.

sively theological nor overtly Christian? The purpose of this chapter is neither to argue about the role of the Christian in the secular academy nor to debate about the manner in which Christian commitments should be defended in a pluralistic setting. It is, rather, to place B. B. Warfield's response to the modern era's relocation of the divine-human nexus in its proper historical context, and thereby to set Warfield up as an example of an evangelical scholar who responded to the problem of the relationship between Christianity and culture in the correct fashion. Whereas the vast majority of Warfield's contemporaries insisted that Christians should integrate faith and learning by bending Scripture "into some sort of conciliation" with the "latest pronouncements" of modern science, philosophy, and scholarship, Warfield countered with the orthodox contention that "the condition of right thinking . . . is . . . that the Christian man should look out upon the seething thought of the world from the safe standpoint of the sure Word of God."[14] Christians, he argued, should not adopt the "very prevalent" yet heretical tendency of looking at the teachings of God's Word "from the standpoint of the world's speculations."[15] Rather, they should repudiate the "habit of 'concession'" manifest in modern reconstructions of religious thinking and assimilate modern learning to Christian truth on the basis of "the fundamental fact of Christianity—that we have a firmer ground of confidence for our religious views than any science or philosophy or criticism can provide for any of their pronouncements."[16]

While the forthcoming discussion forgoes an extensive analysis of Warfield's theological method, it proposes that his solution to the problem of the relationship between Christianity and culture is exemplary not only because it encourages Christians to "seek" and "embrace" truth wherever it is found, but also because it tempers this encouragement with the realization that the seeking and embracing of truth must not be compromised by the pagan tendency to erect "'modern

14. B. B. Warfield, "Heresy and Concession," in Benjamin B. Warfield, *Selected Shorter Writings*, 2 vols., ed. John E. Meeter (Nutley, N.J.: Presbyterian and Reformed, 1970, 1973), 2:676, 677, 674–75 (hereafter *SSW*).

15. Ibid., 2:675.

16. Ibid., 2:675, 677. Assimilating modern learning to Christian truth involves sifting "the good" and "'discarding whatever is at variance with the gospel.'" Cf. 2:675, 672.

discovery' and 'modern thought' . . . into the norm of truth."[17] "No one should greet truth from whatever source with more readiness and more enthusiasm than [the Christian scholar]," Warfield argued, for the believing academic

> has in his hands the norm of truth, in the Word of God. This is the Ariadne clue by means of which he can thread his way through the labyrinths of the world's thought; this is the touchstone by the art of which he may choose the good and refuse the evil. So long as he clings to it he will build up the temple of truth, whencesoever he quarries the stones. When he loses hold of it, however, he descends into the arena and takes his hap with other men; and going his own way, it is not strange that he is often found with his back turned to God.[18]

Truth versus Experience

Warfield's views on the integration of faith and learning were formed in an intellectual environment that was being overwhelmed by controversy over what ideals and values would gain cultural supremacy and dominate in the public square. Gary Scott Smith suggests that, "in the years between the Civil War and World War I, a battle for cultural supremacy broke out on many fronts in America. Humanism, the claims of scientism, and intellectual disdain for the Bible wrestled with theism, both Christian and Jewish, for control of American public life."[19] This cultural battle did not arise in a vacuum, however, but was itself the immediate effect of the crisis of religious authority manifest in the nineteenth-century debate over the essence of Christianity, particularly as it impinges upon the nature of theology and its relationship to religious belief and practice. Whereas orthodox scholars insisted that religion and theology are the parallel products of the objective truth of God "operative in the two spheres of life and thought,"[20] more progressive

17. Ibid., 2:674, 676–77.
18. Ibid., 2:674.
19. Gary Scott Smith, *The Seeds of Secularization: Calvinism, Culture, and Pluralism in America, 1870–1915* (Grand Rapids: Christian University Press, 1985), 39. See especially chap. 3, "The Clash of Worldviews: Secularism vs. Calvinism."
20. B. B. Warfield, "Authority, Intellect, Heart," in *SSW*, 2:668; cf. B. B. Warfield, review of *Foundations: A Statement of Christian Belief in Terms of Modern Thought*, by Seven Oxford

scholars were compelled by cultural accommodation to abandon to science the whole realm of objective truth, and consequently to regard religion and theology as distinct rather than as intimately related entities.[21] Theology, they argued, must not be regarded as that "science of God" which systematizes the objective truths that underlie and produce religious expression.[22] Rather, it must be conceived of as that "science

---

Men, in *Critical Reviews*, vol. 10 of *The Works of Benjamin Breckinridge Warfield* (1932; repr., Grand Rapids: Baker, 1981), 325.

21. Cf. John William Stewart, "The Tethered Theology: Biblical Criticism, Common Sense Philosophy, and the Princeton Theologians, 1812–1860" (Ph.D. diss., University of Michigan, 1990), 79. The developments of the modern era that led to the separation of the epistemological realms of religion and science include: (1) The epistemological skepticism of Kant: cf. William Livingstone, "The Princeton Apologetic as Exemplified by the Work of Benjamin B. Warfield and J. Gresham Machen: A Study of American Theology, 1880–1930" (Ph.D. diss., Yale University, 1948), 117–18; Andrew Hoffecker, *Piety and the Princeton Theologians* (Phillipsburg, N.J.: Presbyterian and Reformed / Grand Rapids: Baker, 1981), 103. (2) The anti-intellectualism of Schleiermacher and the Romantic tradition: cf. Livingstone, "The Princeton Apologetic," 68; Stewart, "The Tethered Theology," 77–79; Lloyd Averill, *American Theology in the Liberal Tradition* (Philadelphia: The Westminster Press, 1967), 37. (3) The absolute idealism of Hegel, the naturalistic standards of evolutionary theory, and the relativizing influence of the historical consciousness: cf. Kenneth Cauthen, *The Impact of American Religious Liberalism* (New York: Harper & Row, 1962), 8–12; Averill, *American Theology in the Liberal Tradition*, 22–24; Ferenc Morton Szasz, *The Divided Mind of Protestant America, 1880–1930* (Tuscaloosa: University of Alabama Press, 1982), 17. (4) The progressive developments within American evangelicalism: cf. Averill, *American Theology in the Liberal Tradition*, 69; William Hutchison, *The Modernist Impulse in American Protestantism* (Cambridge, Mass.: Harvard University Press, 1976), 13, 48; George Marsden, *The Evangelical Mind and the New School Presbyterian Experience* (New Haven, Conn.: Yale University Press, 1970); Iain H. Murray, *Revival and Revivalism: The Making and Marring of American Evangelicalism, 1750–1858* (Edinburgh: Banner of Truth, 1994). According to Kenneth Cauthen these developments fostered the formulation of three principles that together characterize the template of the modern mind. These principles, the endorsement of which led to the emergence of the New Theology, are *continuity* (due to evolutionary theory and Hegel's absolute idealism), *autonomy* (the adoption of an internal rather than an external source of authority), and *dynamism* (because of continuity, all external standards of religious authority are provisional because all things are in the process of dynamic change). Cauthen suggests that the dominating motif of the era—that motif which was responsible for the critical importance of the other two—was that of continuity. Continuity, he contends, manifests itself "in every area of thought and permeates all liberal theology." Cauthen, *The Impact of American Religious Liberalism*, 9. That Warfield would have agreed with Cauthen at this point is clear. For Warfield's take on how the concept of evolution has fostered the virtual obliteration of "a distinguishable supernatural," see B. B. Warfield, "Christianity and Revelation," in *SSW*, 1:26–27; B. B. Warfield, "Christian Supernaturalism," in *Studies in Theology*, vol. 9 of *The Works of Benjamin Breckinridge Warfield* (1932; repr., Grand Rapids: Baker, 1981), 28–33.

22. Orthodox scholars were convinced that just as systematic theology forms "the crown and head" of theological science, so too theology forms "the apex of the pyramid of the sciences by which the structure [of truth] is perfected." Since the subject matter of genuinely theological

of faith" or "science of religion" which supplies—at the behest of the "provisional findings" of modern science, philosophy, and scholarship, or that which is *ultimately* the subjective product of the human soul—merely "the intellectual interpretation" of a really inexpressible subjective experience for a particular time and place.[23] If theology is to sustain vital rather than sterile religious life in each successive age, progressive scholars reasoned, then it must articulate religious truth in a manner that is attuned to the *zeitgeist*, that is, to the progressive activity of the divine within nature, history, and culture.

While orthodox scholars were not completely oblivious to the potential benefits of switching the *discrimen* in theology (or that "imaginative construal" of how God is authoritatively present among the faithful)[24] from an objective to a subjective base, they insisted that such anti-intellectualism could not be sanctioned for two distinct yet interrelated reasons.[25] It could not be sanctioned, they argued, not only because it confounds the objective subject matter of genuinely theological science with "the subjective experiences of the human

science "indirectly" includes "all the facts of nature and history," orthodox scholars concluded that the scope of theological science must not be restricted to that which is merely the subjective product of the human soul. They repudiated, in other words, the modern distinction between religious truth and scientific truth as invalid. B. B. Warfield, "The Idea of Systematic Theology," in *Studies in Theology*, 64, 71, 72–74. On the relationship between the "parts" that constitute the organism of "theology," see B. B. Warfield, "The Task and Method of Systematic Theology," in *Studies in Theology*, 91–92.

23. Warfield, review of *Foundations*, 322–24. The accommodation of Christianity to scholarly conclusions that signal when a new theological interpretation of religious experience is needed is really an implicit appeal to the authority of human nature. This is because what is meant by modern thought "is our own 'science, philosophy, and scholarship'—which seems to be only a naïve way of transferring the claim of infallibility from 'Christianity' and 'its theology' to ourselves."

24. David Kelsey, *The Uses of Scripture in Recent Theology* (Philadelphia: Fortress, 1975), 205–6.

25. One of the potential benefits is the elimination of the need to integrate faith and learning. If it is indeed true that religious truth is merely subjective, then there is no compelling need to relate it to the "objective" conclusions of modern scholarship. Warfield clearly believed that such anti-intellectualism is "the indirect product of unbelief, among men who would fain hold their Christian profession in the face of an onset of unbelief, which they feel too weak to withstand." In this regard, see B. B. Warfield, "Evading the Supernatural," in *SSW*, 2:681. On the rise of anti-intellectualism in American culture, see Richard Hofstadter, *Anti-Intellectualism in American Life* (New York: Vintage Books, 1962, 1963), 55–141; Ann Douglas, *The Feminization of American Culture* (New York: The Noonday Press, 1977), 3–13, 17–43, 121–64.

heart,"[26] but more importantly because it reduces the Christian religion to a natural phenomenon by "casting . . . men back upon their 'religious experience,' corporate or individual, as their sole trustworthy ground of religious convictions."[27] Although orthodox scholars acknowledged that natural religion is valid religion insofar as it expresses the natural religious tendency of the human heart, they claimed that it is inadequate to the needs of fallen sinners, simply because it lacks an effectual soteriological component. Whereas Christianity is sufficient to save precisely because it is based on a supernatural act of God in history, natural religion cannot meet the supernatural need of the sinful soul because it supplies merely the "natural foundation" for Christianity's "supernatural structure."[28] That is to say, it is simply the creature's response to the perception of God in nature and conscience, and as such it is "unequal" to the "unnatural" conditions brought about by the fall of Adam.[29] Since

26. B. B. Warfield, "Apologetics," in *Studies in Theology*, 7; cf. Warfield, "The Idea of Systematic Theology," 56. Obviously, this confusion is the logical consequence of abandoning the whole realm of objective truth to science.

27. B. B. Warfield, "Mysticism and Christianity," in *Studies in Theology*, 658. The attack on the principle of external authority was waged on two fronts: the metaphysical side—"in general, a neo-Kantianism mediated through Albrecht Ritschl"; and the "mystical" side—which stressed "subjective religious experience as the norm and authority of Christian faith." Cf. Livingstone, "The Princeton Apologetic," 175–80; Warfield, "Apologetics," 14–15. On the value judgments that cultivate the religious life of the Christian community, see B. B. Warfield, "The Latest Phase of Historical Rationalism," in *Studies in Theology*, 591–605; B. B. Warfield, review of *Mystik und Geschichtliche Religion*, by Wilhelm Frensenius, in *Critical Reviews*, 357–58; B. B. Warfield, "Introduction to Francis R. Beattie's *Apologetics*," in *SSW*, 2:94. On how the mystic substitutes "his religious experience for the objective revelation of God recorded in the written Word," see Warfield, "Mysticism and Christianity," 651, 655. For a good summary statement of the relationship between Christianity, mysticism, and historical rationalism, see Warfield, review of *Mystik*, 362–65. On the ontology that calls the *semen deitatis* into action, see 359. On the relationship between the adoption of an internal standard of authority and *autonomy*, see Cauthen, *The Impact of American Religious Liberalism*, 12ff.; and Averill, *American Theology in the Liberal Tradition*, 36ff. On the relationship between an internal standard of authority and natural religion, see B. B. Warfield, review of *Mysticism in Christianity*, by W. K. Fleming, and *Mysticism and Modern Life*, by John W. Buckham, in *Critical Reviews*, 366–67; B. B. Warfield, "Recent Reconstructions of Theology," in *SSW*, 2:291, 293; Warfield, "The Idea of Systematic Theology," 57; Warfield, "Mysticism and Christianity," 656, 658.

28. Warfield, "Mysticism and Christianity," 661.

29. Ibid., 659–61; cf. B. B. Warfield, "Faith and Life," in *SSW*, 1:366; Warfield, review of *Mystik*, 362. On how "Christianity is superinduced upon and presupposes natural religion and forms with it the one whole which is the only sufficing religion for sinful man," see 362–63; see also Robert Swanton, "Warfield and Progressive Orthodoxy," *Reformed Theological Review* 23 (October 1964): 76–77. On the inherent "moralism" of natural religion, which involves a

orthodox scholars were convinced that external, supernatural truth "is the very breath of Christianity's nostrils,"[30] it follows that they repudiated the progressive solution to the problem of the relationship between Christianity and culture not simply because it transformed the Christian religion into "a veritable nose of wax, which may be twisted in every direction as it may serve our purpose,"[31] but because it emptied Christian belief of its ability to save fallen sinners from the consequences of sin by throwing them "back on what we can find within us alone."[32] When natural religion in any form "pushes itself forward as an adequate religion for sinners," orthodox scholars maintained, "it presses beyond its mark and becomes, in the poet's phrase, 'procuress to the lords of hell.'"[33]

In light of the crisis of religious authority manifest in the modern debate over the nature of theology and its relationship to religious belief and practice, it follows that the modern era's relocation of the divine-human nexus not only had a tremendous impact on basic understandings of the subject matter of theological science, but thereby also had a revolutionary impact on what the goal of the entire theological enterprise was thought to be. Whereas orthodox scholars were committed to the establishment and systematic explication of a body of truth that was considered to be the objective basis of saving faith, more progressive scholars resolved to adapt theology to the modern *zeitgeist* on the basis of the presumption that the traditional standards of external authority had been discredited by the theological, philosophical, and scientific developments of the modern era. The crisis of religious authority that blossomed into the fundamentalist-modernist

---

trust for salvation in native moral capacities rather than in the sovereign grace of God and as such necessarily deteriorates into a salvifically ineffectual religion of works, see B. B. Warfield, "What Is Calvinism?" in *SSW*, 1:391; see also Warfield's chapter entitled "Autosoterism," in B. B. Warfield, *The Plan of Salvation* (1915; repr., Philadelphia: Presbyterian Board of Publication, 1918), 37–63. On the inherent moralism of all who tend "to reduce to the vanishing-point the subjective injury wrought by Adam's sin on his posterity," see B. B. Warfield, "Imputation," in *Studies in Theology*, 304; cf. B. B. Warfield, "On the Doctrine of the Holy Spirit," in *SSW*, 1:216–18.

30. B. B. Warfield, "Christian Supernaturalism," 29.

31. Warfield, review of *Foundations*, 322. On the explicit meaning of the word "Christianity," see B. B. Warfield, "'Redeemer' and 'Redemption,'" in *Biblical Doctrines*, vol. 2 of *The Works of Benjamin Breckinridge Warfield* (1929; repr., Grand Rapids: Baker, 1981), 396.

32. Warfield, "Mysticism and Christianity," 659.

33. Ibid., 661; cf. Warfield, "Christian Supernaturalism," 38–41.

controversy of the 1920s must be regarded, therefore, as that struggle which was marked, on the one hand, by orthodox theologians' opposition to theological process and change and, on the other, by liberal or modernist theologians' accommodation of Christianity to modern culture.[34] Whereas orthodox theologians insisted that the modern preoccupation with theological reconstruction was part and parcel of a reduction of the Christian religion to a merely natural phenomenon, liberal or modernist theologians argued that orthodoxy's stubborn refusal to make theology relevant to the thought world of the modern era manifested nothing less than gross insensitivity to the immanent activity of the divine within nature, history, and culture, as well as an implicit relegation of the Christian religion to the realm of impotence and meaninglessness. The orthodox refusal to state Christian belief in terms that were amenable to modern thought could be viewed as nothing less, they maintained, than the kiss of death to the religious life of the Christian community.

34. Hutchison, *The Modernist Impulse in American Protestantism*, 2. Historical analysis has established that the New Theology was occasioned by the perceived need "to adjust the ancient faith to the modern world." Cauthen, *The Impact of American Religious Liberalism*, 5. The New Theologians insisted that "the repetition of old answers can serve no purpose. New answers must be framed, and these answers must be couched in the 'terms of modern thought.'" Warfield, review of *Foundations*, 322. As such, the agenda of theological liberalism was driven by the notion that a living faith must come to terms with the modern world. While modern interpreters generally agree upon how to characterize the primary elements of the liberal program, there is no consensus on how to classify the purveyors of theological liberalism. Should "liberals" and "modernists" be lumped together into one category as I have done? Or, should they be differentiated according to the relative priority of their methodological starting point, i.e., according to their starting point in revelation (evangelical liberals) or in science (modernist liberals)? Although most modern interpreters answer this question by distinguishing between evangelical and modernist liberals—for example, cf. Averill, *American Theology in the Liberal Tradition*, 100ff.; Cauthen, *The Impact of American Religious Liberalism*; and Martin Marty, *The Irony of it All, 1893–1919* (Chicago: University of Chicago Press, 1986), 13–80—William Hutchison's insights on the matter deserve thoughtful consideration. Hutchison maintains that "such a differentiation [makes] sense as embodying an opinion about the theological *consequences* of varying modes of liberal advocacy; [but] it [is] not very helpful in clarifying what liberals themselves had *intended*." Few liberals, Hutchison contends, denied that Christian revelation is normative in some sense, and as a consequence few intended to repudiate the essential substance of Christianity. "The deeper difficulty in any sharply drawn distinction between liberals who built on revelation and those who allegedly began with science or culture was that it could not deal with the liberals' crucial contention that this distinction is, from the start, largely invalid. The antinomies that such a system of classification presupposes—between sacred and secular, between a starting point in revelation and a starting point in reason or in science—were precisely what proponents of this movement . . . sought to minimize. . . ." Hutchinson, *The Modernist Impulse in America*, 8–9.

The Authority of Scripture and the Posture of Christian Scholarship

B. B. Warfield's involvement in this cultural as well as theological controversy was triggered by his vigorous opposition to liberalism's heretical attempt not to assimilate modern learning to Christian truth, but to "desupernaturalize" Christianity so as to make it more palatable to the modern mind.[35] Christians must have an attitude "of eager hospitality toward the researches of the world,"[36] Warfield argued, not so that they can determine when a reconstruction of religious thinking is in order,[37] but so they can "*reason* the world into acceptance of the 'truth'" through the superior science of redeemed thought.[38] "The Christian," he maintained,

> by virtue of the palingenesis working in him, stands undoubtedly on an indefinitely higher plane of thought than that occupied by sinful man as such. And he must not decline, but use and press the advantage which God has thus given him. He must insist, and insist again, that his determinations, and not those of the unilluminated, must be built into the slowly rising fabric of human science. Thus will he serve, if not obviously his own generation, yet truly all the generations of men.[39]

While the consensus of critical opinion would have us believe that the aggressive nature of this solution to the problem of the relationship between Christianity and culture is evidence of accommodation to the rationalistic assumptions of Enlightenment philosophy, in fact, it represents the ideal in Christian scholarship for three reasons. It represents the ideal, first, because it is based upon the conviction that the "source and norm of truth"—"the only really solid basis of all . . . thinking"—is found in the Word of God.[40] Although Warfield

35. Warfield, "Christian Supernaturalism," 29.
36. Warfield, "Heresy and Concession," in *SSW*, 2:674.
37. "No one will doubt," Warfield argued, "that Christians of to-day must state their Christian beliefs in terms of modern thought. Every age has a language of its own and can speak no other. Mischief comes only when, instead of stating Christian belief in terms of modern thought, an effort is made, rather, to state modern thought in terms of Christian belief." Warfield, review of *Foundations*, 322.
38. B. B. Warfield, "Christianity the Truth," in *SSW*, 2:213.
39. Warfield, "Introduction to Francis R. Beattie's *Apologetics*," in *SSW*, 2:103.
40. Warfield, "Heresy and Concession," in *SSW*, 2:674, 675.

acknowledged that there are "other sources of knowledge from which [the Christian] may learn what is true," he nonetheless insisted that "there is no source of knowledge which will rank with [the Christian] in authority above the written Word of God, or to which he can appeal with superior confidence."[41] When the Christian comes into contact with "modes of thought and tenets originating elsewhere than in the Scriptures of God," therefore, "the teachings of God's Word" must be esteemed as authoritative "over against all the conjectural explanations of phenomena by men."[42] To do otherwise, Warfield argued—that is, to relinquish authority to the provisional conclusions of modern scholarship by modifying the teachings of God's Word "at the dictation of any 'man-made opinion'"—is to fall prey to "the fruitful mother of heresy."[43]

If Warfield's solution is ideal in the first place because it refuses to give "decisive weight" to modes of thought originating elsewhere than in the Word of God, it is so in the second because it acknowledges that esteeming Scripture as the norm of truth compels believing academics to "seek and embrace" truth wherever it is found.[44] As a Reformed scholar, Warfield was convinced that "zeal in investigation" is one of the "marked characteristics" of Christian scholarship because he recognized that Christians alone have the moral ability to handle the "touchstone" of truth—Scripture—correctly.[45] In the context of the current discussion, this means at least two things. First, it means that Christians zealously pursue truth "in every sphere"[46] because they recognize that the Word of God is not "a substitute for general revelation, but only . . . a preparation for its proper assimilation."[47] Special revelation was not given, Christians maintain, "to supplant a strictly natural knowledge [of God] by a strictly supernatural knowledge," but "so that the general revelation of God may be reflected purely

41. Ibid., 2:674.
42. Ibid., 2:677, 679.
43. Ibid., 2:677, 675.
44. Ibid., 2:677, 674.
45. Ibid., 2:674.
46. Ibid.
47. B. B. Warfield, "Augustine's Doctrine of the Knowledge of God," in *Tertullian and Augustine*, vol. 4 of *The Works of Benjamin Breckinridge Warfield* (1930; repr., Grand Rapids: Baker, 1981), 222.

in minds which now are blinded to its reflection by sin."[48] Second, it means that Christians engage aggressively in the life of the mind because they are confident that Christians alone have the moral ability to reason "rightly," that is, to "see" through the "spectacles" of Scripture.[49] Whereas progressive scholars bend Scripture into conciliation with the latest pronouncements of modern scholarship because they look at the teachings of God's Word from the standpoint of the world's speculations, the regenerate assimilate modern learning to Christian truth because their scholarship is informed by "the better scientific outlook,"[50] that is, by the ability to see revealed truth for what it objectively is, namely, glorious. Believing academics stand calmly "over against the world," therefore, not only because they recognize that "the Christian view of the world" is true, but more importantly because they are convinced that they have no reason to fear the "contention of men."[51] They have the truth, they have the moral ability to discern the truth in all things, and they are confident that everything they encounter will be assimilated to the truth by sifting the good and rejecting the bad.

Finally, Warfield's solution represents the ideal in Christian scholarship because it recognizes that assimilating modern learning to Christian truth is the means to moving the church of God forward in her

48. Ibid. cf. Warfield, "Christianity and Revelation," in *SSW*, 1:27–28.

49. Warfield, "Augustine's Doctrine of the Knowledge of God," 222. For my revisionist interpretation of the role that "right reason" plays in the Princeton tradition, see Paul Kjoss Helseth, "Are Postconservative Evangelicals Fundamentalists? Postconservative Evangelicalism, Old Princeton, and the Rise of Neo-Fundamentalism," in *Reclaiming the Center: Confronting Evangelical Accommodation in Postmodern Times*, ed. Millard J. Erickson, Paul Kjoss Helseth, Justin Taylor (Wheaton, Ill.: Crossway, 2004), 223–50; idem, "'Right Reason' and the Princeton Mind: The Moral Context," *Journal of Presbyterian History* 77, 1 (Spring 1999): 13–28; idem, "B. B. Warfield's Apologetical Appeal to 'Right Reason': Evidence of a 'Rather Bald Rationalism'?" *Scottish Bulletin of Evangelical Theology* 16, 2 (Autumn 1998): 156–77 (an adapted version of this article appears as chap. 2 of the present volume); idem, "The Apologetical Tradition of the OPC: A Reconsideration," *Westminster Theological Journal* 60 (1998): 109–29.

50. Warfield, "Introduction to Francis R. Beattie's *Apologetics*," in *SSW*, 2:100–102. While Warfield acknowledged that there "do exist . . . 'two kinds of men' in the world" who give us "two kinds of science," he insisted that the difference between the science of the regenerate and the science of the unregenerate is not "a difference in *kind*," but a difference in "perfection of performance." The science of the regenerate is of a higher quality than that of the unregenerate, he argued, not because it is "a different kind of science that [the regenerate] are producing," but because the entrance of regeneration "prepares men to build [the edifice of truth] better and ever more truly as the effects of regeneration increase intensively and extensively" (ibid.).

51. Ibid., 2:100, 103.

apologetic task. As we saw in the last chapter, Warfield distinguished between the giving of an "apology" and the task of "apologetics." Whereas an "apology" is a defense of Christianity "against either all assailants, actual or conceivable, or some particular form or instance of attack," the task of "apologetics" is "a positive and constructive science" that undertakes "not the defense, not even the vindication, but the establishment . . . of that knowledge of God which Christianity professes to embody and seeks to make efficient in the world."[52] While "apologies" thus derive their value from that which is incidental to the propagation of the Christian religion—namely, the defense of Christianity against "opposing points of view"—"apologetics" is of the essence of propagation because it has to do with the presentation and validation of the objective content of the Christian worldview.[53] Indeed, apologetics

> finds its deepest ground . . . not in the accidents which accompany the efforts of true religion to plant, sustain, and propagate itself in this world . . . but in the fundamental needs of the human spirit. If it is incumbent on the believer to be able to give a reason for the faith that is in him, it is impossible for him to be a believer without a reason for the faith that is in him; and it is the task of apologetics to bring this reason out in his consciousness and make its validity plain.[54]

When Warfield's solution to the problem of the relationship between Christianity and culture is seen in this light, it becomes clear that assimilating modern learning to Christian truth does not merely sustain the task of apologetics; it *constitutes* the task of apologetics. We must conclude, therefore, that "the men of the palingenesis" ought to engage in the life of the mind not to argue the unregenerate into the kingdom of God, but to establish the integrity of "the Christian view of the world" by urging their

52. Warfield, "Apologetics," 3.
53. Ibid., 15.
54. Ibid., 4. The apologist must validate the truth that is being established, simply because faith, though it is a moral act and the gift of God, "is yet formally conviction passing into confidence." Validation is necessary, therefore, because an intellectual conviction of the truth of the Christian religion is "the logical *prius* of self-commitment to the Founder of that religion." B. B. Warfield, "A Review of *De Zekerheid des Geloofs*," in *SSW*, 2:113. From this it follows that the apologetical task is focused primarily on the labor of the apologist, and only secondarily on that which is beyond his or her control, namely, the mind of the unregenerate.

"'stronger and purer thought' continuously, and in all its details, upon the attention of men."[55] In so doing, they bring the "thinking world" into subjection to the gospel of Christ, and thereby lay the groundwork for the Spirit to work saving faith where he sovereignly chooses, that is, to "give to a faith which naturally grows out of the proper grounds of faith, that peculiar quality which makes it saving faith."[56] Again, while some scholars will likely object that such an approach owes more to Enlightenment philosophy than it does to a consistently Reformed epistemology, Warfield's position in fact is incomprehensible apart from his clear stand within the epistemological mainstream of the Reformed camp. Indeed, such an approach is virtually unintelligible apart from Warfield's forthright endorsement of the classical Reformed distinction between a merely speculative and a spiritual understanding of revealed truth, and as such it has little if anything to do with accommodation to the forbidden fruits of Enlightenment thought.[57]

The Relationship between Warfield and Kuyper

To this point we have seen that Warfield's solution to the problem of the relationship between Christianity and culture represents the

55. Warfield, "Introduction to Francis R. Beattie's *Apologetics*," in *SSW*, 2:102, 103; cf. 104–5.

56. Warfield, "A Review of *De Zekerheid des Geloofs*," in *SSW*, 2:120, 115. What is supplied by the "creative energy" of the Holy Spirit in the new birth is not, Warfield argued, "a ready-made faith, rooted in nothing and clinging without reason to its object; nor yet new grounds of belief in the object presented; but just a new ability of the heart to respond to the grounds of faith, sufficient in themselves, already present to the understanding." Warfield, "Introduction to Francis R. Beattie's *Apologetics*," in *SSW*, 2:99.

57. Cf. George Marsden, "The Evangelical Love Affair with Enlightenment Science," in *Understanding Fundamentalism and Evangelicalism* (Grand Rapids: Eerdmans, 1991), 122–52. Marsden clearly believes that Kuyperians (who "emphasize that any discipline is built on starting assumptions and that Christians' basic assumptions should have substantial effects on many of their theoretical conclusions in a discipline") are less indebted to Enlightenment categories of thought than are Warfieldians ("those who believe in one science or rationality on which all humanity ought to agree"). While defenders of Warfield must concede that he and his colleagues at Old Princeton employed the categories of Scottish common sense realism to buttress their "intellectualism," they need not concede that Old Princeton's emphasis on objective truth and the primacy of the intellect in faith is *ipso facto* evidence of accommodation to Enlightenment categories of thought. Interestingly, the charge of accommodation to Enlightenment categories has also been made against Kuyperians. Cf. Donald Fuller and Richard Gardiner, "Reformed Theology at Princeton and Amsterdam in the Late Nineteenth Century: A Reappraisal," *Presbyterion* 21, 2 (1995): 89–117.

ideal in Christian scholarship for three reasons: it esteems Scripture as the norm of truth; it acknowledges that this esteem compels believing academics to seek and embrace truth wherever it is found; and it insists that the seeking and embracing of truth are the means to moving the church of God forward to joyous conquest. Having thus distinguished between the assimilation of modern learning to Christian truth, on the one hand, and the accommodation of Christianity to modern culture, on the other, we must now consider how to account for the Kuyperian and quasi-Kuyperian pronouncements that pervade Warfield's writings. Given the intensity of the contemporary debate over how Christians should go about integrating faith and learning, such an accounting will amplify the genius of Warfield's conception of Christian scholarship, for it will demonstrate that the aggressive nature of his response to the cultural challenges of his day was informed not by an implicit rationalism, but by the unambiguous affirmation of the supremacy of the Christian worldview.[58]

In his recent analysis of six lectures delivered by Abraham Kuyper (1837–1920) at Princeton Theological Seminary in the fall of 1898, Peter Heslam suggests that despite the apparent differences between Warfield and Kuyper on key issues of religious epistemology, Warfield's conception of Calvinism "was . . . indebted to Kuyper's exposition of it at Princeton" in at least four ways.[59] According to Heslam, Kuyper's Stone Lectures helped Warfield understand that Calvinism

> represented a broad movement in society and culture, not restricted to the church or doctrine; that it emanated outwards from its central source in the religious consciousness; that this religious consciousness represented the purest and most advanced stage in the development of religion; and that Calvinism offered the best prospects for the future of Christianity.[60]

58. For an overview of the broad outlines of the methodological debate between Warfieldians, Kuyperians, and hybrids in between, see Marsden, "The Evangelical Love Affair with Enlightenment Science," 149–52.

59. Peter S. Heslam, *Creating a Christian Worldview: Abraham Kuyper's Lectures on Calvinism* (Grand Rapids: Eerdmans; Carlisle, Pa.: Paternoster, 1998), 255. See also Peter S. Heslam, "Architects of Evangelical Intellectual Thought: Abraham Kuyper and Benjamin Warfield," *Themelios* 24, 2 (Fall 1999): 3–20.

60. Heslam, *Creating a Christian Worldview*, 255.

Heslam then goes on to cite the following quotation as evidence that Kuyper's influence on Warfield was so profound that Warfield eventually came around to acquiescing even in Kuyper's insistence "on the radical influence of worldview on [the] scientific enterprise."[61] Commenting on the publication of a series of lectures delivered by James Orr at Princeton Seminary in 1905, Warfield enthusiastically and, as Heslam would have us believe, uncharacteristically insisted that

> their publication . . . will carry to a wider audience their fine exposition of the fundamentals of Christian anthropology and their vigorous protest against a tendency, apparently growing among us, "to wholesale surrender of vital aspects of Christian doctrine at the shrine of what is regarded as 'the modern view of the world'" (p. vi). What renders this protest most valuable is that it is particularly directed against weak evasions of the issue raised by the conflict between the Christian view of the world and that "congeries of conflicting and often mutually irreconcilable views" which is commonly spoken of as the "modern view." Dr. Orr has the courage to recognize and assert the irreconcilableness of the two views and the impossibility of a compromise between them; and to undertake the task of showing that the Christian view in the forum of science itself is the only tenable one. This task he accomplishes with distinguished success: and this is the significance of the volume.[62]

While Heslam's comprehensive examination of Kuyper's *Lectures on Calvinism* is noteworthy for its incisive treatment of the Dutch theologian's genius, his assessment of the significance of the above quotation cannot be sustained because it is based on the assumption that Warfield and Kuyper in fact disagreed on key issues of religious epistemology. According to Heslam, Warfield and his colleagues at Old Princeton were at epistemological odds with their more consistently Reformed brethren from the Netherlands because the Princetonians were scholastic rationalists whose "infatuation" with Enlightenment categories of thought left them without the epistemological wherewithal

---

61. Ibid.
62. B. B. Warfield, review of *God's Image in Man, and Its Defacement, in the Light of Modern Denials,* by James Orr, in *Critical Reviews,* 136–37.

to affirm the scientific superiority of the Christian view of the world.[63] Warfield's "glowing" review of Orr is regarded as evidence, therefore, not of continuity with the assumptions of the Princeton tradition, but of a deviation from those assumptions, and thus as evidence that Warfield was won over—in principle if not in fact—to the presuppositional views of the Renaissance man from Amsterdam.[64] Though Heslam concedes that Warfield's more mature writings continue to affirm the value of apologetics, he nonetheless insists that these writings manifest a "less triumphalistic," perhaps domesticated Warfield, chastened by the realization that there is more to religious epistemology than the cold analysis of brute facts.[65]

What, then, should we make of Heslam's assessment? Are Warfield's Kuyperian and quasi-Kuyperian pronouncements evidence that he was inspired by Kuyper to move away from the assumptions of Old Princeton in a more presuppositional direction? Two factors, both of which can be found in Warfield's pre-1898 writings, suggest an answer to this question. The first has to do with Warfield's insistence that only regenerated sinners have the ability to see revealed truth for what it objectively is, namely, glorious. Whereas the consensus of critical opinion would have us believe that Warfield stood outside the epistemological mainstream of the Reformed camp because he was indifferent to the subjective and experiential components of religious epistemology, Warfield, in fact, was thoroughly Reformed because these concerns were of critical importance in his religious epistemology despite its apparently rationalistic rigor. As we saw in the last chapter, the justification for this contention is found in the moral, rather than the merely rational nature of his thought. Like his predecessors at Old Princeton Seminary, Warfield was convinced that the operation of the intellect involves the "whole soul"—mind, will, and emotions—rather than the rational faculty alone. He concluded, therefore, that only regenerated sinners can see revealed truth for what it objectively is, for he recognized that it is only in the souls of the regenerate that there is "perfect interaction" between the objective and subjective factors

63. Heslam, *Creating a Christian Worldview*, 190; cf. chaps. 5 and 7, esp. 123–32 and 176–92.
64. Ibid., 256.
65. Ibid.

that impinge on religious epistemology and underlie religious belief and practice.[66]

One of the principal texts that substantiate this claim is an extremely significant yet infrequently discussed essay entitled "Authority, Intellect, Heart" (1896). In this article, published a full two and a half years before Kuyper delivered his Stone Lectures in the fall of 1898, Warfield outlined the anthropological context within which his epistemological views must be interpreted. The key passage, which grounds his endorsement of the classical Reformed distinction between a merely speculative and a spiritual understanding of revealed truth in his clear commitment to the unitary operation of the soul, reads as follows:

> Authority, intellect, and the heart are the three sides of the triangle of truth. How they interact is observable in any concrete instance of their operation. Authority, in the Scriptures, furnishes the matter which is received in the intellect and operates on the heart. The revelations of the Scriptures do not terminate upon the intellect. They were not given merely to enlighten the mind. They were given through the intellect to beautify the life. They terminate on the heart. Again, they do not, in affecting the heart, leave the intellect untouched. They cannot be fully understood by the intellect, acting alone. The natural man cannot receive the things of the Spirit of God. They must first convert the soul before they are fully comprehended by the intellect. Only as they are lived are they understood. Hence the phrase, "Believe that you may understand," has its fullest validity. No man can intellectually grasp the full meaning of the revelations of authority, save as the result of an experience of their power in life. Hence, that the truths concerning divine things may be so comprehended that they may unite with a true system of divine truth, they must be: first, revealed in an authoritative word; second, experienced in a holy heart; and third, formulated by a sanctified intellect. Only as these three unite, then, can we have a true theology. And equally, that these same truths may be so received that they beget in us a living religion, they must be: first, revealed in an authoritative word; second, apprehended by a sound intellect; and third, experienced in an instructed heart. Only as the three unite, then, can we have vital religion.[67]

66. Warfield, "Authority, Intellect, Heart," in *SSW*, 2:669.
67. Ibid., 2:671.

What this text suggests, among other things, is that dismissing Warfield as a scholastic rationalist may not be so easy as it at first appears, for his epistemological views were perhaps more sophisticated than interpreters like Heslam have been willing to grant to this point.

If Heslam's assessment cannot account for Warfield's epistemological assumptions, on the one hand, it also fails to address his pre-1898 opposition to defending the *"minimum"* of Christianity, on the other. In "Heresy and Concession," an article that was published in early 1896, Warfield announced that he was opposed to any approach to doing apologetics that was based on the assumption that the *"minimum"* of Christianity is all "that is worth defending, or all that is capable of defense."[68] What he meant by this opposition is later made clear in his "Introduction to Francis R. Beattie's *Apologetics*" (1903), perhaps his most sustained critique of the Kuyperian approach to apologetics. The apologist's function, he argued, "is not to vindicate for us the least that we can get along with, and yet manage to call ourselves Christians; but to validate the Christian 'view of the world,' with all that is contained in the Christian 'view of the world,' for the science of men."[69] Apologetics, Warfield explained,

> does not concern itself with how this man or that may best be approached to induce him to make a beginning of Christian living, or how this age or that may most easily be brought to give a hearing to the Christian conception of the world. It concerns itself with the solid objective establishment, after a fashion valid for all normally working minds and for all ages of the world in its developing thought, of those great basal facts which constitute the Christian religion; or, better, which embody in the concrete the entire knowledge of God accessible to men, and which, therefore, need only explication by means of the further theological disciplines in order to lay openly before the eyes of men the entirety of the knowledge of God within their reach.[70]

But what, we must ask, was at the heart of this opposition to defending the *"minimum"* of Christianity? Why was Warfield so

---

68. Warfield, "Heresy and Concession," in *SSW*, 2:677.
69. Warfield, "Introduction to Francis R. Beattie's *Apologetics*," in *SSW* 2:104.
70. Ibid., 2:105.

opposed, in other words, to reducing the all-encompassing task of "apologetics" to the level of a bare "apology"? The answer to this question goes to the core of the matter and is found back in "Heresy and Concession," the pre-1898 essay in which Warfield articulates the methodological assumptions that inform his aggressive response to the problem of the relationship between Christianity and culture. In short, Warfield was opposed to defending the *"minimum"* of Christianity because he was convinced that the ability to see revealed truth for what it objectively is extends beyond the scope of Scripture itself to all truth, be it scientific or religious. The basis for this contention is found in his understanding of the authority of Scripture. Scripture, Warfield argued, is not only the "source and norm" of religious truth, but it is the "interpreter" and "corrector" of modern thought as well.[71] It is, in other words, the standard for measuring "right thinking" of all kinds, and as such it is "superior in point of authority" to the provisional conclusions of modern scholarship.[72] Since Warfield was convinced that the view of the world that is mediated through Scripture is objectively, as opposed to merely subjectively or pragmatically, true, he urged believing academics to engage aggressively in the life of the mind not so that they could impose a partisan interpretation of revealed truth upon a credulous public, but in order to establish the integrity of the only view of the world that accords with what is objectively true, that is, with the way things objectively are.

In light of Warfield's pre-Stone inclination to affirm the preeminence of the Christian view of the world in all areas of learning, it follows that the presence of Kuyperian elements in Warfield's writings is evidence not that Warfield was inspired by Kuyper to move away from the assumptions of Old Princeton in a presuppositional direction, but that there was perhaps more in common between the epistemological views of Warfield and Kuyper, of Old Princeton and Amsterdam, than has hitherto been acknowledged. If this revisionist interpretation has any merit, it indicates that the epistemological assumptions that have typically been regarded as the coin of the realm

71. Warfield, "Heresy and Concession," in *SSW*, 2:674, 679.
72. Ibid.

in the Kuyperian camp were in fact always present in the Princeton tradition. More important, it explains why Warfield was confounded by Kuyper's reticence to engage in an offensive apologetic. Given the probable continuity between Warfield and Kuyper on key issues of religious epistemology, we may plausibly conclude that Kuyper's approach to apologetics was "a standing matter of surprise" to Warfield not because Kuyper refused to advance the kingdom by appealing "to the *natural man's* 'right reason' to judge of the truth of Christianity,"[73] as the consensus of critical opinion would have us believe. It was a matter of surprise, rather, because Kuyper was reluctant to do what Warfield believed that the Christian must of necessity do even when there is "no opposition in the world to be encountered and no contradiction to be overcome,"[74] namely, establish the integrity of the grounds of faith by urging "'his stronger and purer thought' continuously, and in all its details, upon the attention of men."[75] It is entirely possible, therefore, that it was Kuyper's perceived indifference to the necessity of establishing the grounds of faith, that is, his perceived tip of the hat to an astonishing fideistic tendency, that led Warfield to conclude that

no mistake could be greater than to lead them [the men of the palingenesis] to decline to bring their principles into conflict with those of the unregenerate in the prosecution of the common task of man. It is the better science that ever in the end wins the victory; and palingenetic science is the better science; and to it belongs the victory. How shall it win its victory, however, if it declines the conflict? In the ordinance of God, it is only in and through this conflict that the edifice of truth is to rise steadily onwards to its perfecting.[76]

73. Jack Rogers, "Van Til and Warfield on Scripture in the Westminster Confession," in *Jerusalem and Athens: Critical Discussions on the Philosophy and Apologetics of Cornelius Van Til*, ed. E. R. Geehan (Nutley, N.J.: Presbyterian and Reformed, 1971), 154.
74. Warfield, "Apologetics," 4.
75. Warfield, "Introduction to Francis R. Beattie's *Apologetics*," in *SSW*, 2:103. This statement will be misunderstood if it is not interpreted in light of Warfield's clear endorsement of the distinction between a merely speculative and a spiritual understanding of the gospel.
76. Ibid.

Implications for the Integration of Faith and Learning

Having proposed a viable explanation for the presence of Kuy-perian and quasi-Kuyperian pronouncements in Warfield's response to the modern era's relocation of the divine-human nexus, it remains to be seen how Warfield's solution is relevant to the contemporary evan-gelical debate about the integration of faith and learning. Warfield's solution is of relevance for three reasons. In the first place, it encour-ages Christian scholars to engage the life of the mind with zeal without allowing naturalistic scholarship to define the objective realm around which the merely subjective "stuff" of religion must orbit. Although Warfield acknowledged that "all truth is God's"[77] and that "men of all sorts . . . work side by side at the common task" of building up the temple of truth,[78] he nonetheless insisted that true interpretations of reality—indeed the best interpretations of reality—are possible only when general revelation is looked at through the spectacles of special revelation. Despite what the consensus of critical opinion would have us believe, Warfield's epistemology here shows remarkable continuity with that of consistently Reformed scholars such as Jonathan Edwards.[79] Like Edwards before him, Warfield was convinced that genuinely Chris-tian scholarship depends on the new birth. Only regenerated sinners can see revealed truth for what it objectively is, he argued, because they alone can discern the spiritual excellence of what is rationally perceived by looking at it through the spectacles of Scripture.[80] Since Warfield was convinced that believing academics alone have the moral ability to "see and savor God in every branch of learning,"[81] he concluded that they must engage the life of the mind with zeal not so that they

77. Warfield, "Heresy and Concession," in *SSW*, 2:674.
78. Warfield, "Introduction to Francis R. Beattie's *Apologetics*," in *SSW*, 2:102.
79. The claim of epistemological continuity between Warfield and scholars such as Edwards can be justified on the basis of Warfield's endorsement of an Augustinian understanding of "right reason." Please see the articles cited in note 49 above.
80. Cf. John Piper, *God's Passion for His Glory: Living the Vision of Jonathan Edwards* (Wheaton, Ill.: Crossway, 1998), 43–45.
81. Ibid., 43. With respect to Edwards's (and, I would add, Warfield's) distinction between speculative rationality (that which grasps "natural things") and spiritual rationality (that which grasps "divine things"), Piper anticipates the predictable objection: "One might object that the subject matter of psychology or sociology or anthropology or history or physics or chemistry or English or computer science is not 'divine things' but 'natural things.' But that would miss the first point: to see reality in truth we must see it in relation to God, who created it, and sustains

can "find a place for theology within the picture of reality defined by scientific naturalists," but to assimilate modern learning to Christian truth through the superior science of redeemed thought.[82]

If Warfield's solution is relevant in the first place because it is fundamentally opposed to both methodological naturalism, on the one hand, and anti-intellectualism, on the other, it is relevant in the second because it suggests that the contemporary division between Warfieldians and Kuyperians has its genesis, at least in part, in the unresolved—and misunderstood—tension between Warfield and Kuyper. When we consider the contemporary debate in light of Warfield's clear stand within the epistemological mainstream of the Reformed camp, it becomes immediately clear that at the heart of the tension between Warfieldians and Kuyperians is the unresolved question of the relationship between regeneration and scholarly activity. Do the regenerate simply see revealed truth differently than the unregenerate, and are the views of the unregenerate thus just as viable as those of the regenerate? Or, do the regenerate see revealed truth for what it objectively is, and as a consequence do they have a rational basis for claiming that the views of the unregenerate do not accord with objective reality despite the fact that they follow logically from their starting premises? While it is certainly true that precisely how general and special revelation should interact in the minds of the regenerate is a question that warrants ongoing consideration, to suggest that the regenerate and the unregenerate look at general revelation in essentially the same manner—to suggest, in other words, that the views of the unregenerate are just as viable as those of the regenerate—is to suggest that the ability to see revealed

---

it, and gives it all the properties it has and all its relations and designs. To see all these things in each discipline is to see the 'divine things'—and in the end, they are the main things" (ibid.).

82. Phillip E. Johnson, *Reason in the Balance: The Case Against Naturalism in Science, Law and Education* (Downers Grove, Ill.: InterVarsity Press, 1995), 97. For an incisive response to evangelicals who "accept not just the particular conclusions that [naturalistic] scientists have reached but also the naturalistic methodology that generated those conclusions," see Johnson's response to Nancey Murphy, "Phillip Johnson on Trial: A Critique of His Critique of Darwin," *Perspectives on Science & Christian Faith* 45, 1 (March 1993): 26–36, in *Reason in the Balance*, 97–110, 235. Johnson insists that "theists who accept a naturalistic understanding of knowledge fatally undercut their own intellectual position," for in so doing they unwittingly endorse the naturalistic distinction between religious truth and scientific truth, and thereby abandon to "science" the whole realm of objective truth.

truth for what it objectively is will have little or no consequence in the prosecution of the task of Christian scholarship. It is to suggest, moreover, that the Christian worldview is only subjectively or pragmatically true, and thus of no more significance than the worldviews of unbelieving academics.[83]

Finally, Warfield's response to the modern era's relocation of the divine-human nexus is relevant because it calls attention to the inherently slippery nature of the enterprise he confidently referred to as "progressive orthodoxy."[84] Though Warfield was convinced that he lived in an age in which the primary responsibility of the church was to establish the integrity of the biblical worldview over and against the critical reconstructions of those who "cheerfully give up the substance, but never the name of Christianity,"[85] he nonetheless "had no quarrel . . . with the notion that men's understanding of Christianity will advance as their understanding of both natural and special revelation is corrected and enlarged."[86] Indeed, he refused to equate the "construction" of theology with the "destruction" of theology,[87] and as a consequence he insisted that the science of theology should proceed into the future "on the basis of the already ascertained truth of the past."[88] Whereas scholars like Mark Noll laud Warfield and his

83. In this regard, I like the following statement by Phillip Johnson because it presents a challenge to believing academics who for one reason or another are reluctant to acknowledge that the Christian worldview makes any appreciable difference in the doing of academic work. Speaking of the contradiction between theism in religion and naturalism in science, Johnson says: "If evidence of divine action in the history of the universe is conspicuous by its apparent absence, then we may still choose to believe that the universe would disappear if God did not constantly uphold it with his mighty (but scientifically undetectable) word of power. Wise metaphysical naturalists will smile at these transparent devices, but they will not openly ridicule them. Why should they—when theists implicitly comply with the naturalistic doctrine that 'religion' is a matter of faith not reason?" (*Reason in the Balance*, 101).

84. Warfield, "The Idea of Systematic Theology," 78.

85. Warfield, review of *Foundations*, 324.

86. Samuel G. Craig, introduction to *Biblical and Theological Studies*, by B. B. Warfield, ed. Samuel G. Craig (Philadelphia: Presbyterian and Reformed, 1952), xliii.

87. Warfield, "The Idea of Systematic Theology," 78.

88. Swanton, "Warfield and Progressive Orthodoxy," 86. "Progressive orthodoxy," Warfield reasoned, "implies that first of all we are orthodox, and secondly that we are progressively orthodox, that is, that we are ever growing more and more orthodox as more and more truth is being established. . . . In any progressive science, the amount of departure from accepted truth which is possible to the sound thinker becomes thus ever less and less, in proportion as investigation and study result in the progressive establishment of an ever increasing number of facts. . . . It is of the very essence of our position at the end of the ages that we are ever more and more

colleagues at Old Princeton for holding, among other things, "that the findings of science should be enlisted to help discover proper interpretations of Scripture,"[89] others like David Hall are convinced that Warfield jettisoned the authority of Scripture because he allowed science to have "at least *theoretical* preeminence over Scripture, at least as an intermediate hermeneutic."[90] He was willing to suggest, in other words, "that if an 'indisputable' result of thorough induction manifestly contradicted an existing doctrine of the church, the theologian *must reconsider* his interpretation of God's word, and see if he has not misunderstood it."[91]

While the question of whether Noll or Hall is correct in his assessment of Warfield is beyond the scope of this chapter, what is of immediate relevance is the question of how those who affirm that "all truth is God's truth" should distinguish "God's truth" from "Satan's error."[92] How, specifically, should those who have the ability to "reason rightly" interact with the conclusions of naturalistic scholarship, and when, more importantly, does their attempt to sift the good and reject the bad cross the almost imperceptible line that separates assimilation from

---

hedged around with ascertained facts, the discovery and establishment of which constitute the very essence of progress. Progress brings increasing limitation, just because it brings increasing knowledge. And as the orthodox man is he that teaches no other doctrine than that which has been established as true, the progressively orthodox man is he who is quick to perceive, admit, and condition all his reasoning by all the truth down to the latest, which has been established as true." Warfield, "The Idea of Systematic Theology," 78–79.

89. Mark Noll, "Charles Hodge and B. B. Warfield on Science, the Bible, Evolution, and Darwinism," *Modern Reformation* 7, 3 (May/June 1998): 18–22; see also idem, *The Scandal of the Evangelical Mind* (Grand Rapids: Eerdmans, 1994), 177–208.

90. David Hall, "Holding Fast the Concession of Faith: Science, Apologetics, and Orthodoxy," A Paper Presented to the 47th Annual Meeting of the Evangelical Theological Society, November 1995, Philadelphia, 10.

91. Theodore Dwight Bozeman, *Protestants in an Age of Science* (Chapel Hill: University of North Carolina Press, 1977), 118. While I agree with Hall that evangelicals "ought to be leery" of surrendering aspects of historic orthodoxy to what he incisively calls "idea-fads of modernity," I am not entirely convinced that allowing accepted *interpretations* of Scripture to be challenged by the *indisputable* conclusions of scientific investigation necessarily entails setting the authority of science over that of Scripture *itself*. Certainly, all but the most progressively inclined will agree that accepted interpretations of Scripture should not be jettisoned cavalierly, if at all. But does it therefore follow that accepted interpretations should never be challenged? Does it follow, in other words, that Christians should discount scientific findings even if those findings will establish *conclusively* that an accepted interpretation of Scripture was never truly scriptural—i.e., true—at all? Obviously, these questions go to the core of the debate between scholars like Noll and Hall.

92. I am indebted to Rev. Ian Hewitson for framing the question in this fashion.

accommodation?[93] Commenting on the inherently conflicted nature of conservative scholarship that makes Scripture "potentially nonfalsifiable" by reading the Bible "through the lens of empirical science," John Mark Reynolds and Paul Nelson articulate a point that all who are concerned about the ultimate authority of Scripture would be wise to consider.[94] "There is something troubling," they argue,

93. These questions are admittedly troublesome in part because no matter how they are resolved the potential for accommodating to the spirit of the age—and thereby of endorsing, either explicitly or implicitly, what J. Gresham Machen called "one of the chief shibboleths of modern skepticism," namely, the notion that religious truth is distinct from scientific truth—appears very real. Machen, "The Relation of Religion to Science and Philosophy," *Princeton Theological Review* 24 (1926): 50. Conservatives who insist on reading Scripture in light of the latest conclusions of modern scholarship are clearly in danger of bending Scripture into conciliation with conclusions that are not *really* true but merely "idea-fads of modernity." As such, they are in danger of acting as if the Christian religion is merely a subjective phenomenon that must be brought into conformity with the prevailing mind of the day, and therefore of thinking like those who are convinced that scientific truth and religious truth occupy different epistemological realms. Certainly this is one reason why arguments that are critical of Old Princeton's openness to certain aspects of evolutionary theory are so forceful. See, for example, Hall, "Holding Fast the Concession of Faith," and David W. Hall, "Angels Unaware: The Ascendancy of Science over Orthodoxy in Nineteenth Century Reformed Orthodoxy," unpublished paper. On Old Princeton's attitude toward evolutionary theory, cf. Charles Hodge, *What Is Darwinism? and Other Writings on Science and Religion*, ed. Mark A. Noll and David N. Livingstone (Grand Rapids: Baker, 1994); B. B. Warfield, *Evolution, Scripture, and Science: Selected Writings*, ed. Mark A. Noll and David N. Livingstone (Grand Rapids: Baker, 2000); Bradley John Gundlach, "The Evolution Question at Princeton, 1845–1929 (Ph.D. diss., University of Rochester, 1995); David N. Livingstone, "Science, Region, and Religion: The Reception of Darwinism in Princeton, Belfast, and Edinburgh," in *Disseminating Darwinism: The Role of Place, Race, Religion, and Gender*, ed. Ronald L. Numbers and John Stenhouse (Cambridge: Cambridge University Press, 1999), 7–38.

But if conservatives who read Scripture in light of modern scholarship are in danger of accommodating the "idea-fads" of the present day, it is entirely possible that those who refuse to bring the non-"idea-fads of modernity" to bear on the interpretation of Scripture are in danger of enshrining the "idea-fads" of an earlier day. They are in danger, in other words, of regarding as true a previous generation's inability to look at general revelation through the spectacles of special revelation, and thus they too are in danger of treating the Christian religion as little more than an essentially subjective phenomenon. How, then, should Christians proceed? Perhaps we should begin by proceeding patiently and cautiously, allowing accepted interpretations of Scripture to be challenged *only* after generations of those who have the mind of Christ and hold the norm of truth in their hands have sorted truth from error on the basis of sound exegesis. I would suggest, moreover, that when we are having difficulty determining which conclusions of modern scholarship are "provisional" and which ones are "indisputable," we would be wise to assume a posture that defers to orthodox interpretations of Scripture. For when we do not assume this posture we act as if the scientific enterprise always and everywhere yields facts instead of interpretations of facts, which is to prejudice believing academics against orthodoxy.

94. John Mark Reynolds and Paul Nelson, "Young Earth Creationism," in *Three Views on Creation and Evolution*, ed. J. P. Moreland and John Mark Reynolds (Grand Rapids: Zondervan, 1999), 69.

about the fact that there is no built-in limit to the amount of accommodation possible. What is meant by the statement "The Bible is true" if accommodation proceeds past a certain point? People holding this view, or any view like it, would need to clarify how far they are willing to stretch language before giving up the initial premise. As the argument stands now, the Bible could theoretically be made to say the opposite of its "plain sense" and still be defended as "scientifically accurate." This is disconcerting.[95]

While no participant in the contemporary debate has any intention of undermining either the integrity or the authority of Scripture, the controversial nature of Warfield's solution to the problem of the relationship between Christianity and culture is a reminder to scholars on both sides of the divide that the line between assimilation and accommodation—between "progressive orthodoxy" and "modernism"—is razor thin and difficult to discern. As such, Warfield's response to the modern era's relocation of the divine-human nexus is finally relevant because it is a call to those who have the mind of Christ and hold the norm of truth in their hands to do scholarship in a manner that accords self-consciously with presuppositions that are consistently Christian.

95. Ibid., 69–70.

❧ 6 ❧

"Wicked Caste": Warfield, Biblical Authority, and Jim Crow

Bradley J. Gundlach

"Nothing is more disheartening," writes distinguished historian Eugene Genovese concerning Southern Presbyterians in the post-Reconstruction era, "than to see such firmly orthodox Christians as [Robert Lewis] Dabney, who stood all his life on *sola scriptura* and turned to the Bible for guidance on every subject, plunge into arguments from sheer prejudice that hardly pretended to be scripturally based."[1] Genovese puts forth the provocative thesis that the pattern of Jim Crow segregation that descended on the South in the last decades of the nineteenth century, while perpetuating the social subordination blacks had endured under slavery, represented a departure—indeed, a *lapse*—from the antebellum proslavery pattern of theological and biblical argument: "The proslavery divines may be criticized severely for theological error, but they cannot fairly be accused of bad faith, much less hypocrisy, in their scriptural defense of slavery. The same cannot be said for their successors' efforts to defend postbellum segregation."[2]

---

1. Eugene D. Genovese, *A Consuming Fire: The Fall of the Confederacy in the Mind of the White Christian South* (Athens, Ga.: University of Georgia Press, 1998), 95.
2. Ibid., 94. This interpretation, Genovese notes (81), revises the common wisdom that segregationism, in reversing the gains of Reconstruction, represented a return to Southern slaveholding ideology, adapted slightly to the realities of emancipation. For the earlier view, see

136

Robert L. Dabney, James Henley Thornwell, and other prominent Southern Presbyterians stand indicted for gross inconsistency in
abandoning their habitual reliance on Scripture and theology when
arguing in support of the color line. Genovese's point, among others,
is that these men knew deep down that the Bible did not support
their attempt to impose a caste system on the freedmen. In the contest between their abhorrence of race mixing and their fidelity to the
Bible, the Bible lost. And that outcome was particularly depressing
in view of the long Southern insistence on a fundamental connection
between socioeconomic system and religion. Dabney argued that biblical Christianity would not survive in the social conditions fostered by
modern industrial capitalism. Orthodox faith needed undergirding by
a society ordered according to biblical teaching: namely, social strati-
fication based on face-to-face relations between masters and personal
servants. While holding no brief for this antebellum social ideology,
Genovese at least admires its consistency and its use of the Bible to
criticize economic and social arrangements. After Reconstruction, he
charges, "many—perhaps a good majority—of the orthodox disgraced
themselves" on the race question by indulging in the rank hypocrisy of
simultaneously touting their orthodoxy and abandoning their previous
habit of close attention to Scripture.[3]

It is, of course, not just the South that stands indicted for institut-
ing a caste system in the years of Jim Crow. As C. Vann Woodward
famously argued, the South modeled its segregation laws on what
certain Northern states, particularly in the old Northwest, had enacted
in the antebellum years to limit and control the African-American presence there. Indeed, the descent of segregationism on the South after

---

H. Shelton Smith, *In His Image, But . . . : Racism in Southern Religion, 1780–1910* (Durham,
N.C.: Duke University Press, 1972).

3. Genovese, *Consuming Fire*, 80, 93. His indictment of these Southern white church
leaders on race is far from his only word on them. Elsewhere he laments the current "neglect of,
or contempt for, the history of Southern whites, without which some of the more distinct and
noble features of American national life must remain incomprehensible. The northern victory
in 1865 silenced a discretely southern interpretation of American history and national identity,
and it promoted a contemptuous dismissal of all things southern as nasty, racist, immoral, and
intellectually inferior." Genovese names Thornwell along with the likes of John C. Calhoun,
Robert E. Lee, and Stonewall Jackson as men deserving of admiration and attention on their
own terms, even as we decry the wicked race system they defended. Genovese, *The Southern
Tradition: The Achievement and Limitations of an American Conservatism* (Cambridge, Mass.:
Harvard University Press, 1994), xi–xii.

Reconstruction represented a distinct turning away from antebellum Southern social patterns, in which blacks and whites had had frequent contact, to the antebellum Northern pattern of separation of the races.[4] And when the federal government abandoned Reconstruction in 1877, the North effectively abandoned "the Negro problem" to the judgment and devices of Southern whites. Labor unrest, concern over a rising flood of "new immigration" from southern and eastern Europe, new scientific theories of human biological and social evolution, and sheer weariness after more than a decade of federal Reconstruction efforts, led the North both to hand race issues back to Southern whites and to agree with them that Southern whites knew best how to handle the black race.

And the story grows yet more depressing when we turn to the churches, both Northern and Southern. With the exception of a handful of heroic voices, Southern white churchmen enacted new rules that relegated blacks to subordinate status within mainline denominations, and then, when African Americans refused to settle for lower-caste status, encouraged them to leave. Black folks flooded out of the white-dominated Methodist, Baptist, and Presbyterian churches of the South, forming independent congregations and denominations under black leadership—something Southern whites had long prevented in antebellum days for fear of the black churches fomenting slave rebellion.[5] Those few blacks who did remain in the white churches had to accept subordinate status—for example, a second-class ordination that limited blacks' ministry to members of their own race and granted them no vote in denominational gatherings; congregations separate from whites but under white pastors and/or white elder boards. Southern Presbyterians instituted such a system of segregation and subordination—and in the 1880s the Northern Presbyterians were considering reunion with the Southern church so ordered.

4. C. Vann Woodward, *The Strange Career of Jim Crow*, 3rd ed. (1955; repr., New York: Oxford University Press, 1974), 17–21.

5. Smith, *In His Image, But*, chap. 5; Andrew E. Murray, *Presbyterians and the Negro—A History* (Philadelphia: Presbyterian Historical Society, 1966), chap. 5. On fears of rebellion through black churches, see John B. Adger, *My Life and Times, 1810–1899* (Richmond, Va.: Presbyterian Committee of Publication, 1899), 165. Adger discusses firsthand the opposition of whites in Charleston, S.C., in the wake of Denmark Vesey's rebellion—which began indeed in a black congregation.

Meanwhile, in the Northern Presbyterian church, a Kentucky-bred son of slaveholders spoke out in print against the drawing of the color line in church and society, and based his socially heretical arguments on the authority of the Bible. His name was Benjamin Breckinridge Warfield, and he had been freshly elected to the top chair in Princeton Theological Seminary. In two articles he wrote for the popular religious press—"A Calm View of the Freedmen's Case," in *The Church at Home and Abroad* (January 1887), and "Drawing the Color Line: A Fragment of History, by a Disinterested Spectator," in the New York *Independent* (July 1888)—and in private correspondence with readers agitated by these articles, Warfield made it clear that for him, in the contest between race feeling and prudential arguments, on the one hand, and scriptural commands, on the other, Scripture must win.[6] When we remember that Warfield spent a good deal of his academic energies defending and establishing the complete authority of the Bible, we find a refreshing counterpoint to the trend that Genovese finds so discouraging among the self-proclaimed defenders of orthodoxy. In this case at least, biblical authority trumped the most pervasive and visceral social prejudices of the day.

Scion of Antislavery Slaveholders

Warfield's commitment to racial justice in society and in the churches shows not only in his undertaking these two articles for the popular religious press, but in his doing so at a time in his career when other duties called with particular urgency. In the late fall of 1886, when he wrote "A Calm View of the Freedmen's Case," Warfield received a call to succeed A. A. Hodge in the chair of didactic and polemical theology at Princeton Seminary. This call required a major career shift: from the New Testament, Warfield's favorite field, to systematics; and from Western Theological Seminary in Allegheny,

6. Benjamin Breckinridge Warfield, "A Calm View of the Freedmen's Case," *The Church at Home and Abroad* (January 1887), 62–65, reprinted in Benjamin B. Warfield, *Selected Shorter Writings*, 2 vols., ed. John E. Meeter (Nutley, N.J.: Presbyterian and Reformed, 1970, 1973), 2:735–42; and Warfield, "Drawing the Color Line: A Fragment of History, by a Disinterested Spectator," *The Independent* (New York), July 5, 1888, reprinted in *Selected Shorter Writings*, 2:743–50.

Pennsylvania (now part of Pittsburgh), where he had been teaching since 1878, to Princeton. He needed to move his household and prepare himself to occupy the most revered academic chair in the Presbyterian church. Numerous correspondents were sending their congratulations and reminding him of the high expectations conservatives entertained of his scholarship, his leadership at this crucial juncture in the life of the church, and his proving a worthy successor to the venerable Hodges. Warfield spent a great deal of time considering the call, especially in view of the change of departments. His correspondence is full of letters from family and friends replying to his thoughts and requests for advice. He was also already engaged to write several biblical commentaries, including one on Revelation, for W. R. Nicoll's new series, *The Expositor's Bible Commentary*.[7] Warfield had work aplenty to occupy his days and evenings; he had a major career change in the works; and on top of that he had family troubles to attend to: in November 1886 his sister-in-law died in childbirth. Warfield made the long trip to St. Louis to comfort his grieving brother. It was on his return to Allegheny from the funeral that he found the letter offering him the coveted chair at Princeton.[8] And yet, beset by all these momentous circumstances, he undertook to write about the plight of America's former slaves.

Since the summer of 1885 Warfield had been a member of the Presbyterian Board of Missions to Freedmen (PBMF), and in that capacity he felt an obligation to work for the betterment of black Americans. It was in fact the PBMF's corresponding secretary who suggested that Warfield write an article on the freedmen's plight.[9] But his election to the board and his interest in the race question were no accident. Warfield came from a Kentucky family deeply committed to, and entangled in, questions of right and justice for the former slaves. For Warfield had been born into a family that found itself in the uncomfortable position of owning slaves and believing slavery a grave evil.

7. William Robertson Nicoll to Warfield (hereafter BBW for correspondence), April 28, 1887 (Warfield Papers, Princeton Theological Seminary [hereafter PTS], box 17). Warfield never did write the commentary on Revelation.

8. James H. Brookes to BBW, December 3, 1886 (Warfield Papers, PTS, box 6); BBW to Caspar Wistar Hodge, December 8, 1886 (Warfield Papers, PTS, box 17).

9. R. H. Allen to BBW, November 10 and 11, 1886 (Warfield Papers, PTS, box 17).

As Warfield wrote to an Ohio critic of his "Freedmen's Case" article in 1887, the draft of which survives among his papers,

> the problem before individual slave holders was far from the simple one that men think, when looking at it from without & from now. I was brought up among slave holders who were sincerely convinced that the holding of slaves was an immense evil & a great sin & I know how impossible it was to extricate oneself from the meshes of the evil & perform duty to all concerned.[10]

In a remarkable passage from that same draft, Warfield detailed his family's antislavery involvement.

> John C. Young, the drawer of the resolutions of the Ky. Synod of 1835 was the husband of my mother's first cousin. My Grandfather R. J. Breckinridge ran on an emancipation ticket in 1849 – at the peril of his life. Cassius M. Clay was the husband of my father's first cousin. My Mother-in-law was an abolitionist of the Garrison type. My grandparents, parents & the parents of my wife sought in every way to do their duty to those whom they felt themselves sinners to hold in bondage. They freed them: they sent them to Liberia; they gave them property & set them up in Ohio, – & they found themselves forced for the negroes' own good to hold them sometimes in bondage. You cannot conceive of the complexity of the individual problems, that arise. But thank God. He has cut the knot which human wisdom could not untie![11]

This striking litany of a slaveholding family's antislavery position bears some drawing out. Among Warfield's antislavery law-kin were

10. BBW to Joseph William Torrence, January 7, 1887 (Warfield Papers, PTS, box 17). Warfield wrote on this draft, "This letter was not sent: but a briefer abstract, conveying the same principles."

11. Ibid. Edgar C. Mayse's dissertation on Robert J. Breckinridge sheds some light on the manumissions Warfield mentions here. Warfield's Great-Uncle William (Robert's brother) liberated eleven of the family's slaves in 1833. They were settled in Liberia by the Kentucky Colonization Society. Robert filed a deed of emancipation for his own slaves in 1835, setting up a gradual emancipation scheme registered at the Fayette County courthouse. Any slaves of his under twenty-one years of age, and any yet to be born to his female slaves, would be liberated on attaining their twenty-fifth birthdays. Edgar Caldwell Mayse, "Robert Jefferson Breckinridge: American Presbyterian Controversialist" (Th.D. diss., Union Theological Seminary, Richmond, Va., 1974), 236–38 (hereafter "RJB" for this Mayse title, RJB for correspondence).

the Rev. John C. Young, president of Centre College in Danville, Kentucky, a leader in the Kentucky Colonization Society,[12] and Cassius M. Clay, a leading advocate of liberal antislavery views. These two worked together with Warfield's grandfather, the outspoken antislavery moderate Robert Jefferson Breckinridge, in a statewide organization called the Friends of Emancipation. In 1849 this group managed to unite the various antislavery positions (conservative, moderate, liberal, and radical) in a bid to write into the new state constitution a provision for gradual emancipation, with financial compensation to the former slaveholders, and facilitating the colonization of the freedpeople in Liberia. The great Whig leader Henry Clay, who years before had considered Breckinridge politically foolish for taking an antislavery stand in politics, supplied a letter in favor of the plan. At the organization's state convention in Frankfort, Breckinridge employed his considerable oratorical powers to whip up the zeal of Kentucky antislavery men. While urging patience and circumspection, Breckinridge attacked slavery as a "great evil, that is weighing down my country," and promised, "I will sacrifice all but honor, to rid my country of it." A few weeks later a Lexington antislavery meeting nominated him for the position of delegate to the constitutional convention, in express opposition to the proslavery nominees in both the Democratic and Whig parties. This was the campaign to which Warfield adverted in the above letter. Though Breckinridge's emancipationism was far from the radical type, incorporating as it did compensation, gradualism, and colonization, the cause aroused bitter hostility and even violence. Duels and fights broke out, one involving Cassius Clay with the sons of a proslavery candidate. Breckinridge's four resolutions against "hereditary slavery" incensed the proslavery element in Lexington. He was barred from speaking in public halls and threatened with mob violence if he attempted to campaign in public.[13] This was likely the threat to Breckinridge's life that Warfield mentions, though he faced the additional peril of cholera. A terrible epidemic swept Kentucky during the campaign, limiting

12. Murray, *Presbyterians and the Negro*, 77; *Encyclopaedia of the Presbyterian Church in the United States of America, Including the Northern and Southern Assemblies*, ed. Alfred Nevin (Philadelphia: Presbyterian Encyclopaedia Publ. Co., 1884), 1053.

13. Ethelbert D. Warfield, "The Breckinridges of Kentucky: A Chronicle of Loyalty," unidentified newspaper clipping, May 22, 1890 (Warfield Family Papers, University of Kentucky).

Breckinridge's efforts to promote his candidacy—but, in a stroke of providence that assured him of the righteousness of his cause and that seems to have lived on in family lore, Breckinridge was the only local candidate not stricken with the disease.[14]

Yet alongside these antislavery credentials stands the fact that Warfield grew up in a household with slaves, among kin who were large slaveholders. These circumstances of birth and rearing in a highly political and influential Kentucky family loomed large in his sense of personal stake in the race issue of his day. The dilemma of the antislavery slaveholder—feeling it wicked to hold people in bondage, but wicked too to release them unprepared into a society unprepared to receive them fairly—beset Warfield's kin and impelled Warfield himself to speak out against segregation and ill treatment of African Americans in the post-Reconstruction era. To appreciate the force of this dilemma, some further particulars of the family's politics and slaveholding are in order.

Warfield was the scion of two prominent Whig/Republican families in the Bluegrass region, a section of Kentucky where those parties enjoyed particular strength and, strikingly, where many of the state's large slaveholders were concentrated.[15] His grandfather Benjamin Warfield was a familiar friend of Henry Clay—a witness, indeed, for Clay's will.[16] The other grandfather, Robert Jefferson Breckinridge, was, in addition to his statewide antislavery efforts, a key supporter of Abraham Lincoln who worked hard to keep Kentucky (a crucial border state during the Civil War) in the Union. At the 1864 Republican national convention in Baltimore, Breckinridge served as temporary chairman and delivered a ringing extempore address for the Republican cause that party leader James G. Blaine long recalled as the best speech he heard there.[17] At the beginning of the secession crisis Breckinridge led a small group of Presbyterian clergymen in

14. James C. Klotter, *The Breckinridges of Kentucky, 1760–1981* (Lexington, Ky.: University Press of Kentucky, 1986), 66–67, 73–76.

15. Charles Hodge, "Emancipation," review of "The Question of Negro Slavery and the New Constitution of Kentucky," by Robert Jefferson Breckinridge, *Biblical Repertory and Princeton Review* 21 (1849): 583.

16. B. B. Warfield, "The Warfields: Kentucky Branch" (Warfield Family Papers, University of Kentucky), 65; Henry Clay Papers, vol. 10.

17. Klotter, *The Breckinridges of Kentucky*, 84–87.

establishing the *Danville Review*, a theological quarterly that also functioned as a starkly pro-Union organ. One pastor went so far as to claim that Breckinridge's essays in the *Danville Review* "were really instrumental in saving California [*sic*] for the Union."[18] Warfield shared his family's strong Republican sympathies, glorying, for example, in the Republican gains in Kentucky in the election of 1880.[19] Those sympathies were all the stronger for the fact that the Breckinridges were notoriously divided over politics: Warfield's mother's cousin was John C. Breckinridge, Democratic vice president under James Buchanan and Constitutional Democratic candidate for president in the campaign of 1860, who as a leading Confederate had to flee the country for several years. Warfield's uncle, William Campbell Preston Breckinridge, served the Confederacy, as a colonel, along with several other uncles and cousins in grey. Uncle Willie became a Democratic U.S. senator after Reconstruction. With secessionism rife among his near kin, Warfield, together with his brother, parents, and grandparents, deepened his Republican convictions. After the war the family never completely patched up its differences.[20]

But these same ardent members of an antislavery, eventually abolitionist, party were themselves large slaveholders. The 1850 Federal Census lists 13 slaves for father William Warfield, 23 for grandfather Benjamin Warfield, and 37 for grandfather R. J. Breckinridge. In 1860 Breckinridge still owned 39 slaves, and William Warfield owned 25. Uncles and great-uncles owned slaves in comparable numbers.[21]

This family prided itself on good treatment of its slaves—solemnizing slave marriages, refusing on general principle to sell them away, providing for the elderly, and, if "black" and "mulatto" notations on

18. "Breckinridge, Robert J.," *Biblical Repertory and Princeton Review*, index volume [1872], 115.

19. Warfield's mother wrote in reply to his letter to her (now lost): "Indeed yes, it was a splended [*sic*] triumph for us Republicans." Mary Cabell Warfield to BBW, November 7, 1880 (Warfield Papers, PTS, box 2).

20. Klotter, *The Breckinridges of Kentucky*, 87; cf. Issa Desha Breckinridge to her husband William C. P. Breckinridge, May 1, 1879: "I did my duty this afternoon by calling on Annie [Mrs. B. B. Warfield, visiting Lexington] – they were all quite polite – but stately – I think I was just as much so – we live too close to be any other way –" (Breckinridge Papers, Library of Congress, Manuscripts Division, bound volume 307). Warfield's mother sometimes referred to the Democratic branch of the family as "the Secesh."

21. Federal Census Slave Schedules, 1850 and 1860, for Fayette County, Kentucky.

the slave census schedules are any indication, not permitting white sons or neighbors to take advantage of slave women.[22] Grandfather Warfield provided for his slaves variously in his will of 1856, including this final stipulation:

> My slaves not given away and which I may own at my death I cannot agree to seperate [*sic*] them from their wives mothers and relations. It is my will therefore that at their Just value (unless they are willing to go they shall not be compelled to remove) my sons in Kentucky take them and keep them: and to be charged with them —[23]

However benign their treatment, though, slaves were still slaves, chattel property under the law, and regularly passed on to the next generation along with other valuables. As legal chattels they were utterly subject to the will of their master or mistress, and even within this highly religious and upright family there were unfortunate incidents. When several young male slaves ran away from the aged Mary Hopkins Breckinridge, Warfield's great-grandmother, in 1848, she took it as a blow of unforgivable ingratitude to a kindly mistress. "Grandma Black Cap," as her family affectionately called her, was an earnest Christian, "a mother in Zion," whose pride and joy it was that three of her sons had gone into the gospel ministry.[24] Two of those ministers, William and Robert (Warfield's grandfather), exchanged several letters over the runaway problem. One of William's letters to Robert shows both the sense of personal affront this Christian mistress felt and the raw fact of power she had over her slaves—as well as showing her minister son's agreement in it.

22. Ibid. William Warfield's 25 slaves in 1860 are: 12 workers in the prime of life (9 men and 3 women), 1 woman aged 90, and 12 children. All are listed as "B" for black—though neighbors have slaves listed as "M" for mulatto. R. J. Breckinridge's slaves are also all "B." On the Breckinridge family's rule of never selling slaves away, see Mayse, "RJB," 46. A bit of evidence on Breckinridge slave marriages is found in R. J. Breckinridge's second wife's papers: he reports that her "servant" (euphemism for slave) Becky has a husband who treats her badly. RJB to Virginia Hart Shelby Breckinridge, December 30, 1852 (Virginia Hart Shelby Breckinridge Papers, Filson Club Historical Society, Louisville, Ky.).

23. Benjamin Warfield's will, dated February 1856, Fayette County (Ky.) Will Book 5:414ff.

24. Klotter, *The Breckinridges of Kentucky*, 39ff.; Mayse, "RJB," 66 n. 85.

I brought out last night your letter to Ma of the 11th. She had not previously heard of the elopement of her negroes. She desires me this morning to write to you on the subject, & say that her wish is that all of them may be sold with the obligation of taking them out of the country, that if this cannot be done, some arrangement may be made by which they may be removed from about Lexington, & that she is determined that in no case shall one of them come on her farm while she lives. . . . I have said as little to her as I well could about these runaways – & nothing, to influence her mind in this matter – judgeing [sic] that there was no call on me to attempt any thing of the kind – but, as you suggest a conference about it, I may as well say here, that I think her notions as above stated are about right in the premises. I am not competent with my limited knowledge of the law, & of the way in which she holds her negroes, to say much on the subject – but I am clear that if in her place, I would not allow any of them to come on the place again, except Harry who ought, I think, to be treated as a child [age 16], perhaps soundly threshed, & put to his business again.[25]

A second sad example from the same family comes in a story about grandfather Breckinridge's pre-conversion days. A family friend recalled,

Grandma Black Cap, in a rather attenuated frame, had the pluck of a battalion. Her son Robert had long threatened that on his sixteenth birthday he would whip old John, the colored carriage driver; which he accordingly did. His mother then took Robert and gave him eye for eye and tooth for tooth, good measure. "I'll let you know sir," quoth she, "that you shall behave yourself, if you are sixteen years old."[26]

25. William L. Breckinridge to RJB, August 15, 1848 (Breckinridge Papers, Library of Congress, Manuscripts Division, box 131). The runaways were "Philip, Reuben, Carey, Wilson, Mike, and Harry, slaves of Mrs Mary H Breckinridge." Robert J. Breckinridge paid some $624 in reimbursement for the "reward, expenses and jail fees" to his agent in the matter—so it appears the runaways were advertised and hunted down in the usual manner. W. S. Pullen to RJB, August 15, 1848 (Breckinridge Papers, box 131). Two more runaway incidents in the family occurred five years later. When a hired-out slave of R. J. Breckinridge's wife, Virginia, ran off, she pondered whether to sell him or free him. Virginia Hart Shelby Breckinridge to RJB, January 5, 1853 (Virginia Hart Shelby Breckinridge Papers, Filson Club). When a female slave of R. J. Breckinridge's ran off, he instructed his wife to hire her out. RJB to Virginia Hart Shelby Breckinridge, January 16, 1853.

26. L. G. Barbour, "The Breckinridges," clipping from the *Presbyterian Monthly* (no volume or date), 426 (Warfield Papers, PTS).

So Warfield's grandfather R. J. Breckinridge, that vociferous anti-slavery advocate, once whipped an old slave just to prove his manhood. His mother whipped him back, making one wonder just how comparable the two whippings were. But we at least see that a teenage boy in such circumstances, even if frowned upon, had it in his power to abuse an old slave.

Slavery was, as Warfield wrote in 1887, a great evil. His slave-holding family believed themselves trapped in the sin of slaveholding, and were not exempt from the temptations of such total power over people. Nor did they rise above their society's belief in racial inequality. In a prolonged, bitter debate with proslavery advocate and fellow Lexingtonian Robert Wickliffe, R. J. Breckinridge defended himself against the charge of advocating "race mixing," calling it "a *base, spurious, degraded mixture, hardly less revolting* than revolution." Wickliffe, seeing the advantages of this line of argument, went on to accuse Breckinridge himself of miscegenation, the worst evil he could think of in connection with the end of slavery.[27] Indeed an important plank in Breckinridge's own antislavery argument was the degrading effect of the presence of a race of inferiors in this free, white land. In his influential "Discourse on the Day of National Humiliation" at the start of the secession crisis (January 1861), Breckinridge suggested that Kentucky, being less dependent on slave labor, was better positioned than the cotton states to begin the removal of the curse of slavery from the South. But for him the scourge of slavery was not simply (or even primarily) the evil perpetrated on the slaves; it was rather the presence of Africans in American society.

> The very instant you enter a confederacy in which all is regulated and created by the supreme interest of cotton, every thing precious and distinctive of you [Kentucky], is jeoparded! Do you want the slave trade re-opened? Do you want free trade and direct taxation? Do

27. Klotter, *The Breckinridges of Kentucky*, 70–73. Wickliffe had once been Breckinridge's friend, and rather treacherously used his intimate knowledge of Breckinridge's pre-conversion days for ad hominem attacks in the antislavery controversy (Mayse, "RJB," 74). Wickliffe had also been the close friend and former law partner of Warfield's other grandfather, Benjamin Warfield (B. B. Warfield, "Warfields: Kentucky Branch," 64). Personal connections and feelings of betrayal inflamed the whole Wickliffe-Breckinridge affair.

you want some millions more of African cannibals thrown amongst you broadcast throughout the whole slave States?[28]

It was clearly not for high regard of black people that Breckinridge opposed slavery.[29]

The most surprising revelation in Warfield's list of antislavery connections is that his mother-in-law, Eliza Pearce Kinkead, was "an abolitionist of the Garrison type." William Lloyd Garrison, editor of the notorious Boston newspaper, *The Liberator*, worked side-by-side with escaped slave Frederick Douglass to convict Christian consciences of the radical, inherent evil of slavery, and to urge immediate, uncompensated abolition, with the added argument that African Americans deserved to participate in American society on terms of civil equality. Garrison's moral urgency and especially the postal delivery of the *Liberator* into slave states, where black folks free and slave might read it and foment slave rebellion, aroused slaveholders in large numbers to defend their "peculiar institution." Garrisonianism prompted Warfield's grandfather Breckinridge to move away from his early, more radical abolitionism.[30] Breckinridge and his brother John traveled to Boston to advocate a moderate antislavery agenda—gradual, compensated emancipation with colonization—calling forth a bitter attack from Garrison in the pages of the *Liberator*. Garrison called

28. Robert J. Breckinridge, "Discourse of Dr. R. J. Breckinridge, Delivered on the Day of National Humiliation, January 4, 1861, at Lexington, Ky.," *Danville Quarterly Review* 1 (1861): 336–37.

29. The context of these remarks demands some notice, however: Breckinridge was trying to sell gradual emancipation to the opposition, many of whom were not slaveholders themselves—poor and middling whites—and whose prejudice against blacks was well known. Elsewhere Breckinridge acted in favor of black empowerment, as when he helped persuade Governor Bramlette near the end of the Civil War to enroll Negro soldiers in the Union forces of the state. Arming blacks, and sending them against slaveholding whites, was an extremely touchy subject—yet Breckinridge came to favor it out of loyalty to the federal government that had directed it. Klotter, *The Breckinridges of Kentucky*, 85; cf. RJB to Gen. S. G. Burbridge, March 26, 1864 (Filson Club, Louisville, Ky.). Also in his favor is the fact that "while in Baltimore he received, for his kind services to the free blacks of Maryland, a piece of gold plate, as a present from more than a thousand of them" ("Breckinridge, Robert J.," *Biblical Repertory and Princeton Review*, index volume, 114). R. J. Breckinridge's brother John once kissed all the children in the room on a visit to Danville, Kentucky. On learning that one of them was a quadroon, he quoted the Scripture, "He hath made of one blood all nations." Barbour, "The Breckinridges," 427.

30. For the ways Breckinridge's antislavery views changed over time, see Mayse, "RJB," chap. 3.

Breckinridge "blasphemous," a spokesman for "the spirit of negro hatred," and accused him of "a most unchristian feeling" toward African Americans. Breckinridge in reply labeled Garrisonian abolitionism "false, pernicious, and immoral," poorly conceived, unlikely to succeed, "stupid and shocking," and likely to produce revolution or war or to split the country.[31] Garrison's position polarized and complicated the antislavery cause, in addition to calling forth a new kind of proslavery argument that even proclaimed slavery a positive good. That Mother Kinkead was a Garrisonian abolitionist is a striking fact indeed, showing that Warfield's relations spanned the spectrum of antislavery conviction.[32]

Warfield in 1887 felt some pride in his family's antislavery connections, even as he recognized their sin in holding slaves. His remarks in the letter cited above suggest also that he shared their basically paternalistic attitude toward blacks. This derived primarily from the experience of master over slave, which his kin took seriously as a position not just of power, but of responsibility. A continuing sense of duty to African Americans seems to have impelled Warfield to write against racial injustice. He believed it his responsibility as one providentially entrusted with a higher status in this world. This sense of duty had a double edge: on the one side, Warfield and his antislavery kin subordinated their personal interests (at least some of them) to their sense of the needs of their underlings; on the other side, they did so from the conscious position of social superiors over social inferiors. The note of paternalism in the Warfields' and Breckinridges' treatment of slavery, their treatment of their own slaves, and later their treatment of race relations with the freedmen, is inescapable. It rings out even in Warfield's letter cited above. But such paternalism does not negate the basic heroism of Warfield's stand against Jim Crow. Indeed, it rather amplifies it, for despite his sense of superiority he advocated complete race equality in the churches, in sheer obedience to God's Word.

31. The whole Garrison-Breckinridge debate is well narrated in Klotter, *The Breckinridges of Kentucky*, 68–70.

32. On Garrison's impact, see Henry Mayer, *All on Fire: William Lloyd Garrison and the Abolition of Slavery* (New York: St. Martin's Griffin, 1998). On proslavery arguments in response, see Larry E. Tise, *Proslavery: A History of the Defense of Slavery in America, 1701–1840* (Athens, Ga.: University of Georgia Press, 1990).

The Freedmen's Case

The first of Warfield's anti-segregationist articles, "A Calm View of the Freedmen's Case," appeared in January 1887 in the new Northern Presbyterian monthly missionary magazine, *The Church at Home and Abroad*. It was an appeal for church people to support the Presbyterian Board of Missions to Freedmen, whose chief work was a combination of education and evangelism through Christian schools for blacks. "We already recognize it as a commonplace," wrote Warfield, "that the greatest work before the American people today is the elevation and civilization of the seven millions of blacks that form so large a section of its fifty millions of souls." But common as this observation was, he argued, Americans did not adequately appreciate the magnitude of the crisis. As the nation was turning "the Negro problem" back to the Southern states, and the Southern states were beginning to reduce African Americans to a state of peonage, Warfield wrote to rekindle the sense of urgency that was ebbing away around him. "The terrible legacy of evil which generations of slavery have left to our freedmen is scarcely appreciated by any of us." Even the most benign experiences of slavery, he said, had rendered its victims morally unfitted for the freedom that emancipation and abolition had suddenly granted them. Slavery had been inherently demoralizing, Warfield contended: "Let us only remember that, by its very nature, slavery cannot allow to its victim a will of his own; that it leaves him master of none of his deeds; that it permits him ownership in nothing, not even his honor or virtue." And worse yet, slavery had encouraged among its victims an *alternative* morality.

> What is virtue in the slave is vice in the freeman, and this reversal of all moral principle is one of the chief characteristics of the terrible institution of human slavery. The task now before us would be easier had slavery only demoralized. As a matter of fact it did worse: it moralized on a false and perverted system.

Nurture, not nature, had degraded the former slaves, unfitting the majority of them for the blessings of free life. Warfield found troubling the "odd divorce between religion and morality" that he observed in his African-American brothers and sisters. While this stark judgment may strike modern readers as condescending or worse, we must note that Warfield blamed not the former slaves but their masters and the evils inherent in the American system of slavery.[33]

By 1887, a new generation of African Americans—a considerable proportion of the black population—had little or no recollection of slavery. But circumstances in the meantime had not created more favorable conditions for them. Warfield believed that the sons of freedmen were now even *worse off* morally than the slaves had been. "The freedman's sons are, morally speaking, a distinct deterioration from the freedman himself." Under slavery, while there had been no inducement to rise, at least the requirements of efficient labor had imposed some outside pressure of discipline on the slaves. Without that outside pressure, blacks needed as inducement to moral restraint the same thing whites did: the hope of rising in society. But sharecropping and tenant farming arrangements trapped the Negro in perpetual squalor and dependency, and were explicitly designed to keep him down. This, Warfield proclaimed, was a dreadful evil.

"The spirit of caste (for it cannot be called by any milder name)," Warfield complained, was universal in the South even among Christians, and now flourished in the North as well. This caste spirit "kills hope," "paralyzes effort," and, in separating the races physically, removes all the influence of moral example that was once available when classes rubbed shoulders. Christians embracing the authority of God's Word, he argued, ought to lead the country in doing away with segregation, heartily embracing the common humanity of the races.

> It cannot be too strongly emphasized that it is not he who feels persuaded that the Negro was made a little lower than man, and who is graciously willing to train him into fitness for such a position, who can educate him into true and self-centered manhood. It is only he who is thoroughly persuaded that God has made of one blood all the nations of the earth, that has the missionary spirit, or that can serve as the hand of the Most High in elevating the lowly and rescuing the oppressed.

33. Warfield, "A Calm View of the Freedmen's Case," 735–37.

When whites justified their encouragement of the black exodus from their churches, saying, as Warfield quoted one delegate to an Episcopalian conference held in the Northern city of Chicago, that "they would be gladly welcomed, and *seats have been set aside for them in all the churches*," and that "'only such a prejudice' exists against the colored people 'as would exist against any uneducated and unrefined people'" (emphasis his), Warfield had had enough. "In what community are special seats set aside 'in all the churches' for the 'uneducated and unrefined'?" he retorted. "Ah, no! we are hand to hand here with the pure spirit of caste . . . which it is painful to see in this nineteenth century anywhere out of India."[34]

The churches alone, Warfield pressed further, could supply what the freedmen most needed: education coupled with preaching, so that moral development might take place alongside intellectual development. "We need Christian schools everywhere," he concluded—and invited Presbyterians to give generously to the struggling Board of Missions to Freedmen.[35]

We find in these observations and arguments the paternalism that we noted earlier: Warfield assumes that American whites will have to do the work of elevating American blacks, leaving unmentioned the efforts and even the responsibility of independent African-American leadership. Since antebellum days the free black communities in Northern cities had operated self-help societies, started independent churches, founded black newspapers, and in many other ways had undertaken to elevate their people.[36] Warfield had attended Princeton Seminary with the extremely capable African-American Presbyterian Francis Grimke, and certainly must have known something of his work. But he appears not to have had in mind the plight of Northern urban blacks—still a small minority of the African-American population in the 1880s. The majority black population, sinking into abject peonage in the rural South, was his chief concern in this article, though he warned of the effects of caste on American society as a whole.

34. Ibid., 737, 739–40.
35. Ibid., 742.
36. See, for example, Ira Berlin, *Slaves without Masters: The Free Negro in the Antebellum South* (New York: New Press, 1971), and James Oliver Horton and Lois E. Horton, *In Hope of Liberty: Culture, Community, and Protest among Northern Free Blacks, 1700–1860* (New York: Oxford University Press, 1997).

Moreover, we find Warfield taking alternative slave morality at face value, not seeing in it the covert declaration of power and self-determination that recent authors have found so fascinating. Warfield's emphasis on the degrading effects of the institution of slavery anticipate the arguments of historian Stanley Elkins in the mid-twentieth century, who likened the slave experience to that of Nazi concentration camps and sought to evince sympathy for racial justice by highlighting the personality disorders (especially the "Sambo" type) consequent upon such experiences. More recent historians have chosen instead to explore the extent to which African Americans, even in the most restrictive of slave circumstances, managed to assert their personhood through acts of individual and collective subversion. What these historians celebrate as self-assertion and insistent, if limited, self-determination—shirking and slowing down of work, lying to the master and overseer, stealing from the oppressor, and the like—Warfield lamented as the moral degradation of a people capable of better things as sharers in the image of God.[37]

Warfield's condemnation of segregation, time-bound though it was, stood out starkly enough to his readers. One wrote in gratitude for Warfield's incisiveness: the superintendent of home missions for the Synod of Kentucky congratulated him "for your contribution which goes to the core of the difficulty."[38] Another, an Ohioan of evident Garrisonian beliefs, contended that Warfield had been too easy on the slaveholders.

37. Stanley M. Elkins, *Slavery: A Problem in American Institutional and Intellectual Life* (Chicago: University of Chicago Press, 1959). As an example of the current interest in slave agency, Ira Berlin writes: "But slaves were never 'absolute aliens,' 'genealogical isolates,' 'deracinated outsiders,' or even unreflective 'sambos' in any slave society. . . . Slaveholders severely circumscribed the lives of enslaved people, but they never fully defined them. Slaves were neither extensions of their owners' will nor products of the market's demand. The slaves' history—like all human history—was made not only by what was done to them but also by what they did for themselves. . . . Slavery, though imposed and maintained by violence, was a negotiated relationship." Ira Berlin, *Many Thousands Gone: The First Two Centuries of Slavery in North America* (Cambridge, Mass.: Harvard University Press, 1998), 2.

38. Samuel Ellis Wishard to BBW, January 6, 1887 (Warfield Papers, PTS, box 17). Wishard shared Warfield's sense of urgency as well as answerability to God: "The problem of the future of this *growing people* is *the problem* of the hour. And in its solution, I am persuaded, is wrapped up the welfare of our own people and nation. If we do our duty by the freedmen we can calmly leave all the issues of the future with him who sitteth in the heavens. If we are recreant to our trust God will take care of these poor helpless ones, but possibly in a way that may grind us to powder."

153

If a great wrong has been done to the black man (though God permitted for his good) shall we please either God or truly intelligent men
on this subject, when we praise or somehow give a good character
to those who were chief in the wrong done, or shall we please God
when we preach repentance to them and to ourselves in proportion
to the complicity of each in the wrong?[39]

This was the letter to which Warfield replied with his list of family antislavery credentials and his admonition that a Northern non-
slaveholder could not fully appreciate the moral dilemma his kinfolk
had faced.

A third correspondent, R. M. Carson, a Kentucky pastor in the
Northern Presbyterian church, trained under Warfield's grandfather
Breckinridge at Danville Theological Seminary during the Civil War,
expressed strong objections to Warfield's condemnation of the spirit
of caste.[40] In a long letter calculated to demonstrate the cumulative
effect of Warfield's logic, Carson pointed out the fundamental principle
of Warfield's view.[41]

I understand you squarely & clearly to lay down absolute ecclesiastical equality in Church Courts – pulpit – etc – etc – as the one &
only solution compatible with the word of God –

I have reflected over this – best I could – but in further prosecution
desire to ask you in regard to some points, and trust you may not
consider it a trenchment [?] upon your *time* – or beneath your notice
in importance, to respond –

But to the point, & briefly –

1 – If Church & Pulpit equality is to be the rule & orthodox
doctrine, where can the line be drawn?

If *this* is adopted, then in *every* particular & in every relation &
every point of social contact, the same equality must logically &
inexorably follow.

39. Joseph William Torrence to BBW, January 4, 1887 (Warfield Papers, PTS, box 17).
40. Carson's basic biographical information is found in *The Presbyterian Ministerial Directory*, ed. Edgar Sutton Robinson (Cincinnati: Ministerial Directory Co., 1898),
1:203.
41. Underlining in original letters is shown here and below in italics.

And from there Carson proceeded to show that in ecclesiastical meetings integrated racially on Warfield's principles ("These Negroes occupy *exactly* equal rights, privileges on floor of Synod – & not the least discrimination must be made on account of color – or even a remote *hint* of anything contrary – as this would be *wicked, unchristian caste*"), blacks must be allowed to occupy key positions of leadership, even the moderator's chair and the chairs of important committees. If this prospect was not shocking enough—raising the specter of the ecclesiastical equivalent of "black rule" that Southern white "redeemers" had recently eliminated in Southern governments—Carson went on to raise the bogey of social equality.

> 3 – But further – A number of these Negro preachers bring their wives with them to Synod – as is so common for white men to do – These Negro ministers & their wives must be treated in *all respects exactly* as the *white* men & their wives are – without the least recognition of any social distinction –
>
> Such a distinction would be very offensive & unkind towards the colored brethren & would be the exhibition of *wicked caste* – It must be *totally* and *utterly ignored*, of course –
>
> 4 – Hence, in the *parlors, bedrooms*, & at the *tables* of the white entertainers of these brethren & sisters in black, all discrimination must be entirely ignored, just *as tho' all* were most estimable & respectable & pious *whites* –

Surely this would convince Warfield that his principles were wrongheaded, playing not only on the visceral revulsion to social mixing common among white Southerners after Reconstruction, but on Warfield's own expressed concern about the moral degradation of African Americans. But in case it did not, Carson pressed relentlessly on:

> 5 – Still further – As often happens, a goodly number of young, unmarried white ministers attend meetings of the Synod & Presbyteries – & very naturally & *properly*, they escort such young ladies as belong to the families where they are entertained – to & from the sessions of the church court – & to church services – The young *black ministers*, of course, may & should also gallantly do the same, with the *young white* ladies of the family where *they* are entertained – To refuse to

be so escorted on account of the *color* of the young ministers would, again, be *wicked caste*, & merit severest condemnation –

And of course this line of argument terminated in the great trump card of racist argument, the threat of miscegenation.

> 6 – Still further, No objection could be raised by any *true Christian* against *marriage* between *black* Christians & *white* Christian ladies, for same reason – To do so would of course be *wicked caste* again ruling above & in opposition to Gospel of X.[42]

In keeping with his custom, Warfield dutifully answered Carson's letter—and that answer rings with his conviction that the authority of Scripture outweighs all human social and cultural commitments. The draft of his letter is so striking that it is worth reproducing in its entirety.

Allegheny 3d March 1887

My dear Brother: –

I owe you thanks for your trouble in writing so fully to me your doubts as to my paper in "The Church."

You have correctly understood me to insist that the Church of Christ can know nothing of social classes or usages in her worship or organization. It may be doubted whether the consequences which you fear will result from this position, either logically follow, or will actually follow, or would be undesirable if they followed. But all this is no concern of yours & mine. For, just because the Church is the pillar & ground of the Truth by which the world is to be saved, the Lord has not left its advising to us but has given us instruction as to how it ought to be behaved in the Church of the Living God. James (ii: 1–13) distinctly forbids attention to be paid in God's house to the social distinctions among men. And Paul gave his work & even life (Eph. iii:1) for the final settlement of the question as regards discrimination on the ground of race: with the result (often declared) that in Christ Jesus there cannot be Greek & Jew, circumcision & uncircumcision, barbarian, Scythian, bondman, free man, but Christ

42. R. M. Carson to BBW, February 19, 1887 (Warfield Papers, PTS, box 17).

is all & alike in all. The matter is therefore for Christians no longer *sub judice*. As James phrases it, it is for us simply, that "if we have respect of persons we commit sin, & are convicted by the law as transgressors." Or as Benezen [?] expresses our duty: "We must own Religion in his rags, as well as in his silken slippers, & *stand by him* too."

For the individual there is, of course, many lines [*sic*] of action open. But I cannot help believing that there is no line so wise or well or so loyal as simply to let God order his own house in his own way & gladly range ourselves by his side. Let us beware lest, in arranging things for oneself & so as to fit our personal prejudices, we build up a kingdom indeed, but not to God or one which He will neither own nor bless. It will no doubt be easier to build a worldly club: but is it as well worth while as to build God's Church? – which nevertheless cannot be builded on other foundations than those that He has laid. –

I am

Most Sincerely Yours
B. B. Warfield[43]

Given his family background in slaveholding and in moderate antislavery sentiment and activity, which included such compromising elements as the desire to rid the nation of the race problem by shipping former slaves back to Africa, vitriolic opposition to Garrisonian abolitionism (except in the case of Mrs. Kinkead), willingness to treat intransigent slaves with the raw exercise of power that slaveholding conferred, express reference to Africans as "cannibals," and Warfield's own words in the Freedmen's Case article describing blacks' ancestors as "the naked savage in the African forests,"[44]

---

43. BBW to R. M. Carson, March 3, 1887 (Warfield Papers, PTS, box 17).

44. The phrase appears in a section where Warfield is addressing those who hold to the old "positive good" proslavery argument, wishing to do their position justice even as he argues against it. The passage reads: "When we grieve over the odd divorce of religion and morality which is so frequently met with among the blacks, let us not indeed blame the slaveholders for it, as if their Christian teaching was at fault, but let us equally remember that slavery itself is responsible for it. I do not forget what contact with Christian masters has done for the thousands of heathen savages which were being continually landed on our shores, up to the very outbreak of the war itself. Let anyone simply compare the average self-respecting Negro in America with the naked savage of the African forests, and thank God for the marvelous change." Warfield, "Calm View of the Freedmen's Case," 736. This passage, in blaming slavery rather than slaveholders,

this radical stand on biblical principle is indeed remarkable. Warfield brushes aside all prudential arguments in the face of biblical command, setting their dubitability against the rock-solid, unanswerable authority of the Word of God. He even suggests that social equality of the races, should it follow even unto race amalgamation, might not be undesirable. When we consider Warfield's close acquaintance with pureblood cattle breeding—his father was an influential author on short-horn cattle culture and Warfield himself worked after college as livestock editor for the *Farmer's Home Journal* (Lexington, Kentucky)—and that his family's attention to breeding extended to participation in the founding of the Sons of the American Revolution and the Daughters of the American Revolution—organizations then dedicated to maintaining white Anglo-Saxon Protestant dominance of American life—this willingness to face unflinchingly the prospect of miscegenation is well-nigh astonishing.[45]

Ecclesiastical Consequences

Warfield's second anti-segregationist article, "Drawing the Color Line," appeared in the liberal-tending New York religious newspaper

prompted Torrence to object that Warfield had let slaveholders off far too easy. Warfield agreed that his words had had that unintended effect—see below.

45. William Warfield, *American Short-Horn Importations: Containing the Pedigrees of All Short-Horn Cattle Hitherto Imported in America* (Chicago: Short-Horn Breeders' Association, 1884); and *The Theory and Practice of Cattle-Breeding* (Chicago: J. H. Sanders, 1889); B. B. Warfield's Alumni File, PTS Special Collections. B. B. Warfield's brother wrote of their family's "sturdy Scotch stock" and "hardy English blood" and described their ancestor John Preston as "one of the noblest progenitors of a line of God-fearing patriots" (Ethelbert Dudley Warfield, *Joseph Cabell Breckinridge, Junior, Ensign in the United States Navy: A Brief Story of a Short Life* [New York: Knickerbocker Press, 1898], 5, 8). B. B. Warfield himself was deeply interested in the family bloodlines; see his extensive genealogical charts in the Warfield Papers, University of Kentucky. One of the earliest surviving manuscripts in the Warfield Papers at PTS announces the gift of a heifer named "Lady Fairy 25 . . . to my grand son, Benjamin Warfield" from R. J. Breckinridge, complete with pedigree (RJB to BBW, October 1, 1860, box 13). Grandfather Warfield, for his part, pioneered short-horn culture in Kentucky; William then followed in his footsteps ("Grasmere: The Home of the Shorthorn," clipping from the *Breeder's Gazette*, ca. 1900, in the possession of Mary Cabell Warfield III of Lexington, Ky.). Numerous letters from William Warfield track the calves bred from "your" (Benjamin's) cattle (box 2). Warfield's uncle Joseph Cabell Breckinridge was an organizer of the Sons of the American Revolution and its president in 1900–1901 (Finding Aid, Breckinridge Papers, Library of Congress); B. B. Warfield and his brother were both members.

the *Independent,* in July 1888. A note in one of his scrapbooks indicates that he wrote the piece as an editorial for the *New Princeton Review,* but it was rejected there as being too strong.[46] This article put into print the biblical argument against segregation in the churches that Warfield had made privately in his reply to Rev. Carson—but it did so under the curious subtitle, "A Fragment of History by a Disinterested Spectator." Warfield wrote forcefully against the sin of racism in society and the churches, but this time chose to do so anonymously.[47]

The occasion for this article was primarily the deliberations in the Episcopal and Presbyterian churches concerning reunion with their respective Southern denominations, and secondarily Warfield's continued interest in the racial arrangements in the new South. Having read in the *Contemporary Review* an "admirable paper" by George Washington Cable that showed "with photographic distinctness and depth of shadow, the disheartening picture" of the descent of black men, women, and children into practical serfdom—and the simultaneous rise of a new generation of Southerners determined on white supremacy—Warfield raised his voice once again in concern for the plight of African Americans.[48]

Warfield was troubled by the triumph of "race antagonism" in church and society in the 1880s, which he viewed not as a return to antebellum patterns, but as something new and worse. "The young men of the 'new South,'" he wrote, "who have had no experience, or who preserve but a faint recollection of slavery, appear to cherish a vehemence of race antipathy to which their fathers were for the most part strangers." This ominous situation had arisen from the loss of routine contact between the races. A new generation had grown up "unsoftened by the intimate association which formerly obtained with the slaves of the household, who constituted almost as much a part of

46. Warfield, "Drawing the Color Line," *Independent,* July 5, 1888. Warfield added the notation about original submission to the table of contents of vol. 6 of his "Opuscula Warfieldii" (scrapbooks containing his smaller publications, PTS Special Collections).

47. Anonymity or pseudonymity when arguing volatile issues was a longstanding tradition—one thinks for example of such Founding Fathers as John Adams ("Novanglus") and James Madison ("Publius"). It remains perplexing, though, how Warfield could describe himself as "a disinterested spectator."

48. Warfield mentions Cable's "admirable paper": "The Negro Question in the United States," *Contemporary Review,* March 1888, 443–68. On Cable's lonely, heroic stand, see Smith, *In His Image, But,* 294.

the family as the children themselves, and who entered heartily into the family life, the family fortunes and the family pride." In the new South, where such familiar contact between the races was no more, whites now smarted from "what they cannot but consider the intolerable impudence of an inferior and menial race" when they encountered African Americans intent on living out their freedom.[49]

Warfield seems here to be recalling slavery in his own father's household, romanticized perhaps in the mists of memory. His description calls to mind the scene from *Gone with the Wind* in which Scarlett O'Hara tells an insufferably anti-black Yankee lady that former slave Uncle Peter is "one of our family." In the 1890s Warfield would repeat such a recollection of slaveholding Christian households as basically happy, presumably again to lament the deterioration in race relations after Reconstruction.[50] It appears, too, a case in point of the difference in racial attitudes between former slaveholders and poor whites that Woodward observes in *The Strange Career of Jim Crow*.

With daily, familiar interchange under conditions of shared personal interest no longer the norm, Warfield argued, a "physical repulsion" between the races was bound to arise, deepening the new white generation's "inherited and passionate conviction that the safety of our State, of society, of the family itself, depends on the stern preservation of their supremacy over the degraded masses that swarm around them." It was bad enough when slaveholders in antebellum days had argued that slavery was necessary to the preservation of Southern (and even Christian) society; now Southern leaders were adding the vitriol of positive hatred for blacks, and cloaking it in a misguided notion of

49. Warfield, "Drawing the Color Line."
50. Margaret Mitchell, *Gone with the Wind* (New York: Macmillan, 1936), 672; anonymous short notice of *Plantation Life Before Emancipation*, by R. Q. Mallard, *Presbyterian and Reformed Review* 3 (1892): 606. Warfield may have been the author of this notice, which calls Mallard's book "certainly delightful reading to one who (like the present reviewer) spent his boyhood on a plantation 'before emancipation.' Dr. Mallard's vivid descriptions of the intercourse between the masters and slaves, and their mutual trust and love on a well-ordered estate, revive many sweet memories and send the heart back into the past, longing for its old joys." Despite this moonlight-and-magnolias sentimentalism, the reviewer insists that "slavery itself" was "that evil of evils," and that slavery's abuses were, alas, more than occasional. Still, he allows that "African slavery in America had many redeeming qualities," especially in civilizing and Christianizing the Africans in a few generations. Even if Warfield did not pen the notice—he did not customarily call his father's cattle farm a "plantation," as the reviewer here calls his boyhood home—he did let it stand under his editorship.

social need.[51] Here Warfield may well have had in mind the arguments of Robert Lewis Dabney, a fine ally in matters of conservative religious doctrine, but an outspoken racist and segregationist as well. It is striking that Warfield never took overt notice of the well-publicized social agenda of this otherwise sturdy doctrinal ally in a sister church. Here he impugns Dabney's cause without confronting him by name, possibly preferring not to get embroiled in a print war on this topic. This may in fact explain his decision to make the article anonymous.

Race antagonism, Warfield went on to say, was now becoming a two-way street. Hatred on the white side was breeding hatred on the black side. "The black masses," he claimed,

> emerged from slavery with no sense of wrongs to avenge, but rather with a lively appreciation of the manifold kindnesses which they had received from their masters, and with a true gratitude for the elevation which they had obtained at their hands through the generation or two that separated them from the dimly remembered savagery of Africa.

(Once again we catch the note of paternalism, together with a very sanguine appraisal of the general experience of slavery rather characteristic of Warfield's class.) But now, freedpeople "have been gradually becoming, under the irritation of continually repeated injustices, great and small, more and more compacted into a sullen mass of muttered discontent, which promises to develop into full-fledged race-antagonism on their side also."[52] Warfield thus observed the growing bitterness of blacks against whites in the South, but unlike most of his race and class, he blamed it not on carpetbaggers and scalawags but on the Southern white population itself.[53] "Thus race seems to be arraying itself increasingly against race"—and both sides are seeking segregation "as the sole hope of the establishment of a *modus vivendi* between them."[54]

51. Warfield, "Drawing the Color Line."
52. Ibid.
53. Cf. Murray, *Presbyterians and the Negro*, 149.
54. Warfield, "Drawing the Color Line."

While most people North and South were content to believe segregation the best expedient, Warfield decried it as a woeful accommodation to the growing evil of race antipathy—and worse, as outright sin in the household of God. At this time the Northern Presbyterian church was considering the possibility of reuniting with its Southern sister communion, each church in 1887 having appointed a committee to look into the possibility. "It soon became apparent," Warfield reported, "that the great difficulty lay in 'the Negro question.'" Southern Presbyterians laid down as nonnegotiable the practice of (he quotes their words) "entire independence of the colored people in their Church organization"—meaning separate congregations, under white oversight, with an eye to creating an African Presbyterian church. White Southern Presbyterians added their intention to provide "the largest measure of aid" to their colored brethren—a claim made bitterly ludicrous, Andrew Murray observes, by the actual record of aid given. But whatever amount of aid might be extended for the purpose of creating racially separate churches, the real problem for Warfield was the goal of separation in the first place. The Northern church offered to reunite with the Southern church by an arrangement that would leave the Southern racial separation intact in the short run, and provide for its full institutional realization in the long run. "Here is an attempt to draw the color line not only unfalteringly but indelibly."[55]

Warfield lamented, "Christian men desert the fundamental law of the Church of the Living God, that in Christ Jesus there cannot be Greek and Jew, circumcision and uncircumcision, barbarian, Scythian, bondman, freeman, under the pressure of their race antipathy." Racism, he proclaimed, struck at the very foundation of the church's organization. This was a highly prophetic thing to say—in the sense of a voice crying in the wilderness—in 1888. And what prompted him to write was the fact that his church, the Northern church, was considering going along with this fundamental sin. Warfield was quick to note the irony of the demands of the Southern church upon the Northern, given the Southern Presbyterian insistence on the "spirituality of the church"—by which they had tried to silence Northern

55. Ibid.

calls for a Presbyterian deliverance against slavery back in the 1830s. "An ecclesiastical body which proclaims itself the champion of the exclusively spiritual functions of the Church, demands, as the price of reconciliation with a sister body, the reorganization of the whole Church organism on the lines of political and social cleavage." Bitter was the irony—but what was far worse, the Northern church seemed willing to oblige. "We notice an apparent readiness of the professed friends of equal rights to betray by indirection the cause which they directly champion." For now it appears that "the General Assembly of the Presbyterian Church is willing to buy reunion with its Southern brethren and the fearful cost of affixing an unjust stigma upon a whole section of its own constituency," namely, the blacks.[56]

The article concluded with a plea for Christ's followers to defend the defenseless and to recognize the common humanity and spiritual virtue of African Americans. It was, all told, a powerful and pointed piece. But again, Warfield's private statements reveal an even deeper conviction than did this publication. In the reply to Rev. Torrence cited above, Warfield declared that racial inequality in the churches was an offense so grave as to prevent ecclesiastical fellowship—an offense worse, scripturally, than slaveholding itself.

> I must confess to you that I am one of those whom you perhaps consider grossly inconsistent, who heartily accord with *both* the deliverances of 1818 & 1845. I do think slavery a gigantic evil & entirely inconsistent with the spirit of the Gospel & a sin in the slave holders: & I do not think it a disciplinable offence or a fit test of communion. It is possible "to sin against Christ" & yet not be subject to exclusion from his table (1 Cor. viii.12, compared with the context & the parallel in Romans xiv, e.g. Ro xiv: 3). . . .
>
> . . . That the Southern Church has not repented of its sin in regard to slavery would be no bar to my union with it: I could unite with it in a free conscience tomorrow. But that it is not awake to its duty to the Freedmen & that organic union with it would injure if not destroy our work among them makes me deprecate & pray against reunion in any near future.[57]

56. Ibid.
57. BBW to Joseph William Torrence, January 7, 1887.

Warfield thus enunciated his belief that the Bible required ecclesiastical separation from segregationists (and, for that matter, from any unrepentant practitioners of systematic preferential treatment), but not from slaveholders. Scripture expressly forbade preferential treatment; it did not so expressly forbid slavery, evil though slavery was. Ecclesiastically speaking, segregationism, not slaveholding, was the greater sin.

Conclusion

That Warfield stood opposed to reunion with the Southern church and the likes of R. L. Dabney, who might be expected to prove staunch allies in the brewing fight with theological liberalism, shows just how strongly he felt about the issue of racism. The Princeton theology had its strongest constituency in the South, as seen in the division of 1837 into Old School and New School. Had the Civil War not precipitated a split of the conservative Old School along sectional lines, Warfield would have found a much larger party within his church to back his efforts against the liberals. Now, if the Northern and Southern churches were to reunite, he would regain that constituency. But even that inducement could not outweigh Warfield's conviction that the unrepentant practice of systemic racism in the church must not be tolerated, out of obedience to "the fundamental law of the church of Christ."[58]

Indeed, Warfield's refusal to compromise on the race question in the church in 1888 stands in stark contrast to what his grandfather Breckinridge did a half-century earlier. R. J. Breckinridge deliberately set aside his own antislavery scruples to join arms with proslavery conservatives in the successful Old School ouster of the liberalizing New School presbyteries in 1837. Breckinridge agreed to silence on slavery in order to gain political advantage to secure what he con-

---

58. He did, however, work closely with Southern Presbyterians in doctrinal matters through non-ecclesiastical means—namely, theological publications. Warfield founded and ran the *Presbyterian and Reformed Review* (1890–1902) as an independent effort of men from various denominational bodies, including the PCUS; the *PRR*'s business manager was the Southern Presbyterian George Summey. In the first decade of the twentieth century Warfield worked with another Southern churchman, William Marcellus McPheeters, as coeditor of another journal, the *Bible Student* (1900–1903).

sidered sound doctrine and polity.[59] Warfield must have known this, and appears to have chosen deliberately not to repeat the shameful deed in his day.

Warfield's stance against racial inequality and segregation is a dramatic find not only for its refreshing departure from the norm, but for the gravity he attached to those sins. In later decades of his life he carried through on these convictions on the Princeton Seminary campus, to the dismay of fellow professor J. Gresham Machen. Machen reported to his mother that in 1911 Warfield had single-handedly reversed the seminary's practice of steering black applicants away from Princeton to all-black church schools, and had "dropped the remark" in his official capacity as chair of the faculty "that if another colored student came there was no objection to having him room in the dormitory." Such a situation arose in the fall of 1913. The seminary registrar, following Warfield's suggestion, housed an African-American seminarian in Brown Hall. "There is nobody here who will make any move against Warfield," Machen complained to his mother. He found Warfield's actions in the matter "domineering"—suggesting that in the policy of racial integration Warfield stood adamant and alone.[60] Clearly for Warfield the seminary, as an institution of the church, was under obligation to follow scriptural injunctions against preferential treatment among Christians. Machen, by contrast, took for granted the ideal of "separate but equal." Here was an instance of a Southern white man of the generation Warfield had warned about: Machen had grown up after slavery, as white attitudes toward blacks were worsening, and his

59. Mayse, "RJB," 111–12. Mayse goes so far as to claim that, thanks to this corrupt bargain over slavery, "Breckinridge's skillful management of the Old School troops was the key to 'victory' over the New School forces."

60. J. Gresham Machen to his mother, Mary Gresham Machen, October 5, 1913, and October 12, 1913 (Machen Papers, Westminster Theological Seminary). In the former letter Machen described the policy of steering black applicants elsewhere: ". . . a change which has recently taken place in the policy of the Seminary with regard to colored students. They have always been received, tho in previous years the registrar has taken occasion to warn them that our course is not so well adapted to their needs as that of the Seminaries which the church provides especially for them . . . . This year the policy of such letters of advice . . . has been abandoned." Former seminary archivist William O. Harris noted in a private letter to me, "Dr. Machen appears not to have known that many negro students lived in Brown Hall during the 19th century. The guide to student rooms in the back of the annual Seminary Catalog indicates this to be the case." Thus the segregationist policy which Warfield overturned must have been fairly recent.

vehemence about segregation shows it. Otherwise, of course, Warfield and Machen were willing comrades in their confessionalism and the battle against theological liberalism.

A second instance of Warfield's continued opposition to racism deserves mention: in 1907, as race hatred produced an epidemic of lynchings in the South, Warfield published in the *Independent* a little poem entitled "Wanted—A Samaritan."

> Prone in the road he lay,
>   Wounded and sore bestead:
> Priests, Levites past that way
>   And turned aside the head.
>
> They were not hardened men
>   In human service slack:
> His need was great: but then,
>   His face, you see, was black.[61]

More striking still are the degree and kind of repentance Warfield hoped someday to see from the churches. He called for a truly color-blind church, or rather one in which color was but another occasion for mutual respect and love. And he was not chary about seeing in slavery and racism a kind of *collective* sin—something again quite unusual for a doctrinal conservative. Such systemic, social sin required systemic, society-wide repentance of a very tangible kind. Again his remarks to Rev. Torrence are revealing.

> We are all sinners in our participation in slavery, & we must repent
> of it by striving to repair our misdeeds in goodness to the slaves' free
> descendants. This is what is on my heart. . . . Our Southern black
> Presbyterians must outnumber & overweigh the white Presbyterians
> on the same ground in connection with the Southern Church before

61. Warfield, writing under the pseudonym Nicholas Worth Jr., "Wanted—A Samaritan," *Independent* (New York), January 31, 1907. "Bestead" means placed or situated. By this time Warfield had begun to indulge in deliberate archaisms in prose as well as poetry—which we might mistake for a wistful arch-conservative temperament, shutting himself off from the modern world, were it not for the widespread vogue of Arts and Crafts and other "antimodern" movements of the time. Cf., e.g., the poetry and prose of Henry Van Dyke, the popular bard of Princeton University.

we dare enter into organic union with them. Let our motto be the salvation of the Freedmen: who are here by the crime of our Fathers against their Fathers: & no reunion with the Southern Church until black & white can sit together in one Presbytery in South Carolina or Louisiana in mutual respect & Christian fellowship.[62]

Warfield was not a flawless opponent of racism, certainly not according to today's standards—but his opposition to Jim Crow, his call for sympathy and fellowship across racial lines, even to the point of social equality and race mixing,[63] was, for its day, prophetic and daring. It finds partial explanation in his duties as a member of the Presbyterian Board of Missions to Freedmen and his family background in antislavery slaveholding, but the leitmotif that runs throughout his consideration of race issues is fidelity to the authority of Scripture.

Warfield read his Bible to say that all races share a common human-ity, common value in the eyes of God, and, by implication from common destiny in the kingdom of God, a common potential. While considering

62. BBW to Joseph William Torrence, January 7, 1887. Note the hint of reparations. In Warfield's day, this question was viable in a way that it may not be today, at the remove of several generations, and Warfield probably did not intend to suggest that civil government undertake reparations for slavery. But he did feel that the church, at the very least, had a moral obligation to work and spend and sacrifice for racial justice, equality, integration, and advancement.

63. Warfield touched on the issue of race amalgamation again in a review of *Encyclopaedia of Religion and Ethics*, vol. 9 (Mu-Ph), by James Hastings, *Princeton Theological Review* 16 (1918): 114–15. He took exception to a Southern Baptist's article on "Negroes" that "cheer-fully contemplates the permanent residence, intermingled in Democratic America, of two races, separated from one another by impassible social barriers, possessed of an ever more intensified race-consciousness and following without regard to the other its own race ideals." To this proposi-tion Warfield retorted: "This is to look upon the negro [*sic*] as . . . just a permanent cancer in the body politic. We may suspect that it is a not unaccountable feeling of race repulsion that impels Dr. Carver to repel with sharp decision the forecast that amalgamation of the races must be the ultimate issue. With continued white immigration and the large death rate of the blacks working a progressive decrease in the proportion of the black population to the white, is it not natural to look forward to its ultimate absorption? That is to say, in a half millennium or so? That is not, however, our problem: for us and our children and children's children the two races in well-marked differentiation will form constituent but disproportionate elements in the one State. What we have to do, clearly, is to learn to live together in mutual amity and respect and helpfulness, and to work together for the achievement of our national ideals and the attainment of the goal of a truly Christian civilization." Here we find Warfield welcoming the notion of race mixing—*but* in a scenario that places it in the distant future and under conditions whereby the black race would basically be absorbed into the white. For the moment he was concerned that the races live and work *together* in harmony: an integrationist vision. Thus he concluded his comments by approving the "exhortation to political and social,—if not yet to racial—amalgamation. After all, we are, for better, for worse, bound up together in one bundle of life."

the former slaves and their descendants at the moment to be, as a class, the moral inferiors of whites, Warfield viewed it as a case of degradation through poor environment, not inherent racial inferiority. The proper course for Christians was not to separate the races—which would only exacerbate the problem—but to address the environmental causes of inequality. Moreover, Warfield laid the evil of degradation entirely to the charge of white Americans who, as a class, had purposely created the degrading environmental conditions. The church had the moral duty to work against such systemic degradation through education, evangelization, and inclusion of all races in church life on a basis of complete equality. If such equality seemed socially undesirable, the answer was to realign one's notions of social good according to scriptural commands.

While Warfield partook of the paternalism and stereotyping common in his day, and seems especially to have ignored the real accomplishments of African-American leadership, this episode is a refreshing example of the way in which the sacred text can provide a standpoint for trenchant social critique. Many leading Presbyterians of equally orthodox convictions did not follow Scripture here, as we noted at the outset. One has to wonder whether it was Warfield's active, leading defense of biblical authority that drove him to his radical anti-racist stance. Perhaps more immediately it was Warfield's specialization in New Testament—his close daily working with the text of Scripture, his care to guard its authority even as he incorporated the new science of textual criticism into his studies[64]—that made the difference. And as we have seen here, his Kentucky background in a family of pro-Union antislavery slaveholders gave him an unusual degree of personal interest and experience in the race question. This background seems to have helped him to see the race issue through sympathetic eyes, and to have made him more receptive to the commands of Scripture. In any case, for Warfield, biblical authority overruled race prejudice in that most intimate of collective social institutions, the church.

64. Warfield of course had co-authored with A. A. Hodge the definitive statement of the doctrine of biblical inerrancy in 1881, "Inspiration," *Presbyterian Review* 2 (1881): 225–60, and would write much more on biblical authority in the 1890s. In the mid 1880s, however, his writings centered on textual criticism and critical exposition; he was encouraged in these efforts by such leaders as Philip Schaff in America and W. R. Nicoll in Britain. See John E. Meeter and Roger Nicole, *A Bibliography of Benjamin Breckinridge Warfield, 1851–1921* (Nutley, N.J.: Presbyterian and Reformed, 1974).

❧ 7 ❧

"The Vital Processes of Controversy": Warfield, Machen, and Fundamentalism

STEPHEN J. NICHOLS

If the Princetonians are known for anything, it is Charles Hodge's famous dictum: "A new idea never originated at Princeton Seminary." By the turn of the twentieth century, the era of Warfield's ascendancy, the theological innovation that so riled Hodge continued to crest. Just a few short years off the horizon, these new ways of thinking about the Bible, God, Christ, humanity, and salvation would eventuate in a full-fledged departure from any semblance of orthodox Christianity, keeping Warfield and his own protégé, J. Gresham Machen, occupied for their entire scholarly careers. In other words, and in keeping with the succession of Old Princeton, Charles Hodge faced merely the incipient birth pangs of what would come to be liberalism, B. B. Warfield battled its developing years, and Machen grappled with it as it quickly matured.

In the early years of his own contest with the emerging new ways and fresh on the heels of the Briggs controversy, Warfield delivered an

I would like to thank Sean Michael Lucas for giving me the suggestion to write on this topic. I am also grateful to Grace Mullen at Westminster Theological Seminary for her invaluable assistance in the Machen Archives, and to Robert Benedetto at Princeton Theological Seminary for his assistance in the Warfield papers.

address before the New York Presbytery on the virtues of the Westminster Confession of Faith. Likening the Confession to the Nicene and Chalcedonian Creeds, he notes that the context of controversy surrounding all of these doctrinal standards in large part accounts for the strength of their mettle. He then colorfully observes, "A higher scientific quality of doctrinal statement is attainable through the vital processes of controversy than through the cool efforts of closet construction." Perhaps Warfield realized presciently in 1897 that his own theologizing for the next two decades would be largely polemical, resulting in his rise as the stalwart defender of the faith against its attacks from modernism and liberalism. Not for Warfield would be the cool efforts of closet theological construction; his would be those vital processes of controversy.[1]

The same processes awaited his successor, J. Gresham Machen. In fact, much can be gained by examining the connections between the thought of Warfield and that of Machen. The biographical similarities between the two are also worth noting. Both Warfield and Machen found their roots in Southern gentility. Relatives included distinguished politicians, successful businessmen, and authors. Warfield's first cousin once removed served as James Buchanan's vice president, and Machen's paternal grandfather was longtime clerk of the United States Senate. Both Warfield and Machen distinguished themselves in their baccalaureate education, Warfield at Princeton and Machen in his beloved Baltimore's Johns Hopkins. Following undergraduate education, both pursued education in Germany and, curiously enough, it was at that time that both succumbed to the call of ministry. They both completed degrees at Princeton Seminary, returning to their alma mater as professors.[2]

---

1. B. B. Warfield, "The Significance of the Westminster Standard as a Creed," in Benjamin B. Warfield, *Selected Shorter Writings*, 2 vols., ed. John E. Meeter (Nutley, N.J.: Presbyterian and Reformed, 1970, 1973), 2:660. The address was delivered November 8, 1897.

2. For biographical information on Warfield, see Mark A. Noll, "B. B. Warfield," in *Handbook of Evangelical Theologians* (Grand Rapids: Baker, 1993), 26–39; James Samuel McClanahan, "Benjamin B. Warfield: Historian of Doctrine in Defense of Orthodoxy, 1881–1921" (Ph.D. diss., Union Theological Seminary in Virginia, 1988), 10–67; and Kim Riddlebarger, "The Lion of Princeton: Benjamin Breckenridge Warfield on Apologetics, Theological Method and Polemics" (Ph.D. diss., Fuller Theological Seminary, 1997), 3–15. For biographical information on Machen, see Ned B. Stonehouse, *J. Gresham Machen: A Biographical Memoir* (Edinburgh: Banner of Truth, 1987); D. G. Hart, *Defending the Faith: J. Gresham Machen and the Crisis of*

Even their writings and thought coalesce. Warfield started his professorial career in New Testament studies at Western Theological Seminary, Allegheny, Pennsylvania, before moving on to Princeton. At Princeton he migrated to the department of didactic and polemical theology, largely viewing his work as that of an apologist. Machen too started in the New Testament department. He was considered for the chair of apologetics but, as a tremor of the coming division between him and Princeton, he was not appointed to the position. Consequently, both men ended up pursuing teaching and writing on similar subjects. Engagement of higher criticism and rigorous biblical scholarship permeate their work, issues of orthodox Christology occupied much of their time and writings, and unswerving commitment to and defense of the Westminster Standards stand as hallmarks of their respective legacies.

Methodological similarities abound as well. Noll observes of Warfield that he "placed less emphasis on the role of religious experience than had his predecessors Archibald Alexander and Charles Hodge"—a judgment made more telling when one considers that the gentlemen being compared are not known as enthusiasts. Hart, in a similar vein, reveals that Machen conspicuously expressed his "discomfort with the Victorian habit of overcoming intellectual doubts by appealing to experience." Thus, both held the view that if orthodox Christianity were to navigate the troubled waters of liberalism successfully, it would do so only by espousing rigorous scholarship. Again, Hart notes, "As Warfield saw it, the task of the minister demanded more, not less, intellectual rigor." Hart makes the connection to Machen, observing that Machen, writing in an especially "intellectually flaccid age," issued a clarion call for robust learning. So Machen declared, "What we need first of all is a more general interest in the problems of theological science"—words that certainly made Warfield leap for joy. Both in content and methodology, Warfield and Machen mirrored each other.[3]

Conservative Protestantism in Modern America (Phillipsburg, N.J.: P&R, 2003), 10–34; and Stephen J. Nichols, *J. Gresham Machen: A Guided Tour of His Life and Thought* (Phillipsburg, N.J.: P&R, 2004).

3. Mark A. Noll, "B. B. Warfield," 34; D. G. Hart, *Defending the Faith*, 26, 33–34. Warfield's inaugural lecture at Princeton Theological Seminary was titled "The Idea of Systematic Theology Considered as a Science" (1887), appearing in a later manifestation as "The Idea of

This is not to suggest that Machen, either consciously or subconsciously, merely parroted his mentor. It is to show, however, that there are many significant connections between these two, connections worth pursuing. Below is such an undertaking, exploring the connections between Warfield and Machen in light of the fundamentalist/modernist controversy. Beginning with an overall look at their association with fundamentalism, the first part of this essay examines that which they held in common with and that which differentiated them from their fundamentalist colleagues. The next two parts analyze Warfield's specific contribution to the controversy in his doctrines of Scripture and Christology, while looking at these same issues in Machen's work. Finally, the essay concludes with a sketch of the legacies of Warfield and Machen, exploring, albeit briefly, the prospects of a reclamation of their programs for contemporary evangelicalism.

Foes from the Right and the Left: The Ambivalent Fundamentalism of Warfield and Machen

Others have well pointed out that the ambivalence of both Warfield and Machen toward fundamentalism and their distance from it are due to specific theological differences. In fact, Noll goes so far as to label Warfield a "Nonfundamentalist," and Machen's own resistance to the classification is well known. Nevertheless, in their own time and repeatedly since then, both figures have been catapulted to the front lines of the fundamentalist defense. Warfield was invited to and did contribute to *The Fundamentals* (1910–15), the multiauthored statement against liberalism and modernism, and he is perhaps most well known as the progenitor of the modern formulation and defense of the doctrine of inspiration and inerrancy, the linchpin doctrine of fundamentalism. As for Machen, his *Christianity and Liberalism* (1923) stands as the high-water mark of the fundamentalist defense. Machen was invited to testify as an expert witness at the infamous Scopes Monkey Trial in Dayton, Tennessee (1925), and when the

---

Systematic Theology," originally in the *Presbyterian and Reformed Review* (1896) and reprinted in B. B. Warfield, *Studies in Theology*, vol. 9 of *The Works of Benjamin Breckinridge Warfield* (1932; repr., Grand Rapids: Baker, 1981), 49–87.

trustees were looking for the first president of the college named for the equally famous prosecutor at the trial, William Jennings Bryan, the offer was extended to Machen, the supremely worthy and natural candidate. While Machen refused both invitations, they speak to his fame as a fundamentalist.[4]

Despite their fame within the camp, both Warfield and Machen were ambivalent about much of what was passing for fundamentalism. Various interpretations have been brought forth to explain this dynamic. Previous scholarship on fundamentalism, represented best in Ernest Sandeen's *The Roots of Fundamentalism*, failed to see how deep the divide ran between Warfield and Machen, on the one hand, and the other fundamentalist camps, on the other hand. Sandeen saw millenarianism, espoused by neither Warfield nor Machen, coupled with inerrancy, almost entirely owing to Warfield, as the essence and scope of fundamentalism. George Marsden, though appreciative of Sandeen's work, demonstrated that a much more nuanced view of fundamentalism was in order. His *Fundamentalism and American Culture* sketches various camps of fundamentalism, all united in what they stood against, to be sure, but not at all together in what they stood for. Marsden's view has led to thoughtful analysis of the exact nature of these differences, shedding much light on Warfield and Machen's thought.[5]

Both Marsden and Noll draw attention to Warfield and Machen's rejection of premillennialism and dispensationalism. Warfield was content to interpret the reference to one thousand years in Revelation 20 symbolically and, in the words of Noll, "was thoroughly unimpressed by the dispensationalism that became so important in American

4. Mark A. Noll, "B. B. Warfield," 32. For Warfield's contribution to *The Fundamentals*, see B. B. Warfield, "The Deity of Christ," in *The Fundamentals*, 2 vols., ed. R. A. Torrey, A. C. Dixon, et al. (Los Angeles: The Bible Institute of Los Angeles, 1917), 2:239–46. For a discussion of the role of Warfield's doctrine of inspiration and inerrancy and his ambivalent relationship to fundamentalism, see George M. Marsden, *Fundamentalism and American Culture: The Shaping of Twentieth-Century Evangelicalism, 1870–1925* (Oxford: Oxford University Press, 1980), 102–23. For Machen's invitation to Bryan, see Stonehouse, *J. Gresham Machen*, 425, and Hart, *Defending the Faith*, 105.

5. Ernest R. Sandeen, *The Roots of Fundamentalism: British and American Millenarianism, 1800–1930* (Chicago: University of Chicago Press, 1970); George M. Marsden, *Fundamentalism and American Culture*. For a treatment of the subtleties within the Presbyterian response to the fundamentalist/modernist controversy, see Bradley J. Longfield, *The Presbyterian Controversy: Fundamentalists, Modernists, and Moderates* (Oxford: Oxford University Press, 1991).

fundamentalism." Machen's views on dispensationalism surface most poignantly in the controversy over the Scofield Reference Bible in the congregations of his fledgling Orthodox Presbyterian Church and his debates with J. Oliver Buswell, his former student, a Presbyterian ministerial colleague, and the president of Wheaton College. Yet, for both Warfield and Machen, eschatology played at best a minor role in their overall scheme of thought. Consequently, while they did not fall in with the increasingly popular dispensational branch of fundamentalism, it is safe to say that this fails to get at the root of the difference between the two of them and other fundamentalists.[6]

Realizing this to be the case, Noll and Marsden also draw attention to differences between Warfield and Machen and the other fundamentalists over Darwin and his theories. Writing in *The Fundamentals*, Henry H. Beach, in his installment titled "The Decadence of Darwinism," describes Darwinism as "deplorable" and as a "wretched propaganda." Another essay in *The Fundamentals*, by an anonymous "Occupant of the Pew," decried the dangerous presence of "evolutionism in the pulpit." While not agreeing with social Darwinism, both Warfield and Machen to differing degrees accepted biological evolution, seeing it not in conflict with the biblical account of creation or with creedal and orthodox Christianity.[7]

Noll accounts for this view in Warfield by drawing attention to Warfield's doctrine of concursus used in his formulation of inspiration. Noll explains it this way: "Just as the authors of Scripture exercised their individual humanity in writing the Bible, even while they enjoyed the full inspiration of the Holy Spirit, so too could all forms of life have developed fully (with the exception of the original creation and the human soul) through natural means." Hart offers a careful analysis of Machen on the subject, noting first that Machen was reluctant to enter the fray over evolution in the 1920s. Hart then, as an explanation for this reluctance, draws attention to Machen's dependence on Warfield for connecting the Genesis narratives to evolution, not jettisoning the

---

6. Noll, "B. B. Warfield," 32. For Machen's involvement in the controversy over the Scofield Bible and his debates with Buswell, see the numerous exchanges in *The Presbyterian Guardian*, 1936 and 1937. See also Stephen J. Nichols, "A Brief Exchange between Lewis Sperry Chafer and J. Gresham Machen," *Westminster Theological Journal* 65 (2000): 281–91.

7. Henry H. Beach, "The Decadence of Darwinism," in *The Fundamentals*, 4:71; By an Occupant of the Pew, "Evolutionism in the Pulpit," in *The Fundamentals*, 4:88–96.

narratives as the modernists were quickly doing. Hart nuances this by noting, "Unlike Warfield, however, Machen drew back from the idea that the human species had evolved from lower forms of life," adding that Machen's "hesitations showed sympathy with fundamentalist hostility to evolution." While it is impossible to conjecture what either Warfield or Machen would make of the contemporary critique of Darwinism coming from the Intelligent Design movement and the work of such scientists as Michael Behe, it is safe to say that they both were quite conversant with the scholarship from the scientific community of their time and the responses from the liberals and modernists on the left and the fundamentalists on the right, and neither theologian felt comfortable going in either direction.[8]

Recently, Kim Riddlebarger has attributed the rift between Warfield—and by extension this would equally apply to Machen—and the other fundamentalists to the Arminianism and revivalism that were widespread in the fundamentalist camps. Appreciating Noll's interpretation of the differences between Warfield and the emerging fundamentalists, Riddlebarger is surprised that Noll "has nevertheless overlooked one of the most important sources of tension between the two: Warfield's animosity to all things Arminian, especially revivalism and 'holiness teaching.'" This accounts, according to Riddlebarger, for Warfield's negative views toward many of the fundamentalist leaders. He further observes that Warfield's critique of Arminianism emerges "as a theological system in its own right." Riddlebarger points to the lengthy reviews by Warfield of John Miley's *Systematic Theology*, Andrew Murray's *The Spirit of Christ*, R. A. Torrey's *What the Bible Teaches*, and Lewis Sperry Chafer's *He That Is Spiritual* as proof of his contention.[9]

8. Noll, "B. B. Warfield," 33; D. G. Hart, *Defending the Faith*, 98; Michael Behe, *Darwin's Black Box: The Biochemical Challenge to Evolution* (New York: Free Press, 1996). For the Intelligent Design movement, see William Dembski, *Intelligent Design: The Bridge Between Science and Theology* (Downers Grove, Ill.: InterVarsity Press, 1999). For more on the issues of creation and evolution in the fundamentalist debate, see David N. Livingstone, "Situating Evangelical Responses to Evolution," in *Evangelicals and Science in Historical Perspective*, ed. David N. Livingstone, D. G. Hart, and Mark A. Noll (Oxford: Oxford University Press, 1999), 193–219; and Ronald L. Numbers, "The Creationists," in *God and Nature: Essays on the Encounter between Christianity and Science*, ed. David C. Lindberg and Ronald L. Numbers (Berkeley: University of California Press, 1986), 391–423.

9. Riddlebarger, "The Lion of Princeton," 210, 212, 213–41.

D. G. Hart's work adds confessionalism to the mix. He argues for a new taxonomy of the fundamentalist/modernist controversy that would move away from this two-party classification to seeing "four different camps in American Protestantism, fundamentalists, evangelicals, mainline Protestants, and confessionalists," fitting Machen, and by extension also Warfield, into the last category. Hart's point is that especially Machen was not for a minimalist Christianity in light of the modernist challenge, but that he was for a thoroughly worked out theology and a maximalist, confessional theology.[10]

As mentioned above, and as this survey reveals, various interpretations have been offered to explain Warfield and Machen's ironic connection to and distance from fundamentalism. Perhaps by way of solving this knotty problem, these various interpretations may be condensed down to differing perspectives of theologizing and of Christianity's relationship to culture. These methodological and philosophical considerations go far in explaining how Warfield and Machen found themselves at odds with the fundamentalists. Exploring these two areas also reveals the contours of Warfield and Machen's theology.

First, consider Warfield and Machen's view on culture. Both received extensive education in the liberal arts, each graduating as valedictorian of his baccalaureate class. Warfield was marked for a career in science. Having served a brief stint as editor of Lexington's *Farmer's Home Journal* in 1871, he pursued graduate studies in science at the University of Heidelberg. While there, he felt the ministerial call and left Heidelberg after the 1871–72 academic year to enroll at Princeton Seminary. Warfield's father, William, had authored the highly respected and widely read book on the scientific breeding of cattle (his own successful business) titled *The Theory and Practice of Cattle Breeding* in 1888. Perhaps the younger Warfield intended a similar trajectory. At any rate, his exposure and education left a mark on his thought and work. The case is repeated for Machen. After his extensive education in the classics, he continued graduate studies in the field at Johns Hopkins, even undertaking graduate courses in banking

10. Hart, *Defending the Faith*, 169. See also D. G. Hart, "J. Gresham Machen: Confessionalism and the History of American Presbyterianism," in *The Practical Calvinist: An Introduction to the Presbyterian and Reformed Heritage*, ed. Peter A. Lillback (Ross-shire, Scotland: Christian Focus, 2002), 357–71.

and international law at the University of Chicago. He reluctantly enrolled in simultaneous degree programs at Princeton University in philosophy and at Princeton Seminary in divinity. He, too, had his share of European studies at Marburg and at Göttingen. Warfield and Machen's counterpart leaders in fundamentalism largely lacked the extensive education and exposure to the liberal arts, language study, and scholarship that these two enjoyed. In fact, some of the early fundamentalists eschewed formal education altogether, blaming it for the malaise of modernity.[11]

Education was not the only factor in Warfield and Machen's relationship to culture; the arts also played a role. This is much more the case for Machen than Warfield. Due to Warfield's wife's longtime invalid state beginning shortly after their marriage, Warfield's world consisted of his home, his classroom in Princeton, and his church, the First Presbyterian Church of Princeton. In fact, Noll observes, "Rarely was he absent from home for more than two hours during the third of a century he taught at Princeton." Conversely, Machen's frequent travels took him to Europe on several occasions, and he regularly took the train north to New York City and south to Philadelphia to take in the sights and venues of the city. Among the early fundamentalists, certain suspicions abounded about the validity of the arts and the Christian's relationship to them. Along these lines, Machen and Warfield's use of alcohol and tobacco certainly marked them off from their fundamentalist counterparts who were at the forefront of bringing in Prohibition with the Volstead Act in 1919 (Machen once quipped, "My idea of delight is a Princeton room full of fellows smoking").[12]

While some fundamentalists were suspicious of culture and retreated from it, Warfield and Machen marked out a different path.

11. See the biographical works on Warfield and Machen cited earlier. For Machen on education, see Nichols, *J. Gresham Machen*, 171–88. On higher education and fundamentalism in general, see Douglas W. Frank, *Less Than Conquerors: How Evangelicals Entered the Twentieth Century* (Grand Rapids: Eerdmans, 1986); Virginia Lieson Brereton, *Training God's Army: The American Bible School, 1880–1940* (Bloomington, Ind.: Indiana University Press, 1990); and Quentin Shultze, "The Two Faces of Fundamentalist Higher Education, in *The Fundamentalism Project*, vol. 2, *Fundamentalisms and Society: Reclaiming the Sciences, the Family, and Education*, ed. Martin E. Marty and R. Scott Appleby (Chicago: University of Chicago Press, 1993), 490–535.

12. "B. B. Warfield," 27. Machen's quote is cited in Stonehouse, *J. Gresham Machen*, 85.

They held to a view of God and his providence that allowed them to accept, though not blindly or unreservedly, the advances of the scientific community. And, they saw no need to shrink before the assaults on Christianity flung from the academy, instead firing back from the ground of a rigorous and well-founded scholarship. For Machen this is evidenced in the obituary written of him by H. L. Mencken. Mencken speaks quite highly of Machen, dubbing him "Doctor Fundamentalis" and even expressing sadness at Machen's death. Mencken's salute to Machen is all the more telling when one considers that not much praise rolled off the typewriter of this consummate contrarian and iconoclast. It is even stronger felt given that Mencken's obituaries for William Jennings Bryan and Billy Sunday were scathing, the respect typically offered the recently departed entirely lacking. Even though he disagreed violently with Machen, Mencken saw in him impeccable scholarship.[13]

Warfield's scholarship is clearly seen in his approach to theology. In his "The Idea of Systematic Theology," Warfield painstakingly spells out what systematic theology is and is not. Along the way, he engages theology as a science and its relationship to all of the other sciences. He first speaks of the supremacy of theology as a science over the other sciences. He also points out, "It is not so above them, however, as not to be also a constituent member of the closely interrelated and mutually interacting organism of the sciences." He then adds, "Theology, thus, enters into the structure of every other science." Warfield's engagement of the natural sciences reflects an overall perspective on the Christian's relationship to culture that quite differs from the typical fundamentalist program.[14]

While Warfield and Machen did not retreat from culture, neither did they espouse triumphalism over culture or the establishment of a "Christian culture"— another distinction from their fundamentalist colleagues. Though a triumphalist note rings throughout much of fundamentalism, the salient example is found in the revivalist Billy

13. H. L. Mencken, "Doctor Fundamentalis," *The Evening Sun*, January 18, 1937. For a discussion of Mencken's obituary on William Jennings Bryan, "In Memoriam: W. J. B.," see Terry Teachout, *The Skeptic: A Life of H. L. Mencken* (New York: HarperCollins, 2002), 212–22. Warfield, "The Idea of Systematic Theology," 68–69.
14. Warfield, "The Idea of Systematic Theology," 68–69.

Sunday. In addition to driving home rather flamboyantly the gospel message during his crusades, Sunday also rallied for the war effort, raising substantial funds and peppering his sermons with anti-German rhetoric. One of Sunday's recent biographers notes that "he became the leader of those who wanted to keep biblical, conservative Christianity alive in an increasingly secular society." Warfield and Machen likely would not disagree with Sunday's aim. They would choose theological and ecclesiastical means to achieve it, however, as opposed to Sunday's choice of political means.[15]

Warfield and Machen's understanding of the Christian's relationship to culture is only one prong of the methodological or philosophical differences with the other fundamentalists. The second concerns their theologizing. Both Machen and Warfield were quite capable as exegetes and familiar with the biblical scholarship of their day. Both were conversant with the history of doctrines, though Warfield excelled beyond Machen in this area owing to their respective specialties, and they both possessed the skills of organizing and synthesizing the data from Scripture and historical theology into cogent and compelling systematic expression. Facile in the languages of the Bible, the Latin of the church fathers, medievalists, and Reformers, and the French and German of current European biblical scholarship, Warfield and Machen brought a depth and a dimension to their work that were simply lacking among fundamentalists unable to work in any language other than English and dependent primarily on the English Bible for exegesis.

Warfield and Machen's theological method, centered on the Bible, avoided a naïve biblicism. This is perhaps most clearly seen in Warfield's

15. Lyle W. Dorsett, "Sunday, William Ashley, Jr." in *Biographical Dictionary of Evangelicals*, ed. Timothy Larsen, David Bebbington, and Mark A. Noll (Downers Grove, Ill.: InterVarsity Press, 2003), 653. See also Lyle W. Dorsett, *Billy Sunday and the Redemption of Urban America* (Grand Rapids: Eerdmans, 1991). Dorsett notes that Sunday also failed in a bid for the presidency as a Republican, later followed by a failed candidacy for vice president in the fold of the Prohibition Party. This is not to suggest that Machen eschewed political involvement. He corresponded with numerous public officials on such topics as the location of roads in national parks to New York's Lusk laws. He testified before the United States Congress against the establishment of the Department of Education and before the Philadelphia City Council against jaywalking laws. Machen's libertarianism, and especially his anti-prohibitionist stance, ran counter to other fundamentalists. While Machen advocated personal political involvement, he did not advocate political activity by or in the church. For more on Machen's politics, see Nichols, *J. Gresham Machen*, 137–52.

review of R. A. Torrey's *What the Bible Teaches* (1898). Himself an exception among the fundamentalists, Torrey was a graduate of Yale University and Yale Divinity School, having attended German universities for one year. As an associate of D. L. Moody, Torrey served first at the Moody Bible Institute before moving on to the Bible Institute of Los Angeles, the forerunner of Biola University. Warfield's review hinges on one central criticism, Torrey's claim of an inductive methodology. Warfield was not against the inductive method. Far from it, he hails the method as "the chief gain that has been made by doctrinal study of late years." He then equates the inductive method with "the new discipline of 'Biblical Theology,'" offering a rather extensive definition:

> Whereas there has been a tendency hitherto to formulate doctrine on the basis of a general impression derived from a cursory survey of the Scriptural material or on the basis of a specific study of a few outstanding texts isolated from their contexts, and then to seek support for it in more or less detached passages; it is becoming more usual now to rise from the thorough understanding of the teaching of complete sections of Scripture to larger and larger groups until an insight into the doctrinal whole is attained—in the unity of its historical development and the harmony of its varied expression.

Warfield is essentially contrasting "proof-texting" with his preferred truly inductive or biblical theology method. Warfield then directs his criticism at Torrey, noting that his method is largely proof-texting and that "Mr. Torrey's method is altogether alien to this truly inductive process." Because of Torrey's method, Warfield offers the following judgment of the finished product: "If we are to regard it as a contribution to dogmatics, we must needs look upon it as moving over the surface of its subject—as incomplete, insufficient and occasionally erroneous." He adds that Torrey's "exposition runs much on the surface of things and is rather external and at points even shallow." Not all of the review sounds such a negative note. Warfield commends Torrey's setting forth of the doctrine of the personality of the Holy Spirit, desiring that Torrey's "three paragraphs on it be bound as a frontlet between the eyes of every Christian teacher." And, Warfield ends the review by lauding the many things Torrey "has learned and knows how to teach the Christian world, and we gladly," he concludes, "put ourselves in these at his feet." Despite his mixed review, one point comes through quite clearly: differing methods of theologizing and hermeneutics were at work among the fundamentalists.[16]

Warfield's own theological method comes through most clearly in the above mentioned "The Idea of Systematic Theology." Warfield considered systematic theology not only the chief of the sciences but also "the crown and head" of other related disciplines such as "Apologetical Theology," "Exegetical Theology," and "Historical Theology." The theologian, however, must not neglect careful work in all of these areas, exegetical theology entailing both hermeneutics and biblical theology. Warfield's own thought and writing bear this out. While much has been made of Warfield's apologetics, his work as a historical theologian proves equally fruitful. Warfield gives just a brief glimpse into the benefit of historical theology in the essay under consideration. He notes the scope of the discipline: "Historical Theology investigates the progressive realization of Christianity in the lives, hearts, worship, and thought of men." The result is a "full account of Christianity" and "a body of facts," derived from "Christian organization, worship, living and creed-building, as well as the sifted results of the reasoned thinking and deep experience of Christian truth during the whole past." "Systematic Theology," Warfield argues, "does not fail to strike its roots deeply into this matter furnished by Historical Theology," adding, "it knows how to profit by the experience of all past generations in their efforts to understand and define, to systematize and defend revealed truth; and it thinks of nothing so little as lightly to discard the conquests of so many hard-fought fields." For Warfield, historical theology was no mere luxury; it was a necessity.[17]

16. R. A. Torrey, *What The Bible Teaches* (Chicago: Fleming H. Revell, 1898). For biographical information on Torrey, see William Vance Trollinger Jr., "Torrey, Reuben Archer," in *Biographical Dictionary of Evangelicals*, 674–76. Warfield's review first appeared in *Presbyterian and Reformed Review* 39 (July 1899): 562–64. It is reprinted in Mark A. Noll, ed., *The Princeton Theology, 1812–1921: Scripture, Science and Theological Method from Archibald Alexander to Benjamin Breckenridge Warfield* (Grand Rapids: Baker, 2001), 299–301. See also Timothy P. Weber, "The Two-Edged Sword: The Fundamentalist Use of the Bible," in *The Bible in America: Essays in Cultural History*, ed. Nathan O. Hatch and Mark A. Noll (New York: Oxford University Press, 1982), 101–20.

17. For a treatment of Warfield as a historical theologian, see McClanahan, "Benjamin B. Warfield," esp. 113–45.

Machen's own theologizing reflects Warfield's. Once asked to review a doctrinal statement by Charles Gallaudet Trumbull, contributor to *The Fundamentals* and editor of *The Sunday School Times*, Machen responded that he preferred not to attempt creedal formation, opting instead to assent to the Westminster Standards. Like Warfield before him, Machen's theologizing preferred to sink its roots in the past. He also learned from Warfield the primacy of systematic theology. In a letter to Ethelbert D. Warfield, B. B. Warfield's brother, Machen expresses his concerns over the fate of systematic theology at Princeton, himself entertaining the notion of moving from the New Testament department to that of systematics. Machen writes, "I regard the department of systematic theology as the centre around which everything else in the Seminary revolves," adding, "The development of the department of systematic theology has been the greatest achievement of Princeton Seminary . . . stressing of anything else at the expense of systematics would mean the destruction of the real Princeton Seminary." Ethelbert Warfield, president of Wilson College, sent a brief, but intriguing reply: "I should have been glad to see you to make the transfer [from New Testament to systematic theology], for exactly the same reasons that I urged a similar transfer on my brother in 1887." The reference is to Warfield's move from Western Seminary, where he taught New Testament, to Princeton, where he taught theology. Though Machen never made the move, the letter reveals his view of systematic theology.[18]

Evidence of Machen's abilities as an exegete and apologist may be found in his two scholarly books, *The Origin of Paul's Religion* (1921) and *The Virgin Birth of Christ* (1930), both works hailed in their day as monuments of scholarship, as well as in his numerous articles. His abilities in the languages were without question, as his *New Testament Greek for Beginners* (1923) enjoyed and continues to enjoy wide use as a textbook. Unlike his mentor, Machen is not typically considered a systematic theologian first. Nevertheless, like his mentor's work in

18. Charles G. Trumbull to J. Gresham Machen, December 19, 1928 (Machen Archives, Montgomery Library, Westminster Theological Seminary [hereafter WTS]); Machen to Trumbull, December 23, 1928; Trumbull to Machen, January 3, 1929; Trumbull to Machen, January 9, 1929. Machen to Ethelbert D. Warfield, April 15, 1921; Warfield to Machen, April 21, 1921. See also Machen, "The Creeds and Doctrinal Advance," in *God Transcendent*, ed. Ned B. Stonehouse (Grand Rapids: Eerdmans, 1949), 157–67.

theology, Machen's reflects the same commitment to careful work in the text, in the history of Christian thought, and in the formulation and expression of doctrine, all the while demonstrating a sharp apologetic edge. Machen himself viewed all of these as contributing to the essence of Princeton Seminary. Amidst the controversy at Princeton in the late 1920s, he writes, "We have seen that Princeton Seminary stands in the first place for the complete truthfulness of the Scriptures as the Word of God, and in the second place for the Westminster Standards as containing the system of doctrine that the Scriptures teach." He then adds the apologetic angle: "In the third place, Princeton Seminary holds that both these things—the full truthfulness of Holy Scripture and the system of doctrine that our Standards set forth—need, and are capable of, intellectual defense."[19]

As Warfield and Machen were parallel in methodology, it should not be surprising to find them of a piece when it comes to their specific work in theology. While numerous areas show this to be true, two specific areas, their views on Scripture and Christology, are examined below.

"Seeking New Paths": Warfield and Machen's Response to Liberal Bibliology and Christology

Quite the opposite of Hodge's dictum that "a new idea never originated at Princeton Seminary," Friedrich Loofs, commenting on the state of theology and especially Christology in Germany in the early twentieth century, notes that "all learned Protestant theologians in Germany, even if they do not do so with the same emphasis, really admit unanimously that the orthodox Christology does not do sufficient justice to the truly human life of Jesus, and that the orthodox doctrine of the two natures in Christ cannot be retained in the traditional form. All our systematic theologians," he adds, "are seeking new paths in their Christology." The new paths in Christology taken by the German theologians were first forged in the field of biblical studies. It is not surprising, then, that these two areas are center stage

19. Machen, "The Attack upon Princeton Seminary: A Plea for Fair Play," (Princeton: privately published, 1927), 11.

183

in the polemical work of both Warfield and Machen. While defense of an orthodox view of Scripture is associated most closely with Warfield and a defense of orthodox Christology is associated most closely with Machen, in fact both wrote extensively and perceptively on both subjects. Further, one can see the contours of Warfield's criticism reverberate in the work of Machen. Commenting on Machen, but equally true of Warfield, D. Clair Davis once noted, "Nevertheless [Machen] believed with Martin Luther that if you are not faithful at the precise point where the gospel is under attack, then you are not really faithful to the gospel at all." The points of Scripture and Christ were where orthodox Christianity faced attack. Rather than seek new paths, Warfield and Machen were quite content with the old ones. Nevertheless, they cleverly used the methodologies of their liberal counterparts, such as textual criticism, not to debunk orthodox tradition as liberalism did, but to vindicate it.[20]

The first area concerns Scripture. While the fundamentalists agreed that the crisis of modernism was that of the authority of the Bible, they were not in agreement as to the response to this crisis. An acute area of difference between Warfield and Machen, on the one hand, and other fundamentalists, on the other, is their view of textual criticism and a nuanced view of inspiration and inerrancy. Warfield's first full treatment of the topic came in 1886 while he was still at Western Seminary. In 1881, along with Archibald Alexander Hodge, Warfield published his legendary article "Inspiration." From the beginning, Warfield insisted that inspiration, which demanded inerrancy, be restricted to the original autographs. This immediately raised the issue of textual criticism and the trustworthiness of the biblical manuscripts, given that the original autographs are no longer extant. The product of Warfield's thought on these matters is *Textual Criticism of the New Testament*, published in 1886. Reflecting on Warfield's thought and legacy in this area, Moisés Silva observes, "The contemporary debate regarding inerrancy appears hopelessly vitiated by the failure—in both

---

20. The remarks are from Loofs's Oberlin lectures, as cited in B. B. Warfield, "The Twentieth Century Christ," first appearing in *The Hibbert Journal* 12 (1914), reprinted in *Christology and Criticism*, vol. 3 of *The Works of Benjamin Breckinridge Warfield* (1929; repr., Grand Rapids: Baker, 1981), 372. D. Clair Davis, "Machen and Liberalism," in *Pressing Toward the Mark: Essays Commemorating Fifty Years of the Orthodox Presbyterian Church*, ed. Charles G. Dennison and Richard C. Gamble (Philadelphia: Orthodox Presbyterian Church, 1986), 247.

conservative and nonconservative camps—to mark how carefully nuanced were Warfield's formulations." Silva further draws attention to the "carefully qualified" Princetonian doctrine, marking Warfield's textual criticism and skillful exegesis as the qualifiers.[21]

Warfield's bold move as a textual critic led him to publish in the quite conservative *Sunday School Times* an article in which he denies the validity of the longer ending of Mark (Mark 16:9–20). As Kim Riddlebarger notes, this article quickly met opposition, causing Warfield to be "vilified at the time for taking a 'liberal' position in his views on the 'spurious' ending of Mark's gospel." Riddlebarger points also to Warfield's favorable view of the so-called Westcott-Hort method as putting the Princetonian under further suspicion. Even today, Warfield's thought on textual criticism is met with concern. Theodore Letis argues that it was Warfield's work on criticism in the 1880s that opened the door to the liberalism of the 1910s. Again, Riddlebarger, arguing that Letis's work is "repeatedly marred by such hyperbolic assertions," draws different conclusions. He notes that Warfield did employ the new method, but also adds, "Warfield is not breaking with the past in a 'wholly new' manner, as much as he is attempting to use the new method as a means of advancing the traditional Princeton apologetic."[22]

Warfield was driven by a deep commitment to the original divinely inspired text. As he notes in *Textual Criticism of the New Testament*, "The Nature of the New Testament as a Divine book, every word

---

21. "Inspiration," co-authored by A. A. Hodge and Warfield, first appeared in *Presbyterian Review* 2 (April 1881): 225–60, and is reprinted in Noll, *The Princeton Theology, 1812–1921*, 218–32. Warfield, *Textual Criticism of the New Testament* (New York: Thomas Whittaker, 1886). See also the various essays in Benjamin B. Warfield, *The Inspiration and Authority of the Bible*, ed. Samuel G. Craig (Philadelphia: Presbyterian and Reformed, 1948). Moisés Silva, "Old Princeton, Westminster, and Inerrancy," in *Inerrancy and Hermeneutic: A Tradition, A Challenge, A Debate*, ed. Harvie M. Conn (Grand Rapids: Baker, 1988), 68–69; this essay also appears in adapted form as chap. 3 of the present volume.

22. B. B. Warfield, "The Genuineness of Mark 16:9–20," *Sunday School Times* 24, no. 48 (December 2, 1882): 755–56. In the article, Warfield offers a detailed analysis of the various manuscript witnesses and a scholarly review of the key issues, leading him to conclude that "this passage is no part of the Word of God." He acknowledges that this means that "we have an incomplete document in Mark's Gospel." He then adds, "The important point for us is that, although a Gospel comes to us mutilated, *the* Gospel does not" (emphasis his). Riddlebarger, "The Lion of Princeton," 71–82. For the work of Theodore Letis, see "B. B. Warfield, Common-Sense Philosophy and Biblical Criticism," *American Presbyterian* 69, 3 (Fall 1991).

of which is precious, bids us be peculiarly and even painfully careful here." Then, he shows why this careful path is to be chosen, adding that one is to be "careful not to obtrude our crude guesses into the text"—referring to the work of conjectural emendation emanating from the higher criticism of liberal scholars—"and careful not to leave any of the guesses of the slips of the scribes in it"—referring to the naïve trust in the transmission of the English Bible largely emanating from conservatives. Earlier in the work, Warfield is quick to point out that while there are a large number of variant readings, "The great mass of the New Testament, in other words, has been transmitted to us with no, or next to no variation." Consequently, he undertakes the task of criticism with both "a sense of duty" and "the inspiration of hope," declaring, "The autographic text of the New Testament is distinctly within the reach of criticism in so immensely the greater part of the volume, that we cannot despair of restoring to ourselves and the church of God, His Book, word for word, as he gave it by inspiration to men." Warfield's high view of the Bible as the inspired, authoritative, inerrant text, in other words, drove him to his work as a textual critic, and did not cause him to shy away from the task, as was the case with those content with the English Bible.[23]

Letis's work, as well as the criticisms of Warfield's contemporaries, fails to account for the differences in the starting point, application, and results of the method of criticism in Warfield's work from that of liberal critics. Warfield's advocacy of textual criticism is of quite a different strain than that of higher criticism or the so-called modern criticism of the Bible. The latter starts with the presupposition of human reason as the arbiter of revelation; Warfield begins with the presupposition of Scripture's truth, the "fact" that marks off his starting point. Warfield saw this as the dividing line between orthodox and liberal Christianity. The orthodox view begins with the notion that Christianity is a supernatural religion, entailing that its divine origin demands its truthfulness. Liberalism, on the other hand, starts from the premise

---

23. Warfield, *Textual Criticism of the New Testament*, 208, 14–15. Warfield does not ignore the role of providence in the transmission of Scripture. Rather, he notes that the New Testament has been copied with great care, "a care which has doubtless grown out of true reverence for its holy words,—such has been the providence of God in preserving for His church in each and every age a competently exact text of the Scriptures" (12).

that Christianity is a natural religion, entailing that, as a product of human thought, it necessarily reflects human fallibility and is necessarily bound to the culture. But, given that Christianity is supernatural and therefore its revelation is true—and here is where Warfield's doctrine of concursus comes back into play—the exegete or theologian is not then relieved of the duty of textual criticism, just as one interpreting the text is not relieved of the duty of hermeneutics.[24]

Warfield was followed by Machen. Again, for Machen the dividing line was also found in Christianity's supernatural origin. Like Warfield, Machen also saw value in textual criticism, as evidenced in his inaugural lecture at Princeton, "History and Faith" (1915), and his *Origin of Paul's Religion* and *The Virgin Birth of Christ*. Hart draws attention to the impetus behind Machen's methodology, arguing that he espoused a scholarship that countered "the conventional and unthoughtful piety of American Protestantism." Hart then concludes, "Rather than eschewing the methods and findings of higher criticism, as many conservatives did, Machen used the new learning both to defend historic Christianity and to attack the complacency of mainstream Protestantism." Machen's treatment of the Lucan narrative of the virgin birth illustrates the point. Interacting with the work of Adolf von Harnack, Machen undertook an intensive study of the phrases and wording of Luke. Harnack argued that Luke avoided the use of sources in the composition of Luke 1–2. Machen, perhaps surprisingly, argued against his thesis. Machen's detailed analysis of the text led him to conclude what he considered to be two "really important facts": "The birth narrative formed an original part of the Third Gospel; and in the second place [the birth narrative] is genuinely primitive and Palestinian." In other words, Luke employed a prior source. This same conclusion, however, led others to see the birth narrative as a later interpolation, therefore eviscerating Luke's account as an authentic witness to the virgin birth. Undeterred, Machen again undertook an intensive study to argue for the integrity of the Lucan

24. The Bible's divine origin is key to Warfield's understanding of inspiration. See the essays previously cited, as well as "The Biblical Idea of Revelation," reprinted in Warfield, *The Inspiration and Authority of the Bible*, 71–102. Here he begins by declaring, "The religion of the Bible is a frankly supernatural religion," before proceeding to develop a doctrine of revelation (71).

narrative, responding to objections and offering a point-by-point study of the connection of chapters 1 and 2 to the rest of the book.[25]

Comparing Warfield and Machen's approach to the challenges of their day with that of other fundamentalists both then and now shows that they avoided simply arguing to the choir or arguing from experience. This is not to suggest that Machen and Warfield stood alone in their approach. W. H. Griffith Thomas asserted, "We do not question for an instant the right of Biblical criticism considered in itself. On the contrary, it is a necessity for all who use the Bible to be 'critics' in the sense of constantly using their 'judgment' on what is before them." What often won out in the popular rhetoric of fundamentalism, however, was not the detailed, page-after-page and chapter-after-chapter discussion of the views of various critics weighed against the evidence, as one consistently finds in Warfield and Machen, but instead the rather simplistic or even subjective arguments, as can be found in the popular hymn "He Lives," written in 1887: "You ask me how I know he lives? He lives within my heart." Both Machen and Warfield recognized that the scholars of modernism were posing formidable challenges that needed to be met with equal or better scholarship. Machen once observed, "We cannot agree at all with those who despise the adversaries in this great debate, who think that the 'critics' are to be disposed of with a few general words of adjectival abuse." He then added that while the liberal scholars are wrong, "they are wrong in a grand and imposing way; and they cannot be refuted either by a railing accusation or by a few pious words."[26]

The area of Christology is also informative. As mentioned earlier, Machen is more than likely thought of first as the supreme defender of orthodox Christology. Nevertheless, one finds that Warfield is not

25. Hart, *Defending the Faith*, 37. Machen, *The Virgin Birth of Christ* (New York: Harper & Brothers, 1930), 118, 119–68. Machen's work on the virgin birth extends back to his first published article, "The New Testament Account of the Birth of Jesus," *Princeton Theological Review* 3 (1905): 641–70. Warfield treats Harnack similarly in "The Essence of Christianity," *The Harvard Theological Review* 7 (1914): 538–94, reprinted in *Christology and Criticism*, 393–444.

26. W. H. Griffith Thomas, "Old Testament Criticism and New Testament Christianity," in *The Fundamentals*, 1:128. Other essays in *The Fundamentals* reflect the spectrum of the fundamentalist response. Some offer a rigorous engagement of higher criticism, while others simply refer to personal experience or the sublimity of the text as the only argument for its veracity. Machen, "The Attack upon Princeton Seminary," 11–12.

too far behind. Upon further examination, one sees that elements of Machen's defense find earlier manifestations in his mentor's work. Warfield's contribution to *The Fundamentals* was "The Deity of Christ." James McClanahan further observes, citing from Warfield's article "The Supernatural Birth of Jesus," "Warfield said that the three pillars on which the structure of Christianity rests were 'the supernatural, the incarnation, and redemption.'" Warfield then relates that the particular doctrine of the virgin birth "takes its significant place and has its significant part to play with respect to each one of them." For Warfield, the supernatural birth of Christ is necessary to New Testament Christianity; he argues that it is not an invention of the biblical writers, a point that Machen takes up at length in *The Virgin Birth of Christ*. Warfield further argues that the orthodox doctrine of the incarnation, demanding both Christ's full deity and his full humanity, is "the cardinal point upon which the whole of this supernaturalistic Christianity, commended to us by the New Testament, turns"; Christianity, therefore, "is formed by its doctrine of incarnation." As he continues, Warfield notes that the incarnation, however, was merely a means to an end: redemption. He concludes, "It cannot be denied that the supernatural birth of Jesus enters constitutively into the substance of that system which is taught in the New Testament as Christianity—that it is the expression of its supernaturalism, the safeguard of its doctrine of the incarnation, the condition of its doctrine of redemption." This, Warfield argues, is New Testament Christianity. Anything less is something quite different.[27]

In "The Essence of Christianity," Warfield, engaging the current works of Harnack and Ernst Troeltsch among others, notes that the essence of Christianity has to do with the historical Christ as its namesake. It is not a "form which religion has spontaneously taken in the course of developing religion," as Troeltsch and the history of religions school were arguing. It is instead "a 'historical religion'; and its content is to be ascertained not by reference to what we may think 'the ideal religion,' but by reference to the character given it by its Founder." In the same essay, Warfield repudiates the notion that

27. McClanahan, "Benjamin B. Warfield," 115. Warfield, "The Supernatural Birth of Jesus," first appeared in *The American Journal of Theology* 10 (1906): 21–30, and is reprinted in *Christology and Criticism*, 447–58.

Paul invented a "new gospel" quite apart from the true teachings of Christ. At the center of the gospel shared by Christ and Paul is the message of redemption, the essence of Christianity. Warfield then concludes, "It may be within the rights of those who feel no need of such a redemption and have never experienced its transforming power to contend that their religion is a better religion than the Christianity of the Cross. It is distinctly not within their rights to maintain that it is the same religion as the Christianity of the Cross."[28]

Those even vaguely familiar with Machen's classic text *Christianity and Liberalism* will recognize the footprints of Warfield's thesis on its pages. In his chapter on Christ, Machen also engages the issue of the connection between Christ and Paul, though he does so much more extensively in *The Origin of Paul's Religion*. Machen concludes, with Warfield, that it was not just the faith that Christ displayed that captivated Paul, but faith *in Christ*: "Jesus was not for Paul merely an example for faith; He was primarily the object of faith." He adds, "Christianity from the beginning was a means of getting rid of sin by trust in Jesus of Nazareth." But the reference to Christ's humanity should not deter one from seeing Machen's emphasis on Christ's deity. In a memorable line he quips, "Liberalism regards Jesus as the fairest flower of humanity; Christianity regards him as a supernatural Person." This emphasis on the Person of Christ, Machen continues, "runs all throughout the New Testament."[29]

Earlier in the book, Machen observes, "In the sphere of religion, in particular, the present time is a time of conflict; the great redemptive religion which has always been known as Christianity is battling against a totally diverse type of religious belief." Christianity is one thing, liberalism is something quite different. As Warfield said earlier, it is not within the rights of liberals to call their religion the Christian-

---

28. Warfield, "The Supernatural Birth of Jesus," 429, 432, 444. Warfield makes a similar point in "Christless Christianity," in *Christology and Criticism*, 366.

29. Machen, *Christianity and Liberalism* (New York: Macmillan, 1923), 81, 91, 96. Both Warfield and Machen saw that underlying the emaciated view of Christ and his work is an overly exalted view of humanity. See Warfield, "The Supernatural Birth of Jesus," and Machen, *Christianity and Liberalism*, 54–68. The liberal view of Christ as, in Machen's words, the "fairest flower of humanity" is exemplified in Harry Emerson Fosdick. See his "Shall the Fundamentalists Win?" (1922), reprinted in *American Protestant Thought in the Liberal Era*, ed. William R. Hutchison (New York: Harper & Row, 1968; repr., Lanham, Md.: University Press of America, 1984), 170–82.

ity of the cross. Machen's indebtedness to Warfield on these topics is revealed not only here, but elsewhere as well. It is quite clear, however, what was at stake for both men throughout the fundamentalist/modernist controversy: a Christless Christianity is no Christianity at all. And, both men saw the dangers lying ahead for the church as it sought out these new paths.[30]

Mighty Defenders of the Faith: The Legacy of Warfield and Machen in Fundamentalism

In a flyer looking more like a broadside for a prize fight than an advertisement for a speaking engagement, onlookers are enjoined to attend a "Great Fundamentalist Rally" to hear Professor Machen, "renowned as a mighty defender of the Integrity and Authority of the Holy Scriptures" and a "Mighty Preacher of the Word of God"—all of which is in bold print. One last exhortation appears at the bottom: "Hear These Mighty Messages" as "A Great Revival of Faith in God's Gospel is Stirring Our Land"—again appearing in bold. While the particulars of the advertisement might have caused Machen to wince a bit, its broad stroke could not be truer: it is quite likely that no more mighty defenders of the faith rose to the occasion in early twentieth-century America than Warfield and Machen. Perhaps that sentiment best sums up their contribution to the fundamentalist movement as well as their ongoing legacy.[31]

At the time of Warfield's death, Machen's battle royal with liberalism was just heating up. At that time, however, it was quite clear that a sea change was occurring around both men. Warfield died on February 16, 1921. The next day, in a letter to his mother, Machen wrote that "Princeton will seem to be a very insipid place without him," adding, "There is no one living in the church capable of occupying one

---

30. Machen, *Christianity and Liberalism*, 2. For Warfield, see "Christless Christianity" and "The Twentieth Century Christ," 313–67, 371–89. For Machen, see his essays on the deity of Christ in *The Christian Faith in the Modern World* (New York: Macmillan, 1936).

31. The "rally" was held at Calvary Baptist Church, Brooklyn, New York, on February 11, 1924. A copy of the advertisement is in the Machen Archives. I am indebted to Rich Michael for pointing this piece out to me. See C. Richard Michael, "The Fundamentalist-Modernist Controversy and the Work of J. Gresham Machen: Lessons for Evangelicalism Today" (M.A.B. Thesis: Lancaster Bible College Graduate School, 2003).

quarter of his place. To me, he was an incalculable help and support in a hundred different ways. This is a sorrowful day for us all."[32]

A few days later, on February 20, Machen wrote another letter to his mother relaying the events of the funeral. Here, Machen's grief at Warfield's loss is much more poignant, causing him at one point to exclaim, "I feel very black without him." Machen's estimation of the loss to Princeton and the common cause he shared with Warfield is equally poignant, as he relates: "It seemed to me that the old Princeton—a great institution it was—died when Dr. Warfield was carried out. The present Princeton, except for some survivals, is inexpressibly cheap and vulgar." He then quite sentimentally recalls:

> I am thankful for that one last conversation I had with Dr. Warfield some weeks ago. He was quite himself that afternoon. And somehow I cannot believe that the faith which he represented will ever really die. In the course of the conversation, I expressed my hope that to end the present intolerable condition there might be a great split in the church in order to separate the Christians from the anti-Christian propagandists. "No," he said, "you can't split rotten wood." His expectation seemed to be that the organized church, dominated by naturalism, would become so cold and dead, that people would come to see that spiritual life could be found only outside of it, and that thus there might be a new beginning.[33]

Warfield's final conversation with Machen had a prophetic ring to it. Princeton further marginalized Machen until he had no real choice but to resign and begin anew with Westminster Theological Seminary, established as it was in the spirit of the grand institution of Old Princeton. Further, Machen's defrocking from the Presbyterian Church in the United States led to his forming the Orthodox Presbyterian Church (OPC). These two institutions—Westminster Seminary and the OPC—constitute Machen's legacy, but they also, if only in an indirect way, can trace their origins to Warfield. Machen learned from his mentor the necessity of rigorous scholarship in ministerial education. He learned it firsthand as a pupil and then as a colleague.

32. Machen to Mary Gresham Machen, February 17, 1921 (Machen Archives, WTS).
33. Machen to Mary Gresham Machen, February 20, 1921 (Machen Archives, WTS).

Machen also learned from Warfield that seminaries and other such institutions were merely a means to an end—the edification and building up of the church.

If this is the case, then any reclamation of Warfield, or of Machen for that matter, would have to go beyond a simple retrieval of an argument for inerrancy, or of a statement of inspiration, or of a case for the virgin birth. A true reclamation would involve wrestling with the fundamental relationship of the church to culture, avoiding, as with liberalism, mere adaptation, while also avoiding, as with fundamentalism, withdrawal. Recently, Millard Erickson observed that Warfield and Machen's thought in this area, as well as that of Charles Hodge, has left a lasting legacy. Erickson notes, "What are the fortunes today of those churches that followed the ideas of Charles Hodge, Benjamin B. Warfield, and J. Gresham Machen versus those that followed the teachings of Henry Preserved Smith, Charles Briggs and Harry Emerson Fosdick?" He then answers his own question:

> The former were persons who advocated what I call a "classical" theology, and the churches that followed that theology are for the most part growing and thriving. The latter theologians tied their theology more closely to the culture of the time, and the churches that followed in that stream are in decline, strangely unappealing to people of today.[34]

A reclamation of Warfield and Machen would also entail a commitment to the type of theologizing represented in their work. Firm commitment to exegesis, as well as to tradition, runs somewhat counter to typical contemporary evangelical sensibilities, but they were quite crucial to both Warfield and Machen. Since their time, the fields of biblical theology, systematic theology, and historical theology have all become increasingly more specialized. While it is difficult for contemporary scholars to keep up with each of these fields, there is much to be gained by the mutual interchange between these disciplines, as marked by the work of Warfield and Machen, over and against the entrenchment one sees in the contemporary scene. Finally, Warfield

34. Millard J. Erickson, "Evangelical Theological Scholarship in the Twenty-First Century," *Journal of the Evangelical Theological Society* 46, 1 (2003): 26.

and Machen were not ultimately for a generic Christianity revolving around a bare minimum of theological definition. Instead, they were for a thorough-going, detailed theology. For Warfield and Machen, a Christianity without theology—substantive theology, that is—is not Christianity at all.

In that letter to his mother on February 20, 1921, Machen, almost in the form of a mission statement, declares, "Nearly everything I have done has been done with the inspiring hope that Dr. Warfield would think well of it." Such was his devotion to his mentor. For sixteen years after Warfield's death, Machen continued to fight, almost with a dogged determination to see Old Princeton carry on. But, perhaps the line most worth remembering in Machen's letter is the one cited earlier regarding Warfield's true legacy, "Somehow I cannot believe that the faith which he represented will ever really die."

~ 8 ~

Warfield and C. A. Briggs:
Their Polemics and Legacy

GARY L. W. JOHNSON

Odium theologicum is a rather ugly sounding Latin expression that was used in days gone by to refer to the bitter doctrinal rivalries that were fairly common among theologians of all stripes. These ardent polemical debates did at times degenerate into acrimonious personal attacks that amounted to character assassination. Because of this we are prone—living, as we like to assume, in our postmodern "kinder and gentler" time—to dismiss the need for polemics simply because the language used in such clashes strikes us as so offensive. Sir Henry Wotten, an English poet who also served as foreign ambassador during the reign of the House of Stuart (mostly remembered for his quip that an ambassador was "an honest man sent abroad to lie for the good of his country"), had engraved on his tombstone a line taken from his book *A Panegyric to King Charles*, which read: *disputandi pruritus ecclesiarum scabies*—"an itch for disputation is the mange of the churches." Unfortunately, as the late Robert D. Preus points out, some people mistakenly conclude that there is some inevitable connection between orthodoxy and bitter invective and plain belligerence.[1]

---

1. Robert D. Preus, *The Theology of Post-Reformation Lutheranism: A Study of Theological Prolegomena I* (St. Louis: Concordia, 1970), 33. Preus provides us with some cautionary words on how polemical theology is to be conducted. See also Roger Nicole, "Polemic Theology:

The heated exchange, for example, that took place between the highly acclaimed Arminian John Wesley and his equally celebrated Calvinistic opponent Augustus Toplady quickly comes to mind. Both men were stalwart evangelicals (in the sense that they both affirmed the centrality of the Reformation doctrine of *sola fide*). Both had the courage of their convictions, and each man did his best to articulate and defend his position. One cannot read Wesley's or Toplady's diatribes without being impressed with each man's rhetorical, literary, and even satirical skills. But their exchange is nonetheless so marred at times by its acidity of language as to rightly be considered scandalous and a glaring blemish on both men's careers.[2] But, this kind of exchange was common and even considered fashionable at the time!

This is not to say, however, that the issues over which the two men crossed swords were unimportant or that even the intensity with which they argued was in itself inappropriate. J. I. Packer, in his stimulating article "Calvin the Theologian," writes of the role of polemics in Calvin's *Institutes*:

> The harsh controversial passages, which cause modern readers much offence, are actually essential to its design. Just as the Bible, being the proclamation of God's truth to an intellectually warped world, is necessarily polemical at point after point, so Calvin, as a Christian and a minister, could not but be a fighting man, and the Reformation, as a renewal of biblical faith amid ecclesiastical paganism, could not but be a fighting movement, and the *Institutio*, as a Reformation manifesto and apologia, could not but be a fighting book. John Calvin was a peace-loving person who found controversy a tedious burden, and who worked tirelessly to bring Protestants together, yet any account of him which minimized the intensity of his commitment to the conflict of God's Word with human error, as well as sin, would be an injustice. We may not dismiss Calvin's polemics as mere appendages to his positive teaching, as unnecessary as they

---

How to Deal with Those Who Differ from Us," in *Standing Forth: Collected Writings of Roger Nicole* (Ross-shire, Scotland: Christian Focus, 2002), 9–26.

2. See George Lawton, *Within the Rock of Ages: The Life and Work of Augustus Montague Toplady* (Cambridge: James Clarke & Co., 1983). This is an excellent piece of historical research on the controversy between Wesley and Toplady.

were unpleasant. Rather, we must reckon with Calvin's insistence that some notions ought to be fought to the death.[3]

Wesley and Toplady would have agreed wholeheartedly. Indeed, polemics, which is what Wesley and Toplady were engaged in, should be conducted in an open arena and undertaken in a serious fashion. After all, the purpose of polemics is not argument for argument's sake, but the critical evaluation of truth claims. Granted, how we do polemics is a legitimate concern.[4] But if we value, as we should, the truth of the Christian faith, then we are going to have to engage in polemics.

Polemical theology serves a noble and important role only when doctrine is highly valued. If doctrine is devalued or considered to be an awkward encumbrance—like some embarrassing relative we wish would not make an appearance at family gatherings because he or she makes everyone else uncomfortable—then, of course, polemics will always be held in contempt. In a very provocative article entitled "Theological Pluralism and the Unity of the Spirit," the late Jacques Ellul, speaking of what he refers to as the attitude of agnostic tolerance (this has become commonplace in those Christian circles that identify with the claims of postmodern epistemology), makes this telling observation:

3. J. I. Packer, "Calvin the Theologian," in *John Calvin: A Collection of Distinguished Essays*, ed. G. E. Duffield (Grand Rapids: Eerdmans, 1966), 154.

4. The blog sphere is one example of how polemics are often done in shrill tones. One recent example took place when Guy Prentiss Waters's book, *The Federal Vision and Covenant Theology: A Comparative Analysis* (Phillipsburg, N.J.: P&R, 2006), was subjected to a tortured review by a Presbyterian minister from the same denomination as Waters, but one who so disliked Waters's book that he concludes by declaring that Waters will fall under "God's harshest judgment" for writing it! This kind of invective can manifest in even the best of us. John Frame, a highly respected Reformed theologian (and one of my former professors) got caught up in the debate that still swirls around Norman Shepherd and declared of some of Shepherd's critics (many of whom were former colleagues on the faculty at Westminster Theological Seminary) that they were "stupid, irresponsible, and divisive. Theological professors who make such comments, in my judgment, do not have the intellectual, theological or spiritual maturity to prepare students for gospel ministry." Frame issued a back-handed apology saying that his language was inflammatory, but stood by the substance of his criticism; cf. his preface in *Backbone of the Bible: Covenant in Contemporary Perspective*, ed. P. Andrew Sandlin (Nacogdoches, Tex.: Covenant Media Press, 2004). One of the professors criticized was O. Palmer Robertson, who has written his first-hand personal observation of the Shepherd case in *The Current Justification Controversy* (Unicoi, Tenn.: The Trinity Foundation, 2003).

At the present time it is not, on the whole, so much a disposition toward intolerance that confronts us. Instead, I see around me a broad tolerance reigning everywhere except within the "sects." It does not appear, however, to be a positive tolerance and a progress of the human spirit beyond the intolerance of the past but rather what I would call a "tolerance by default." That is to say, when we consider the reaction against intolerance in the preceding centuries, we are perturbed by the vast number of ideologies, by the scientific critiques, and by the uncertainties of life in the modern world; and we adopt a rather skeptical attitude, somewhat disabused of previous illusions and, even in the churches, somewhat agnostic. There is nothing absolute, there is not a jot or tittle in the Bible of which we can be sure, there is nothing left of absolute truth. As a consequence we can "tolerate." This attitude implies an absence of doctrinal formulations (for example, the incredible theological poverty and mediocrity of the "theologies of liberation"!).

As for dogmas, we consider them unworthy of interest because, at bottom, they are nothing more than opinion. A diversity of opinion seems entirely acceptable, and this "tolerance by default" is as much evident in the theological sphere or among ministers of the churches as it is among the faithful.[5]

Polemics are, in fact, essential to the gospel. One cannot read Paul's epistle to the Galatians, for example, without detecting this refrain (see Gal. 2:5, 14; 4:16; 5:7). Because true Christianity is important, it must be preserved from error. The history of the Christian church often discourages people because there is so much controversy. But theological controversy is to be expected. The establishment of truth and the exposure of error are never reached without conflict and controversy; and, as B. B. Warfield pointed out long ago, there are, regrettably, those in our midst who fear controversy more than error.[6]

Benjamin B. Warfield was involved in a number of theological controversies during his lifetime, but none was more significant than the

5. Jacques Ellul, "Theological Pluralism and the Unity of the Spirit," in *Church, Word, and Spirit: Historical and Theological Essays in Honor of Geoffrey A. Bromiley*, ed. J. E. Bradley and R. A. Muller (Grand Rapids: Eerdmans, 1987), 216.

6. B. B. Warfield, "Christianity the Truth," in Benjamin B. Warfield, *Selected Shorter Writings*, 2 vols., ed. John E. Meeter (Nutley, N.J.: Presbyterian and Reformed, 1970, 1973), 2:216.

one he undertook with Charles Augustus Briggs of Union Theological Seminary in New York. For almost three decades, Warfield and Briggs engaged in a theological *affaire d'honneur* over issues that focused primarily on biblical authority and the Westminster Standards.

Both men echoed the complaints of Job and charged the other with "moving the boundary stones" (Job 24:2) of the Bible's infallibility. For Briggs, Warfield moved it *outside* of that which the Bible claimed for itself, a position that Briggs contended was not recognized by the Reformers and their true theological descendants. Warfield saw Briggs as moving the boundary stones also—but in the *other* direction. Briggs moved the stones to *restrict* the Bible's authority and infallibility—and Warfield argued that the Reformers and their descendants rejected such a concept of limited infallibility.[7] Both took their respective views very seriously, and this is reflected in their polemical writings.

The Polemics of C. A. Briggs

Charles Briggs was, in the words of one recent historian,

—the suave, elite, intellectual bent on leaving his indelible mark upon history and the church. As early as the 1870s, Briggs began to deconstruct traditional orthodoxy with respect to revelation and history. Briggs averred that the doctrine of the infallibility of the Bible had been invented by Francis Turretin and swallowed by Archibald Alexander, Charles Hodge, and other benighted Princeton fellows. To this myth manufactured by Briggs, he added the historical confusion—even contradiction—of the Biblical narratives: Briggs maintained that the Bible could only be authoritative for "faith and practice," *not* for history, geography, and other subjects. This view of 'limited inspiration' arose from Briggs's enthrallment with biblical theology of a rationalistic variety. From the rise of the German Enlightenment, the Bible was regarded as a cultural relic yearning to be set free from hide-bound traditionalists—benighted pietists

7. Warfield specifically addresses this concept in the January 1894 issue of *The Presbyterian and Reformed Review* under the title "Professor Henry Preserved Smith on Inspiration." This was later published as *Limited Inspiration*, International Library of Philosophy and Theology (Philadelphia: Presbyterian and Reformed, 1962). Smith defended Briggs and his views and, like Briggs, was suspended from the ministry in the Presbyterian church.

with confessional or dogmatic attachments to a book that never mingles with fallible, ordinary men and women. Scriptural infallibility and inspiration, he believed, was repressive and reactionary. A truly "modern" approach to the Bible jettisoned the dogmatic approaches of the precritical era and opened the Scriptures with truly scientific methods. Biblical supernaturalism was an outdated handicap. Reliable Biblical history was an impossibility given the prejudices of all writers of history (Biblical writers included). Everyone had an agenda—even the writers of the books of the Bible. Biblical theology was Briggs's theology of liberation of the day and he himself was its greatest critical advocate.[8]

Briggs contended that men like Warfield were "clamoring against the truth of God."[9] The issue with Briggs—the one major issue he opposed with all of his being—was the doctrine of the complete inerrancy of Scripture. This doctrine, Briggs contended, had cost the church the loss of thousands, and unless it was completely overthrown, it would cost the church hundreds of thousands.[10] He went on to declare, "No more dangerous doctrine has ever come from the pen of men."[11] One cannot read a single book penned by Briggs in which he does not pronounce anathema against this doctrine. Not only did he denounce the doctrine, but he denounced in very harsh language those who held and taught this doctrine. Briggs was convinced that the Bible did not

8. James T. Dennison Jr., *The Letters of Geerhardus Vos* (Phillipsburg, N.J.: P&R, 2005), 33–34.

9. C. A. Briggs, *The Bible, the Church and the Reason* (New York: Charles Scribner's Sons, 1892), 130.

10. Ibid., 159. Briggs took a very optimistic attitude on the possibility of a Protestant/Catholic reunion, and his later works (*Church Unity* and *Theological Symbolics*) show that he was very much in favor of it. However, he expressed shock and outrage by the encyclical letter *Providentissimus Deus* of Pope Leo XIII (1893) that affirmed in very strong language the complete inerrancy of the Bible. "It is indeed the irony of history that Rome has undertaken the defense of the inerrancy of Holy Scripture at the very time when it has been abandoned by most Protestants." *Church Unity* (New York: Charles Scribner's Sons, 1909), 430. Cf. Baron Friedrich von Hugel, the acclaimed Roman Catholic philosopher and mystic, and his *Essays and Addresses on the Philosophy of Religion* (London: J. M. Dent and Sons Limited, 1926), 104, where he makes reference to this and to his *valiant friend* Charles Augustus Briggs.

11. C. A. Briggs, *Whither? A Theological Question for the Times* (New York: Charles Scribner's Sons, 1889), 73. Briggs's words are in reference to the article on "Inspiration" by A. A. Hodge and B. B. Warfield that appeared originally in *Presbyterian Review* 2 (April 1881): 225–60.

teach its own inerrancy. "The Scriptures," he writes, "nowhere claim to be free from errors. From Genesis to Revelation no such claim can be found in any sentence or in any word."[12] He was further convinced that the doctrine was of recent vintage, declaring that if the Presbyterian church of his day officially adopted this dogma, then no man of science or scholar of history could ever be a Presbyterian.[13] "This doctrine of the inerrancy of the original autographs of Holy Scripture stands like a wall of rock in the path of the scientific study of the Bible. It is impossible for anyone who holds it to do any thorough Biblical work."[14]

Briggs's opinion of the Princeton theologians and men like his colleague at Union, W. G. T. Shedd, makes for sad reading. He obviously considered the debate over inerrancy and the right of higher criticism a fight to the death.[15] The two could not co-exist. On this, at least, Briggs and Warfield agreed.

It should be noted that it was *not* the Princeton men who first drew blood in this battle. The call to arms against the invasion of higher criticism did indeed involve the Princetonians. But it should be remembered that Princeton directed its early attack *not* against Briggs, but against the likes of William Robertson Smith and the German higher critics. Briggs, however, took this as a personal attack against his own views. That the Princetonians had not singled Briggs out in the early going is evident by Briggs's own correspondence with A. A. Hodge while the two men were co-editors of the *Presbyterian Review*. In 1882 A. A. Hodge let it be known that he would resign from the affair. Briggs wrote urging him to reconsider, assuring him that they both had the same objectives.

> If you will only have a little more patience with me . . . and trust me
> a little longer and not allow yourself to be influenced by anything
> whatever against me and my cause. I believe that you will be greatly
> rewarded, you will find that the positions that I will take will *conserve*
> all that you will deem essential in the Inspiration of the Scripture

12. Briggs, *The Bible, the Church and the Reason*, 107.
13. Ibid., 94.
14. Ibid., 105.
15. Briggs, *Church Unity*, 327.

and the standards of the Church and that the Higher Criticism that I will advocate will be one that will be seen to be of very great value for the defense and advocacy of the Scriptures themselves. I want to establish the Higher Criticism on a permanent basis in relation to the Church doctrine of Inspiration and I am sure that I can do it without disturbing the Westminster doctrine of the Scriptures in the slightest degree: And after that I wish to resume my Westminster studies and do something of permanent value for Historical Presbyterianism.[16]

Briggs's letter to Hodge is important for two reasons: (1) It was written *after* the Hodge/Warfield article on Inspiration, (2) therefore, Briggs understood Hodge's position when he assured Hodge that he would seek to "conserve" all that Hodge deemed important in the doctrine of Scripture.

A. A. Hodge died in 1886, and in 1889 Briggs dropped his bomb in his famous *Whither?* This book reveals that Briggs had no intention of "conserving" anything remotely resembling Hodge's doctrine of Scripture. Not only would Briggs break radically with Hodge on this matter, he would attack Hodge's doctrine without restraint. Writing in the preface, Briggs declares:

The book is polemical. It is necessary to overcome that false or-thodoxy which has obtruded itself in the place of the Westminster orthodoxy. I regret, on many accounts, that it has been necessary for me to attack so often the elder and younger Hodge, divines *for whom I have great respect and admiration*. Their names will always rank among the highest on the roll of American theologians. It has also been necessary to expose the errors of my younger associates in the editorship of the *Presbyterian Review*, and other divines, my friends and colleagues. The reader will see that this polemic has nothing in it of a *personal* or partisan character; it could not be avoided in the line of discussion that has been undertaken; for it is the theology of the elder and younger Hodge that has, in fact, usurped the place of the Westminster theology in the minds of a large proportion of the ministry of the Presbyterian Churches, and now stands in the way of progress in theology and of true Christian

16. Briggs to Hodge, October 1882 (Hodge Papers, cited by Lefferts A. Loetscher, "C. A. Briggs in the Retrospect of a Half a Century," *Theology Today* 12 (1955): 35.

orthodoxy; and there is no other way of advancing in truth except by removing the errors that obstruct our path.[17]

The "younger associates" referred to here were Francis Patton and B. B. Warfield. Briggs's "colleague" was the Old School Presbyterian theologian W. G. T. Shedd.[18] Briggs did, to some degree, curb his "personal" criticism of these men in this particular book. He even declared that it was *not* his wish to exclude these men and their view from the church, saying he was, after all, a "broad churchman."[19]

But Briggs had thrown down the gauntlet, and the Princeton men, especially B. B. Warfield and W. H. Green, were quick to respond. Briggs's subsequent writings would reflect more than a polemical disagreement over doctrine. He would attack with vicious strokes the men who held the doctrine.

Briggs's first line of attack centered on the question of scholarship. Even in *Whither?* Briggs questioned the scholarship of A. A. Hodge and B. B. Warfield by stating that the Hodge/Warfield position was questioned by scholars "wiser and greater than they."[20]

In 1892 Briggs declared that no true biblical scholar can hold to inerrancy.[21] Later Briggs wrote:

17. Briggs, *Whither?* ix, x, emphasis added.

18. In 1874 W. G. T. Shedd replaced the ailing Henry B. Smith (not to be confused with Henry Preserved Smith) as professor of systematic theology. Smith had been one of Briggs's staunchest supporters. Shedd, however, would prove to be one of his strongest critics. Alan Gomes recently wrote: "Two years before his retirement, Shedd published his greatest work, *Dogmatic Theology*. The system was initially released as two volumes. During his retirement Shedd worked on miscellaneous publishing projects, most notably the production of the supplemental third volume to his *Dogmatic Theology* in 1894. Also during his retirement, he provided significant input in two debates that were agitating the Presbyterian church: the charge of heresy against Dr. Charles Briggs occasioned by his inaugural address and the proposal to revise the Westminster Confession in a more latitudinarian direction. In both instances, Shedd—not surprisingly—championed the conservative cause in arguing for the removal of Briggs and in opposing the revision of the Westminster standards." Cf. the revised and edited, one-volume edition of W. G. T. Shedd, *Dogmatic Theology*, ed. Alan W. Gomes (Phillipsburg, N.J.: P&R, 2003), 18.

19. Briggs, *Whither?* 8.

20. Ibid., 64. Briggs also declared that the view of Hodge and Warfield "is worth much less than the authority of the much greater and more honored divines." Briggs, *Defense of Professor Briggs before the Presbytery of New York* (New York: Charles Scribner's Sons, 1893), 35.

21. Briggs, *The Bible, the Church and the Reason*, 215. On pp. 236–47, Briggs gives the names of more than a hundred scholars who favor higher criticism, and says, "It ought to be plain to every intelligent person, that the traditionalists are in such a hopeless minority that

It is quite true that some able and honest men are opposed to the principles and methods of the Higher Criticism. But every one of these is opposed to criticism on dogmatic grounds, because it imperils the dogmas of his school and party. The same set of men have opposed every advance of modern science and modern philosophy. Such men are not true biblical scholars.[22]

In Briggs's mind, the *major* reason for not holding to the higher criticism was traceable to a deficiency in scholarship.[23] Briggs, while paying lip service to Charles Haddon Spurgeon as a great preacher, could at the same time declare, "He was not a master of Christian theology, and, therefore, so soon as he went out of his sphere to teach men wiser than himself he made a sad failure among those who were nearest to him in denominational affinities."[24] All those who opposed higher criticism, therefore, were not real scholars. They only "pretend" to be.[25] These men, in Briggs's estimation, really have "little if any technical knowledge of Holy Scripture itself."[26] Not only do they lack scholarship, but they are, in fact, *ignorant*, and not only of Scripture but of the Westminster Confession.[27] Princeton is singled out as the

---

it is extremely improbable that they will ever be able to overcome the weight of scholarship throughout the world which is so overwhelmingly on the critical side" (247).

22. C. A. Briggs, *General Introduction to the Study of Holy Scripture* (1900; repr., Grand Rapids: Baker, 1970), 108.

23. J. Gresham Machen, who would eventually assume Warfield's mantle at Princeton, may well have had Briggs in mind when he wrote: "In general, I have found from that day to this that the really able men do not by any means share the contemptuous attitude toward conservative scholars which seems to be regarded as a mark of learning in certain circles in America. That may serve to give comfort to us believers in the truth of the Bible. On the other hand, I have never been able to give my self the comfort which some devout believers seem to derive from a contemptuous attitude toward the men on the other side of the great debate; I have never been able to dismiss the 'higher critics' *en masse* with a few words of summary condemnation. Much deeper, it seems to me, lies the real refutation of this mighty attack upon the truth of our religion, and we are not really doing our cause service by underestimating the power of the adversaries in the debate." *J. Gresham Machen: Selected Shorter Writings*, ed. D. G. Hart (Phillipsburg, N.J.: P&R, 2004), 557.

24. Briggs, *Defense*, 79. Briggs later commended Spurgeon by writing, "It is the merit of C. H. Spurgeon that he has recently called attention to the neglected Puritan commentators and expressed his great obligation to them." Briggs, *General Introduction to the Study of Holy Scripture*, 468.

25. Briggs, *Defense*, 108.

26. Ibid., 110.

27. Ibid., 610.

chief culprit and called "blind guides."[28] Those who fear higher criticism are really "uncertain in their faith."[29]

Briggs's attack on inerrancy and those who defended it involved, as far as Briggs was concerned, more than scholarship. Briggs accused them of being "the enemies of truth,"[30] and "hypocritical and traitorous companions who make a show of using the principles and methods of the scientific study of the Bible either for the purpose of discrediting them, or else as advocates and partisans of traditional and sectarian opinions."[31]

Briggs considered his new discipline of "Biblical Theology" vastly superior to the older type of systematic theology, which in his mind belonged in the museum of antiquities. Here is one of Briggs's typical statements.

> No one who has studied through the literature of Christology can do other than say that the researches of recent scholars have put the whole subject in such new lights that the writings of the older scholars have become for the most part antiquated. There are doubtless many still living who are unwilling to accept any theological opinions which have not been stamped with the approval of the antiquarians. For such the author does not write. The readers he desires are the open-minded and truth-loving, who would see the Christ as the apostles saw him, and who will not be restrained from the heavenly vision by the pretended perils of the Higher Criticism and of Biblical Theology, or by the supposed safer paths of traditional and ecclesiastical theology. . . . The author has done his best to turn away from the Christ of the theologians and of the creeds and of the church, and to see the Messiah as he is set forth in the writings of the apostles.[32]

Briggs considered the representatives of this antiquated way of doing theology personified in men such as Hodge, Shedd, and Warfield. They are "Theological Bourbons," who never learn from past

28. Ibid., 162.
29. Ibid., 80.
30. Ibid., 9.
31. Ibid., 10.
32. C. A. Briggs, *The Messiah of the Apostles* (New York: Charles Scribner's Sons, 1895), ii.

defeats.[33] One of Briggs's favorite terms for describing his opponents is "obstructionists."

> They would force evangelical critics to choose between truth and scholarly research on the one side, and Christ and tradition on the other. But there are many far better scholars who are Christian critics, and they will not be deterred from criticism themselves, or allow others to be deterred, by these reactionary alarmists. The issue is plain, the result is not doubtful: the obstructionists will give way in this matter, as they have already in so many other matters. Holy Scripture will vindicate itself against those who, like the friends of Job, have not spoken right concerning God in presuming to defend Him.[34]

Briggs could even blame the defenders of inerrancy for keeping people *away* from the Bible.[35]

When one remembers that Briggs had said he was a "broad churchman" and did not want to exclude these men and their views from the church, his personal criticisms seem uncalled for and extremely harsh. After all, he did recognize these men as true Christians—or did he? Briggs could go so far as to call them "hissing serpents" (citing Matt. 23:33) and "dogs" (with reference to Phil. 3:2).[36] Is it any wonder that Warfield, in reviewing Briggs's *General Introduction to the Study of Holy Scripture*, could write:

> If Dr. Briggs could only have found, amid the blocks of "twenty years" and "a quarter of a century," which he has told us from time to time he has given to the study of this or that branch of research, another twenty years or so which he might have given to cultivating the art of self-restraint, on the one hand, and the art of orderly and proportional presentation, on the other, his remarkable industry and his great talents might have received their crown in a corresponding usefulness. As it is, as there is hardly a page he has written that we can read without instruction, there is hardly a page we can read without offense.[37]

33. Ibid.
34. Ibid., 273; see also p. 11.
35. Briggs, *Church Unity*, 323.
36. Briggs, *The Bible, the Church and the Reason*, 278.
37. Warfield, "Review of *General Introduction to the Study of Holy Scripture*," by C. A. Briggs, *The Presbyterian and Reformed Review* 11 (1900): 359. A very similar assess-

Briggs carried his debate with the Princeton men and others such as W. G. T. Shedd[38] into the arena of personal attacks. He called their beliefs "abnormal, immature and defective," and said they were "very poor Christians."[39] Their theology was described as an "ill-formed and sickly child,"[40] which Briggs considered "a dyspeptic and diseased" form of Christianity.[41]

Briggs despised their doctrine of inerrancy and therefore denied them not only the claim to scholarship, but, it would seem, even the right to the name "orthodox." This is all the more amazing when one considers that Briggs declared the great distinguishing principle of his hoped-for Christian unity between the Catholic and Protestant churches to be "sanctification by love."[42] Clearly, Briggs had no love for the doctrine of inerrancy or for those who espoused it.

The Polemics of B. B. Warfield

Warfield stands in marked contrast to Briggs in a number of ways, especially in how he did polemics. Most notably, Warfield did not engage in the kind of malicious name-calling that was characteristic of Briggs.[43] In the words of George Marsden, he was "a hard-hitting and

---

ment of Briggs was made by Warfield's colleague Geerhardus Vos in his review of Brigg's *The Messiah of the Gospels* and *The Messiah of the Apostles*, which appeared in the pages of *The Presbyterian and Reformed Review* 7 (1896): 718–24. Vos remarked upon Brigg's rejection of historic Christianity, "Such wholesale condemnation of historic Christianity we have long been accustomed to from certain quarters where the contempt of so-called tradition is equaled by the lack of historic information, but in the case of a scholar and student of history like Dr. Briggs it is inexcusable." As cited in *A Geerhardus Vos Anthology*, ed. D. E. Olinger (Phillipsburg, N.J.: P&R, 2005), 9.

38. Briggs could refer to Shedd as "my beloved colleague" (*Whither?* 209), and yet group him with all who opposed him with the aforementioned defamation. Shedd's theology, claimed Briggs, would have been declared heresy in the seventeenth century. Briggs, *The Bible, the Church and the Reason*, 215.

39. Briggs, *General Introduction to the Study of Holy Scripture*, 667.

40. Briggs, *The Bible, the Church and the Reason*, 11.

41. Briggs, *Church Unity*, 10.

42. Ibid., 449.

43. Warfield took exception to L. J. Evans, a staunch defender of C. A. Briggs, for a snide remark Evans made about A. A. Hodge and himself, but Warfield chose to focus on the insult as directed at Hodge: "He [Evans] calls the joint authors of a tract he did not like by the opprobrious name of 'our *par nobile fratrum dogmaticorum*' (p. 57). We cannot believe either that Dr. Evans the scholar did not know, or that Dr. Evans the Christian minister meant to apply to the sainted Dr. Hodge, the implications of this language (Horatii *Sermonum*, Lib. Ii, 3, 243).

sometimes brilliant polemicist in a day of increasingly polite theology," and "had by this time established his reputation, for better or worse, as the John L. Sullivan of the theological."[44] Warfield could be blunt and relentless in his critique of his theological opponent, but he maintained a sense of fair play and gamesmanship even when the issue at stake was very dear to him. Bernard Ramm captured the essence of the man when he wrote:

> Warfield must be considered one of the greatest book reviewers of theological literature the Christian church has ever had. A Southern gentleman of the highest order, he always wrote with grace and polish. However, as one progresses through the review, he realizes that a first-class mind is at work, and soon through the gracefulness of spirit and politeness of vocabulary comes a devastating criticism. So remarkable were these reviews that the Oxford Press produced one whole volume of them—*Critical Reviews*. It is in these reviews that some of the most devastating criticisms of liberal theology made from the evangelical side are to be found.[45]

This is not to say that Warfield never used sarcasm to show his disdain. In his review of Yale professor George B. Stevens's *The Christian Doctrine of Salvation*, Warfield shows he gave little quarter for sloppy and misdirected theological guides.

> We shall not profess to have found the volume pleasant reading. The polemic tone in which it is cast from beginning to end, strident from the commencement, finishes by becoming rasping. It is not obvious

---

We must think he had simply mounted again his high rhetorical horse, and his charger had run away with him." *Limited Inspiration*, 4.

44. George M. Marsden, *Understanding Fundamentalism and Evangelicalism* (Grand Rapids: Eerdmans, 1991), 122.

45. Bernard Ramm, *The Evangelical Heritage: A Study in Historical Theology* (Grand Rapids: Baker, 1973), 98. Hugh Kerr, who once held the same chair at Princeton as Warfield, makes a similar observation, then adds, "Book reviewing is, I think, one of the most important means of theological communication." Warfield somehow managed to publish more than 780 of them in various publications, of which 318 were "very substantial critical reviews." Hugh Thomson Kerr, "Warfield: The Person behind the Theology," Annie Kinkead Warfield Lecture for 1982, at Princeton Theological Seminary, ed. William O. Harris (1995), 21, as cited by Kim Riddlebarger, "The Lion of Princeton: Benjamin Breckinridge Warfield on Apologetics, Theological Method and Polemics," Ph.D. diss., Fuller Theological Seminary, 1997. Of all the dissertations that I have read on Warfield, this is among the best.

that the opinions thus endlessly controverted have been sympathetically appreciated. It is not even obvious that the trouble has been taken thoroughly to understand them. Certainly they are not always stated in their completeness; and they are not seldom refuted in mere caricature. The reader acquires an unpleasant feeling as he proceeds in the volume that the language of scorn, rising even to vituperation, is now and again depended upon to do the work of argument. Dr. Stevens does not like the doctrine of "penal satisfaction." Not liking it, he is entitled to argue against it, and (if he can) to refute it. It may be questioned, however, whether its refutation is advanced by declaring that it makes God a Shylock (p. 410) whose most distinguishing characteristic is "his appetite for revenge" (p. 331 *et seq.*). And it seems more than questionable whether this procedure is justified by the open declaration that the advocates of such a doctrine are past arguing with. Take, for example, this sentence: "It seems to me that one who can adopt the principle which underlies the penal theory of our Lord's sufferings—that God is so just that He cannot forgive the guilty until He has first punished the innocent—thereby renders himself inaccessible to all considerations of equity and morality" (p. 383). In Dr. Stevens' view sin itself, in its most complete development, does not reduce man to so hopeless a condition (p. 316): he remains always accessible to appeal and open to conviction. It is inconceivable that he really considers his Christian opponents in worse case than the worst of sinners. His language is the language of simple vituperation.[46]

Although Warfield could be charitable when reviewing a book that lacked theological depth and substance, he had what borders on contempt for what Riddlebarger identified as "popular works by highly visible leaders with Arminian and revivalist leanings and who were associated with the emerging fundamentalist movement."[47] Among those whom Warfield singled out were Charles Trumbull, R. A. Torrey, Andrew Murray, and a young Lewis Sperry Chafer. This "coterie" (one

46. B. B. Warfield, "Review of *The Christian Doctrine of Salvation*," by George B. Stevens, in *Critical Reviews*, vol. 10 of *The Works of Benjamin Breckinridge Warfield* (1932; repr., Grand Rapids: Baker, 1981), 128.

47. Riddlebarger, "The Lion of Princeton," 224.

of Warfield's favorite terms, according to Marsden[48]) would all play significant roles in founding major evangelical institutions.[49]

Warfield, always the conscientious Calvinist, was of the opinion that confessional Calvinism was Christianity in its purest form. He declared in his critical review of the acclaimed Methodist theologian John Miley's systematic theology:

> It is just as well that the world should come to know with the utmost clearness that these Evangelical doctrines are unconformable with Arminianism. It is just as well that the world should realize with increased clearness that Evangelicalism stands or falls with Calvinism, and that every proof of Evangelicalism is a proof of Calvinism.[50]

He therefore looked with great disfavor on any hybrid system that would seek to dilute confessional Calvinism.[51]

48. George M. Marsden, *Fundamentalism and American Culture: The Shaping of Twentieth Century Evangelicalism, 1870–1925* (The Oxford University Press, 1980), 98.

49. Many of the leading twentieth-century evangelical educational institutions became centers for the teaching of the victorious Christian life—well into the 1960s at least. Among these are Columbia Bible College, founded by one of Trumbull's closest associates, Robert C. McQuilken; Prairie Bible Institute; Moody Bible Institute, founded by R. A. Torrey; Wheaton College; and Dallas Theological Seminary, founded by Lewis Sperry Chafer. See Douglas W. Frank, *Less Than Conquerors: How Evangelicals Entered the Twentieth Century* (Grand Rapids: Eerdmans, 1986), 113.

50. Benjamin B. Warfield, "A Review of *Systematic Theology*," in *Selected Shorter Writings*, 2:316. Warfield often displayed a playful sense of humor in the midst of the theological fray, stating in this review, "Let us only remark in passing that it passes the comprehension of our Calvinistically warped mind to understand how so close a thinker can, on the one hand, hang the whole weight of depravity on a 'law of nature,' or, on the other, deny the condemnability of a state of depravity which inevitably produces sin in every action into which it issues" (313).

51. Note how Warfield argues for this Reformational understanding of the term "evangelical": "The question, however, was a pressing one, whether the Evangelical elements thus taken up could consist with the Arminian principle. Calvinists earnestly urged that the union was an unnatural one, and could not be stable: that either the Evangelical elements ought to rule to the exclusion of the unharmonizable Arminian principle, in which case we should have consistent Calvinism; or else the Arminian principle would inevitably rule to the exclusion of the Evangelical doctrines forced into artificial conjunction with it, and we should have consistent Arminianism. After a century of conflict, Dr. Miley's admirably reasoned volumes come to tell us frankly that the Calvinists have been right in these contentions. Arminianism, he says, has no logical place in its system for a doctrine of race sin, either in the sense of the participation of the race in the guilt of Adam's first sin, or in the sense of the infection of the race with a guilty corruption. Arminianism, he says, has no logical place in its system for a doctrine of penal substitution of Christ for sinners and of an atonement by satisfaction. If the Arminian principle is to rule, he says, the doctrine of race sin must go, and the doctrine of vicarious punishment must go. And, as he thinks that the Arminian principle ought to rule, he teaches that men are not by

Charles Gallaudet Trumbull, whom Warfield politely identified as "the accomplished editor of *The Sunday School Times*," came under close scrutiny by Warfield in a series of articles that the Princetonian penned near the end of his life.[52] Trumbull never claimed to be a technical scholar or theologian and this becomes evident in his popular writings, especially when he seeks to establish his Wesleyan-derived notion of the Victorious Life in the sixth chapter of Romans. Warfield found Trumbull's handling of the passage appalling and "crass," concluding that Trumbull and the rest of the Victorious Life writers "do not impress us on the philological side."[53]

Andrew Murray and R. A. Torrey fare no better. Riddlebarger observed that, as in the case of Trumbull, "Warfield had little patience with these two Victorious Life advocates. Enthusiastic minds like Mr. Murray's need to exercise special care in adopting forms of statement from other writers." Because of the author's lack of such care, "we meet every now and then in the book with a phrase or doctrine the implications of which have scarcely been thought through by him." As a prime example of this, Warfield selects "the crude trichotomistic anthropology," which is adopted by Murray in one place, "only to be laid aside" elsewhere. In another place, Warfield, uncharacteristically engaging in a bit of *ad hominem* argumentation, points out that Rev. Murray sounds like a "fully developed Schleiermacherite." In yet a third example, Warfield contends that "every now and then we strike against a sentence delivered as if it contained the very kernel of the gospel, which quite puzzles us." The Princeton theologian, by now obviously exasperated, concludes that Murray's "book is marred everywhere by such straining after novel and striking forms of statement,

---

nature under the condemning wrath of God, and that Christ did vicariously bear the penalty of sin. Thus, in his hands, Arminianism is seeking to purify itself by cleansing itself from the Evangelical elements with which it has been so long conjoined" (ibid.).

This stands in marked contrast to present-day efforts to define evangelicalism as something that developed outside the boundaries of the Reformed tradition. See *The Variety of American Evangelicalism*, ed. Donald W. Dayton and Robert K. Johnson (Pasadena, Calif.: Wipf & Stock, 1997).

52. These appeared in *The Princeton Theological Review* in the years 1918–1921 and were later collected as part of *The Works of Benjamin B. Warfield*, vols. 7 and 8, entitled *Perfectionism*.

53. Warfield, *Perfectionism*, 8:569.

a vice, we may add, very common with books of this class."[54] One thing is clear: B. B. Warfield was not very impressed with the work of Andrew Murray.

Some ten years later, when Warfield reviewed Reuben Archer Torrey's book *What the Bible Teaches* (1899), the Princetonian's caustic tenor in treating "books of this class" was, as Riddlebarger again observes, again quite evident. Torrey (1856–1928) was a Congregational Minister and a graduate of Yale, who became superintendent of the Moody Bible Institute in 1889. Though yet to rise to his full prominence, as he would do in the first decade of the twentieth century, Torrey was in many ways the closest successor to Dwight Moody, and was, as George Marsden notes, already "a world-touring evangelist," and "one of the principal architects of fundamentalist thought." As Warfield sized Torrey up, he chidingly noted, "There are many things that Mr. Torrey has yet to learn concerning the great doctrines that the Bible teaches."

While Torrey's book promises to "give us a thorough and complete study of all that the Bible has to say concerning the great doctrines of which it treats," it does not deliver on its promise. "Needless to say, Mr. Torrey's useful volume hardly fulfills to the letter this great promise."[55]

In 1919 Warfield reviewed Chafer's popular book *He That Is Spiritual* in *Princeton Theological Review*.[56] Warfield pulled no punches, and it is doubtful if Chafer ever received a more devastating analysis

54. B. B. Warfield, "Review of *The Spirit of Christ: Thoughts on the Indwelling of the Holy Spirit in the Believer and in the Church*, by Rev. Andrew Murray," *The Presbyterian Review* 10 (April 1889): 334-35. This review has been recently reprinted in Benjamin B. Warfield, *The Person and Work of the Holy Spirit* (Amityville, N.Y.: Calvary Press, 1997), 171–72; the quotations cited come from p. 171.

55. B. B. Warfield, review of *What the Bible Teaches* (1899), by R. A. Torrey, *Presbyterian and Reformed Review* 39 (July 1899): 562–64. For this analysis of Warfield's take on the men associated with Keswick, such as Murray and Torrey, I am indebted to Riddlebarger, "The Lion of Princeton," 227–28.

56. Curtis I. Crenshaw and Grover E. Gunn III, in their trenchant critique *Dispensationalism Today, Yesterday, and Tomorrow* (Memphis: Footstool Publications, 1985), 410, mistakenly place Warfield's review in *Bibliotheca Sacra* and compound their error by adding that this journal, at the time Warfield wrote the review, was published by Princeton. *Bibliotheca Sacra* originally was the property of Andover Seminary. After a period of floating from one institution to another (Princeton not being one of them), it became the property of Dallas Theological Seminary in 1934. See John Hannah, "The History of *Bibliotheca Sacra*," *Bibliotheca Sacra* (July-September 1976).

of his views than the one that Warfield delivered. George M. Marsden sums up Warfield's review:

> The essence of Warfield's criticism was, as he put it in a review of a work by young Lewis Sperry Chafer, that the Keswick teacher was plagued by "two inconsistent systems of religion struggling together in his mind." One was Calvinist, so that he and his "coterie" (one of Warfield's favorite words) of evangelists and Bible teachers often spoke of God's grace doing all; but behind this Calvinist exterior lurked the spectres of Pelagius, Arminius, and Wesley, all of whom made God's gracious working subject to human determination. The resulting synthesis, Warfield said, was "at once curiously pretentious and curiously shallow."[57]

Despite his contribution to *The Fundamentals* in 1909 (he wrote the article on "The Deity of Christ"), Warfield was not the kind of fundamentalist that developed in the early decades of the twentieth century.[58] Noll remarks:

57. Marsden, *Fundamentalism and American Culture*, 98, quoting B. B. Warfield, review of *He That Is Spiritual*, by Lewis Sperry Chafer, *The Princeton Theological Review* 17 (April 1919): 322–27.

58. Despite the massive amount of literature on the subject, the idea still persists in some quarters that Warfield is to be grouped with a kind of fundamentalism that he deliberately criticized. A recent book portrays him in a decidedly distorted fashion as the following badly garbled assessment displays.

"Towards the end of the nineteenth century a group of fundamentalist scholars connected with Princeton University, New Jersey developed a doctrine called the inerrancy of scripture. Through this theological device such theologians as James Orr, Charles and Archibald Hodge and B. B. Warfield attempted to provide an incontestable philosophical foundation for the truth of scripture. However, though they wished, through the assertion of the doctrine of inerrancy, to protect the infallibility of scripture, they were in danger of making faith in a particular theological dogma more important than the revelation of Christ. Some theologians have suggested that to make scripture, instead of God, the locus of truth may be a form of religious positivism which borders on idolatry. However, the doctrine of inerrancy still exercises a powerful hold on much of the evangelical church today." William Raeper and Linda Edwards, *A Brief Guide to Ideas* (Grand Rapids: Zondervan, 1997), 339.

Warfield was, by his own words, an orthodox Calvinist, and not a "fundamentalist." Harold O. J. Brown has made this very important distinction: "The major difference between Protestant orthodoxy and fundamentalist Protestantism lies in the fact that orthodoxy is doctrinally comprehensive, while fundamentalism is highly selective. Orthodoxy, with its creeds and confessions, presents a broad range of doctrines it considers vital, and integrates them into a dogmatic system. Fundamentalism is a derivative of orthodoxy; it selects a small number of doctrines as fundamental and fights for them: two important examples are the doctrine of biblical inerrancy and, for many fundamentalists, the doctrine of the pre-millennial return of Christ. Although these doctrines are

The rise of Fundamentalism placed the Princeton theologians in an ambiguous situation. They certainly applauded the fundamentalists' adherence to scriptural infallibility, and they heartily approved the fundamentalistic insistence upon a supernatural faith. Yet they were squeamish about the anti-intellectual tendencies and the snap theological judgments that often characterized the movement.[59]

Another distinguishing feature of fundamentalism that Warfield held in contempt was the dispensational premillennialism that was deemed to be the centerpiece of the movement. From its inception with Archibald Alexander, the old Princetonian attitude toward premillennialism has been described in the words of David B. Calhoun as one of "tolerant dissatisfaction."[60] Warfield's attitude toward chiliasm (as premillennialism has been referred to historically) is typical of leading Reformed theologians of the period. W. G. T. Shedd and Robert Lewis Dabney on the American scene, as well as the Scotsman James Orr, and the Dutchmen Abraham Kuyper and Herman Bavinck, all wrote critically of premillennialism.[61]

Chafer, it must be admitted, was not a product of this Reformed tradition. Although ordained as an evangelist in the Northern Presbyterian church, he received no formal theological training (something he actually thought was to his advantage).[62] His circle of friends, for

---

part of the historic Christian tradition, by fighting selectively for them while virtually neglecting others, fundamentalism has become a very distinctive and somewhat one-sided branch of Protestant orthodoxy. In its preoccupation with a small number of doctrines, it resembles many of the classical heresies. Because of its combativeness, Protestant fundamentalism has succeeded in attracting the attention of the media and the general public, and by doing so has sometimes come to be mistaken for Protestant orthodoxy, of which it is only an important but somewhat unrepresentative part." Harold O. J. Brown, *Heresies: The Image of Christ in the Mirror of Heresy and Orthodoxy from the Apostles to the Present* (Garden City, N.Y.: Doubleday, 1984), 29.

59. Mark Noll, *The Princeton Theology, 1812–1921* (Grand Rapids: Baker, 1983), 299.

60. David B. Calhoun, *Princeton Seminary*, vol. 2, *The Majestic Testimony, 1869–1929* (Edinburgh: The Banner of Truth, 1996), 183.

61. Cf. W. G. T. Shedd, *Dogmatic Theology*, 3 vols. (1894; repr., Grand Rapids: Zondervan, 1971), 2:642; Robert Lewis Dabney, *Discussions*, 4 vols. (1890–92; repr., Edinburgh: The Banner of Truth, 1982), 1:210; James Orr, *The Christian View of God and the World* (1893; repr., Grand Rapids: Eerdmans, 1948), 334; Herman Bavinck, *The Last Things: Hope for This World and the Next*, ed. John Bolt, trans. John Vriend (Grand Rapids: Baker 1996), 94–98.

62. C. F. Lincoln, writing the "Biographical Sketch" of Chafer in volume 1 of Chafer's *Systematic Theology*, 7 vols. (Dallas, Tex.: The Seminary Press, 1948), 1:5, records Chafer as saying, "The very fact that I did not study a prescribed course in theology made it possible for

the most part, were among the likes of Harry Ironside, James Gray, R. A. Torrey, and especially C. I. Scofield, whose influence was undoubtedly the single greatest factor in molding Chafer's thought. All of these men, in addition to being in the forefront of the Victorious Life teaching, or the Keswick movement, were ardent premillennialists of the dispensational stripe. It would not be an exaggeration to say that, as far as they were concerned, premillennialism constituted the *essence* of what it meant to be a "Bible-believing Christian."[63] Warfield found this emphasis (and scheme) completely unacceptable. Furthermore, he had no patience for those fellow Presbyterians (such as Chafer) who would seek to graft this branch of fundamentalism on his beloved Reformed tree. More recently, those with close ties to this school of thought have singled out Warfield (and Charles Hodge) because Old Princeton did not espouse a form of young earth creationism.[64]

---

me to approach the subject with an unprejudiced mind to be concerned only with what the Bible actually teaches."

63. This situation later became exacerbated within the ranks of those who followed J. Gresham Machen to establish Westminster Theological Seminary. Premillennialists, especially those sympathetic toward dispensationalism, broke away under the leadership of J. Oliver Buswell, Allan A. MacRae, and Carl McIntire to found Faith Theological Seminary and the Bible Presbyterian Church (I also studied at Faith; the school has long since disappeared, but did for a while produce a number of graduates who influenced the evangelical world, most notably the late Francis Schaeffer); see Timothy P. Weber, *Living in the Shadow of the Second Coming: American Premillennialism, 1875–1982* (Grand Rapids: Academie Books, 1983), 168.

Added to this was the very strained relationship that Warfield and Machen had with Charles Erdman. Erdman served on the faculty of Princeton Theological Seminary during this period as professor of English Bible. He, along with the president of the school, J. Ross Stevenson, was not sympathetic to the Old Princeton tradition and was successful in eventually changing Princeton's theological identity. Both men vigorously opposed Machen's appointment to the chair in apologetics. What is significant is that Erdman had also served on the revision committee for the *Scofield Reference Bible*. For Machen's perspective on Erdman, see "Statement to the Special Commission of 1925" in Hart, ed., *J. Gresham Machen*, 291–309. See also the fascinating introduction by Stephen J. Nichols, "A Brief Exchange between Lewis Sperry Chafer and J. Gresham Machen," *Westminster Theological Journal* 62 (2000): 281–91. The nature of the differences between Old Princeton and what became Dallas Theological Seminary is clearly delineated.

64. The creationist group known as Answers in Genesis has gone out of its way to blame Charles Hodge and Warfield for the eventual demise of Old Princeton because of a concession these two were supposed to have made to Darwinian evolution. Warfield in particular is treated very shabbily and is portrayed in a decidedly distorted fashion. Take, for example, this statement: "The (otherwise) great Presbyterian theologian Charles Hodge admitted that long ages of earth history appeared to be at odds with the straightforward Mosaic narrative, but nevertheless, he bowed to the authority of 'science' and so accommodated his understanding of the Bible. Thus, even though he railed against Darwinism as rank atheism, the nose of the camel was already in the tent. His successor at Princeton,

Warfield, Briggs, and Their Legacy Today

Briggs and Warfield spent much of their careers engaged in polemics. Warfield actually held the chair of didactic and polemical theology at Princeton; Briggs began his career as professor of Hebrew and cognate languages but ended, strangely enough, as professor of irenics. In this capacity Briggs sought to lay the foundation for a Protestant/Catholic reunion; as such, Briggs still engaged in polemics, continuing to single out the Princetonians in particular as the object of his scorn. Typical of the present-day evangelical mind-set, Briggs did not like creeds and did not want to be limited in his freedom to disagree with them. He really wanted a confession/creed that was as broad as possible and one that would allow all Christians—Catholics and Protestants—liberty of opinion.[65] In a statement guaranteed to get the attention of Warfield, Briggs declared, "Another great barrier to the reunion of Christendom is subscription to elaborate creeds. This is the great sin of the Lutheran and Reformed Churches."[66] Car-

---

B. B. Warfield (who was conservative enough to sign the well-known 'Fundamentals' document), took this 're-adjustment' of the Scripture to its next logical step, calling himself a 'Darwinian of the purest water'." Carl Wieland, *http://www.answersingenesis.org/tj/v12/i3/summer.asp*. The Fundamentals "document" was never signed by Warfield or anyone else. The *Fundamentals* were, as reliable historians know, a series of essays on the distinctive doctrines of the Christian faith published between 1910 and 1915. The remark about Warfield calling himself a "Darwinian of the purest water" is reprehensible and completely inexcusable. Warfield made that statement about himself as a boy! In fact, the context of that remark reads like this: "His early tastes were strongly scientific. He collected bird's eggs, butterflies and moths, and geological specimens; studied the fauna and flora of his neighborhood; read Darwin's newly published books with enthusiasm; and counted Audubon's works on American birds and mammals his chief treasure. He came to Princeton the same year that James McCosh arrived from Scotland to become one of the most famous of its presidents. That Dr. McCosh did not succeed in making him a Darwinian, as in the case of so many of his fellow-students, finds its explanation in the fact, as he himself has told us, that knowing his *Origin of Species* and *The Variations of Animals and Plants Under Domestication* 'almost from A to Izzard' he was already a 'Darwinian of the purest water' before coming under McCosh's influence—a position which he later repudiated, not without warrant as even biologists have come more and more to admit." See Samuel G. Craig's biographical sketch in *B. B. Warfield: Biblical and Theological Studies* (Philadelphia: Presbyterian and Reformed, 1968), xii.

65. Briggs, *Whither?* 239.

66. C. A. Briggs, *Church Unity*, 191. On the same page, Briggs threw in this draconian remark: "There are some who will continue to cling to the Westminster Confession; others to the decrees of the Council of Trent; others to the Heidelberg Catechism, and others to Luther's Catechism. Let them retain their darlings and . . . conserve their beloved opinions."

ried away by the grand optimism of the times, Briggs could boldly proclaim:

> The antitheses of the sixteenth century are to a great extent antitheses of one-sidedness, which the modern world has outgrown. The world has moved since then. The world has learned many things. We have new views of God's universe. We have new scientific methods. We have an entirely different psychology and philosophy. Our education is much more scientific, much more thorough, much more accurate, much more searching, much more comprehensive. All along the line of life, institution, dogma, morals new situations are emerging, new questions pressing for solution; the perspective is changed, the lights and shadows are differently distributed. We are in a state of enormous transition, changes are taking place whose results it is impossible to foretell—reconstruction is in progress on the grandest scale. Out of it all will spring, in God's own time, a rejuvenated, a reorganized, a truly universal Christianity, combining in a higher unity all that is true and real and worthy in the various Churches which now divide the world.[67]

Briggs died before the outbreak of World War I and did not live to see how completely misguided he was in his exorbitant enthusiasm. Warfield, during the same time period, maintained a constant vigilance in his efforts to defend confessional Calvinism against all foes, and it did not matter to him whether they were theological liberals (like Stevens), confessional revisionists with their ersatz Reformed theology (like Briggs), or even Bible-believing fundamentalists (like Chafer and Torrey). Briggs is pretty much a forgotten figure today. Other than the famous *A Hebrew and English Lexicon of the Old Testament* that he produced along with Francis Brown and Samuel Driver, his books are no longer in print, and his name rarely surfaces in today's theological discussions except in an occasional Ph.D. dissertation. However, even though Briggs might not be referenced as such, his views do have a following, and a significant one at that. In other words, views that were championed by him in his lifetime are alive and well today. No doubt some of those I have linked to

67. Ibid., 435.

Briggs will protest that they have never heard of him, much less been influenced by his writings. But this is like the claim that we often hear today from well-meaning individuals who espouse an identical understanding to doctrines closely associated with Jacobus Arminius (i.e., libertarian free-will, conditional election, resistible grace), and yet protest that they have never read him and therefore should not be identified as Arminian. Nevertheless, in theological parlance they are classified as "Arminian," protest notwithstanding.

How are Briggs's views represented today? To begin with the most obvious, Briggs's overt rejection of the Old Princeton understanding of inerrancy has a wide following among professed evangelicals today. One might even suggest that it is the majority view.[68] But there are other areas where Briggs's perspective would find safe haven as well. The late Stanley Grenz is a prime example. Grenz specifically contrasts his view of Scripture with that of Warfield,[69] and blames the Old Princeton theology for making propositional truth the touchstone for theology as over against pietism's (Grenz calls it "classic evangelicalism") emphasis on having a relationship with God.[70] Grenz also makes a very Briggs-like shift by following the lead of Schleiermacher in positing *three* sources or norms for theology: Scripture, tradition,

68. Attesting to this is the work by Jack Rogers and Donald McKim, *The Authority and Interpretation of the Bible* (San Francisco: Harper & Row, 1979). More recently, the group identified by the label "postconservative evangelicalism" has jettisoned the doctrine as formulated by Warfield. Roger Olson, who is credited with coining the label, openly dismisses the doctrine; see his "Why 'Inerrancy' Doesn't Matter," *The Baptist Standard* (March 26, 2006): 1–2. Dave Tomlinson, in a book that is popular in what is called "the Emergent Church," offers a section titled "Inerrancy? A Monumental Waste of Time." Tomlinson goes on to declare, "I have no intention of arguing against this doctrine; I simply marvel that anyone should think it plausible or necessary to believe in such a thing." Dave Tomlinson, *The Post-Evangelical* (London: Triangle, 1995), 105. Finally, James D. G. Dunn, a leading scholar for the so-called New Perspective on Paul, echoes Briggs's assessment by declaring inerrancy "exegetically improbable, hermeneutically defective, theologically dangerous, and educationally disastrous." James D. G. Dunn, *The Living Word* (Philadelphia: The Fortress, 1988), 107.

69. See Stanley Grenz, *Renewing the Center: Evangelical Theology in a Post-Theological Era* (Grand Rapids: Baker, 2000), and the book he coauthored with John Franke, *Beyond Foundationalism: Shaping Theology in a Postmodern Context* (Louisville: Westminster John Knox Press, 2001). It was disappointing to see Grenz relying so heavily on the work of Rogers and McKim in assessing Warfield, and this despite the fact that Grenz alludes to the work of John Woodbridge and his devastating work *Biblical Authority: A Critique of the Rogers/Kim Proposal* (Grand Rapids: Zondervan, 1982).

70. Grenz, *Renewing the Center*, 84.

and culture.[71] Briggs so firmly endorsed this idea that he devoted a book to the subject: *The Bible, the Church and the Reason* (1892). Elsewhere, Briggs wrote:

> Three fountains of divine authority are not and cannot be contradictory, because they are three different media for the same divine Being to make His authority known to mankind. We may compare them with the three great functions of government: the legislative, the executive and the judicial, which in the best modern governments conspire to express the authority of the nation. The Bible is the legislative principle of divine authority, for it is the only infallible *rule* of faith and practice. The Church is the executive principle of divine authority. It makes no rules save those which are executive interpretations and applications of the rules contained in apostolic teaching. The Reason is the judicial principle of divine authority to the individual man. The Reason, when it judges, must be followed at all costs. There is liability to mistake, in individuals and in ecclesiastical bodies, in interpreting the decisions that come through these three media. Two may usually be used for verification of any one of them.[72]

Briggs grew to dislike what he called "the scholastic" element in Reformed theology. He wrote:

> The *scholastic* spirit seeks union and communion with God by means of well-ordered forms. It searches the Bible for well-defined systems of law and doctrine by which to rule the Church and control the world. It arises from an intellectual nature, and grows into a more or less acute logical sense, and a taste for systems of order. This spirit exists in all ages and in most religions, but it was especially dominant in the middle age of the Church and in Latin Christianity.

71. Grenz, *Revisioning Evangelical Theology: A Fresh Agenda for the 21ˢᵗ Century* (Downers Grove, Ill.: InterVarsity Press, 1993), 70. D. A. Carson correctly observes, "This is, to say the least, decidedly unhelpful. Quite apart from the extraordinary complexities of linking Scripture and tradition in this way, the addition of culture is astonishing. One might hazard a guess that Grenz has read enough to recognize that the interpreter cannot escape his or her own culture, and therefore has put down culture as a norm or source of theology, without recognizing the minefield he has created for himself. . . . His openness to Tillich's method of correlation is not reassuring. With the best will in the world, I cannot see how Grenz's approach to Scripture can be called "'evangelical'" in any useful sense." D. A. Carson, *The Gagging of God: Christianity Confronts Pluralism* (Grand Rapids: Zondervan, 1996), 481.

72. Briggs, *Church Unity*, 244.

It is distinguished by an intense legality and by too exclusive attention to the works of the law, and a disproportionate consideration of the sovereignty of God, the sinfulness of man, and the satisfaction to be rendered to God for sin. In biblical studies it is distinguished by the legal, analytic method of interpretation, carried on at times with such hair-splitting distinction and subtlety of reasoning that Holy Scripture becomes, as it were, a magician's book. Through the device of the manifold sense the Bible is made as effectual to the purpose of the dogmatician for proof texts as are the sacraments to the priests in their magical operation. The doctrinal element prevails over the religious and ethical. Dogma and institution alike work *ex opera operato*.[73]

What is most surprising at this juncture is that Briggs's sentiments are now resonating in those circles usually identified with the theological concerns closely linked with Old Princeton. Andrew Sandlin, a leading voice in Reformed circles that identify with theonomy, parrots Briggs in his negative assessment of scholasticism.[74] Guy Waters has recently written this in regard to Sandlin:

Sandlin argues for what he has termed a "catholic Calvinism." He divides the Reformed world into three parts: the Truly Reformed, the Barely Reformed, and the Catholic Reformed. He comments that the Truly Reformed are "fervently committed to the scholastic, Reformed orthodoxy of the 16th and 17th centuries." To them, Sandlin contends, "the great crisis of the modern church [is] a deviation from this formulation of *doctrine* or *theology*." They are "particularly

---

73. Briggs, *General Introduction to the Study of Holy Scripture*, 570.
74. Despite the monumental efforts of Richard Muller, David Steinmetz, W. J. van Asselt, R. Scott Clark, and W. Robert Godfrey (to mention only a few) to correct it, the view of Protestant scholasticism that reaches back to Briggs and runs well into the twentieth century continues to paint a distorted picture of "Calvin against the Calvinists," usually to advance a particular theological agenda. Regrettably, many ill-informed evangelicals build on this faulty foundation. See, for example, how Stanley Grenz and John Franke use the term in their *Beyond Foundationalism: Shaping Theology in a Postmodern Context*. This view has been rebutted by Richard A. Muller, "Giving Direction to Theology: The Scholastic Dimension," *Journal of the Evangelical Theological Society* 28, 2 (1985): 183–93. "Protestants," Muller writes, "commonly assume that scholasticism represents a profoundly medieval and Roman Catholic phenomenon. Scholasticism is dry. It is a useless jumble of metaphysical issues totally unrelated to piety. It was set aside by the Reformation. It cannot be evangelical and, for Protestantism, is therefore rightly dead. . . . There can be only one complaint with this view of scholasticism. It is false" (183).

suspicious of any [theological] development within the last hundred years," a suspicion that Sandlin contends extends to virtually anything theological "later than the seventeenth century."

Who are the Catholic Reformed? Sandlin attempts to chart a *via media* between what he conceives to be the doctrinally rigid TRs and the evangelistically but pragmatically minded BRs. He cites, as representative among the Catholic Reformed, a concern regarding "incessant dispute over comparatively secondary doctrines to the exclusion of the energetic preaching of the gospel." It holds a suspicion of "Protestant scholastic confessionalism" as an optimal solution to contemporary theological challenges, and argues for a resurgence of the "great gains of . . . the patristic and medieval eras." It is the "scholastic formulations" of many Reformed doctrines, Sandlin argues, that have contributed to "the general lack of acknowledgement of the broad, orthodox, catholic tradition."[75]

As noted, Briggs took a very jaundiced view of the Protestant scholastics (and, by extension, Old Princeton) whom he sought to

---

75. Waters, *The Federal Vision and Covenant Theology*, 296–97. The initials "TR" (the Truly Reformed) are frequently used today with decidedly pejorative overtones. A recent example of this is seen in John Stackhouse's rather contumely remark: "A second dangerous trend is heading in the other direction, toward a traditionalism, even a creedalism, that is satisfied that God has broken forth all the light from his Holy Word that he is ever going to break. If the previous danger is that of speculation, we now encounter the danger of formalism. It arises in evangelicalism nowadays with certain devotees of certain brands of Reformed orthodoxy, often dubbed the 'Truly Reformed' by those who have felt the sting of their criticism. These warriors not only claim to speak authoritatively and univocally for what is in fact a multistranded Reformed tradition, but presume then to go on to speak for all evangelicals (as in the Alliance of Confessing Evangelicals)." As evidence, he cites in a footnote, "So the several books by David F. Wells." See *Evangelical Futures: A Conversation on Theological Method*, ed. John G. Stackhouse Jr. (Grand Rapids: Baker, 2000), 49 n. 17.

Warfield had to deal with this attitude in his day as well. In reviewing a book by the acclaimed church historian Philip Schaff, Warfield detected this and wrote: "We have all long known that Dr. Schaff was no Calvinist. He represents himself as an adherent of the 'Evangelical Union Theology'—or 'the Mediating Theology'—which he thinks occupies a position so much above that of Lutheranism and Calvinism, and even of Rationalism and Supranaturalism, that they are reconciled in it. The only Calvinism for which he felt sympathy was that which he describes as 'moderate or progressive Calvinism,' telling us that it 'omits or softens the five knotty points of Dordt'—i.e., of course, has ceased to be Calvinism at all. Calvinists, it seems, are to be divided hereafter into a hard, strict, reactionary party which absurdly insists on being what it calls itself—in some sense at least, Calvinistic; and a 'moderate or progressive' party, which rejects every distinguishing doctrine which characterized ecumenical Calvinism!" B. B. Warfield, review of *Theological Propaedeutic* (1892), by Philip Schaff, *The Presbyterian and Reformed Review* 5 (1894): 180.

vilify for corrupting the Reformed faith, especially as this developed into covenant theology. Briggs declared that the Puritans were influenced too much by the Old Testament in proportion to the New Testament, and this, Briggs goes on to lament, led to a full-blown covenant theology.[76] Briggs singled out as the chief culprits the great Puritan divine John Owen and the noted theologian Francis Turretin, whose *Institutio* was used by Charles Hodge as a text in theology at Princeton. Briggs claimed that this polluted form of Reformed theology entered American Presbyterianism via Princeton Seminary. Over time, and after his departure from the Presbyterian church, Briggs developed an intense dislike for the Westminster Confession. The Westminster divines, he contended, followed the theology of the Synod of Dordt, which made the Westminster Confession savor of "scholastic Calvinism." On *all* the major points established at Dordt, the Westminster Confession followed suit. This, in Briggs's mind, was a major flaw.

The Westminster divines, he further contended, had a very defective view of sin that stemmed from their defective psychology. They were "excessive in their elaborate statements, and rigid and polemic in their doctrine." They followed the scholastic Calvinists in building their doctrine of the atonement by overemphasizing the idea of *purchase* and *satisfaction*. The Westminster divines' doctrine of justification is warped by their "high Calvinism," and they are not clear on sanctification. Briggs especially objects to the doctrine of man and the divine decrees as taught by the Westminster Confession.[77]

Another high-profile contemporary evangelical who displays a "Briggsian" mind-set is John Armstrong, who once actively promoted the kind of conservative Reformed theology associated with the likes of Charles Hodge, B. B. Warfield and J. Gresham Machen. But, he does so no longer. Armstrong has gone on record as endorsing the views of both N. T. Wright and Norman Shepherd on justification. He has also embraced the postmodern epistemological proposals of

---

76. Charles A. Briggs, "The Principles of Puritanism," *The Presbyterian Review* 5 (1884): 662

77. C. A. Briggs, *Theological Symbolics* (New York: Charles Scribner's Sons, 1914), 319. Even earlier, Briggs contended that "it would have been better for us if the Westminster Divines had stopped with sections 1, 5, 6, 8, and that sections 2, 3, 4, 7 had never been framed." Briggs, *Whither?* 33; cf. 99.

Stanley Grenz and John Franke.[78] Like Briggs, Armstrong has grown to dislike Reformed theology as set forth in the Westminster Standards and the Second London Confession, asking,

> Why do conservative Reformed Christians treat only certain confessional traditions such as the Westminster Confession or its cousin the London Baptist confession, as if only these confessions and catechisms were the proper confessional grounds for the Reformed faith and thus for contemporary understanding of the Bible and classical Christian thought, if they even care about classical thought? These important creedal standards of the 17th century are not the only standards for orthodoxy, for all time and all cultures, and few have ever treated them in this manner. Therefore, why do ordinary Christians hardly ever hear this from many of the conservative Reformed spokesmen? (There are few if any conservative Reformed spokeswomen, which is another question for another time.)[79]

Or again, speaking of "Reformation romantics" who give the Reformation priority of place in their theology, Armstrong says, "I pray that Reformation romantics will soon see the silliness of their near worship of the early Protestant era."[80] Sounding very much like Briggs, Armstrong declares, "The danger modern Reformed and Lutheran conservatives face is very real at this point. They have a strong tendency to judge everything by their creeds."[81] In Armstrong's opinion,

78. Armstrong edited *The Reformation & Revival Journal* from 1992 to 2005, when he changed the name of the journal to *ACT III* to better reflect his own theological change of mind. Armstrong documented these changes in his theology in his *Reformation & Revival: The Weekly Messenger* articles "FAQ: Imputation, Justification and the Gospel" (April 5, 2004) and "I Stand Corrected: Norman Shepherd and the Doctrine of the Covenant" (March 22, 2004). See also his *Viewpoint* series: "How I Changed My Mind: Theological Method," *Viewpoint* 7, 4 (Sept.–Oct. 2003), "How I Changed My Mind About Faith and Understanding," *Viewpoint* 7, 5 (Nov.–Dec. 2003), "How I Changed My Mind: How Doctrine and Faith Relate," *Viewpoint* 8, 1 (Jan.–Feb. 2004), and his Web postings under the title "Questions I Ponder as a Reformed Christian" *http://johnharmstrong.typepad.com* (June 2, 2006).

79. Armstrong, "Questions I Ponder as a Reformed Christian," May 16, 2005.

80. Ibid., May 3, 2005.

81. Ibid., June 2, 2006. Another example of this outlook is from a minister in the Presbyterian Church in America, Jeffrey Meyers, a zealous defender of the Federal Vision, who declares in a review of Waters, *The Federal Vision and Covenant Theology*: "To the consternation of strict confessional Presbyterians, Waters included, the reason so much of this is resonating with people is because the sixteenth and seventeenth-century confessions and catechisms are no longer sufficient guides for the modern church. . . . If we want to be an enclave of ecclesiastical

most conservative Reformed Christians are addicted to "the narrow use of their creedal tradition."[82] Like Briggs, Armstrong uses pejorative language to describe this "tribe" as motivated by "fear, insecurity and the need for approval and control."[83]

Perhaps even more surprising than Armstrong's affinity for Briggs's views is that of Peter Enns, professor of Old Testament at Westminster Theological Seminary in Philadelphia. Enns's recent book *Inspiration and Incarnation: Evangelicals and the Problem of the Old Testament*, has come under closer scrutiny, especially from those sympathetic to the concerns of Old Princeton.[84] Enns argues that while he stands in the noble tradition that goes back through men

---

romantics living in the 17th century, a tribe of irrelevant theologues, then by all means let's continue to multiply conferences and books on the glory of Westminster. Let's continue to demand subscription to every jot and tittle of our precious unreformable tradition. Let's attack anyone who suggests updates and changes. If, however, we desire to minister to people in our world, we need to stand on the shoulders of our glorious forefathers in the faith and do what they did—preach, write, and formulate answers from the Bible for the people of our generation! . . . I do not believe that I am required to believe and confess all the details in the confessions and catechism. Nor am I bound to their *form*. The chapter on the covenant, for example, is filled with problems. So much progress has been made in the last century on the biblical theology of the covenants. There are still things to be learned from the Bible, which necessitates updating and correcting our theological formulations. The *form* of the Shorter and Larger Catechisms (definitions, definitions, definitions, *ad nauseam*) has led to much of the warfare that seems to be endemic to Presbyterianism and is pedagogically questionable for little children. I know that statement is controversial, but as good as one might think the Catechisms are, they are cultural artifacts of the 17th-century scholasticism." *http://web.mac.com/jeffmeyers* (July 19, 2006). As documented, Briggs made very similar statements, and so did Alexander Campbell and Barton Stone, who left the Presbyterian ministry to form what became "The Church of Christ" and "The Disciples of Christ." Their motto "no creed but the Bible" actually meant "No creed but the Bible . . . as I interpret it!"

82. Armstrong, "Questions I Ponder as a Reformed Christian," June 19, 2006.
83. Ibid.
84. See the reviews by Paul Helm, *http://reformation21.com* (April 25, 2006); D. A. Carson, *Trinity Journal* (May 2006); B. C. Ferry in *New Horizons* (Oct. 2005); Greg Beale, "Myth, History, and Inspiration: A Review Article of Peter Enns, *Inspiration and Incarnation. Evangelicals and the Problem of the Old Testament* (Grand Rapids: Baker, 2005)," *Journal of the Evangelical Theological Society* 49, 2 (2006): 287–312; and idem, "Did Jesus and the Apostles Preach the Right Doctrine from the Wrong Texts? Revisiting the Debate Seventeen Years Later in the Light of Peter Enns' Book *Inspiration and Incarnation*," *Themelios* (Summer 2006). The book was also reviewed in a more positive vein by M. Eschlebach in *Journal of the Evangelical Theological Society* 48, 4 (2005): 811–12; T. Longman, "Divine and Human Qualities of the Old Testament," *Modern Reformation* 14 (2005): 33–34; M. Daniel Carroll R. (Rodas), *Denver Journal: An Online Review of Current Biblical and Theological Studies* 8 (2005). John Armstrong gave the book a hearty endorsement while reprimanding Enns's critics; see his "Interpreting the Bible: The False Assumptions of Modernism," *http://johnharmstrong.typepad.com* (Sept. 29, 2005).

such as J. Gresham Machen, the founder of Westminster Theological Seminary, to the likes of Warfield, he is nonetheless attempting to advance that tradition in light of new discoveries and more recent scholarship. Enns is well aware that his proposals on the doctrine of inspiration will raise eyebrows, especially coming as they do from someone at an institution founded to carry on the Old Princeton tradition.

Sensing that he is walking on thin ice, Enns notes:

> Although not universally true, many can attest that a strong element of suspicion exists among evangelicals both toward the types of evidence we have looked at and toward those who engage it. This is partly understandable, since a great deal of the history of modern biblical scholarship does not show evidence of being overly concerned with the doctrinal and practical implication of exegetical work. This is not a comment on the personal faith of these scholars, only that the necessary conversation between evidence and doctrine did not take place—or if it did, it was largely destructive.
>
> But the evidence we have at our disposal transcends such labels as liberal or conservative. Evangelical biblical scholars and students of the Bible (which includes informal study as well as college or seminary) regularly find themselves having to interact with the important developments in recent generations. And this is why the suspicion needs to come to an end. I am not suggesting that we throw caution to the wind and bow to every trend. Part of the academic quest is to be critical of evidence until such time that certain conclusions seem to present themselves naturally. But the attitude of an academic quest is very different from judgmental suspicion, which is a predisposition against new and different ideas that challenge existing ones.
>
> In some respects what drives this suspicion is fear that what is new will necessarily threaten the old, which is often uncritically equated with the gospel itself. I agree that modern biblical scholarship has handled some issues in ways that could certainly lead in that direction, and so fear is understandable. But fear cannot *drive* theology. It cannot be used as an excuse to ignore what can rightly be called evidence. We do not honor the Lord nor do we uphold the gospel by playing make-believe. Neither are those who engage the kinds of issues discussed in this book necessarily on the slippery slope to unbelief. Our God is much bigger than we sometimes give him credit

for. It is we who sometimes wish to keep him small by controlling what can or cannot come into the conversation. The result is—what would have been soundly condemned by Christ himself and any New Testament writer—polarization and power plays among the people of God, the body of Christ, his ambassadors who are called by him to be his ministers of reconciliation to the world. The issue is not whether we disagree; that is healthy provided it does not become an end in itself. The problem is that true Christians erect a wall of hostility between them, and churches, denominations, and schools split.

It has been my experience that sometimes our first impulse is to react to new ideas and vilify the person holding them, not considering that person's Christian character. We jump to conclusions and assume the worst rather than hearing—*really* hearing—each other out.[85]

These remarks are not only difficult to harmonize with the views of Old Princeton, but are equally out of line with the apologetic thrust of Cornelius Van Til, the famed founder of "presuppositional" apologetics and longtime professor at Westminster. How so? Enns appeals to evidence outside the Bible in order to corroborate the Bible, saying in effect that the Bible has to harmonize with Ancient Near East texts and other extra-biblical evidence in order to establish its character and relevance. Van Til would have totally disapproved.[86]

Briggs made a similar claim about the nature of the evidence for which the biblical scholar must account, and he clearly anticipates Enns in affirming the priority of this "solid" evidence which incorporates "myth" and "legend" but is nonetheless given "inspired" status.

Legends constitute the form in which historical material is handed down from generation to generation in oral transmission, especially in times prior to written literature. Holy Scripture uses a great abundance of these legends. The popular imagination embellishes them; changes them in many ways as to time, place, and circumstances; and only preserves the substance of the truth and fact. As an illustration

---

85. Enns, *Inspiration and Incarnation*, 171.

86. Van Til argued, as one of his former students correctly put it, that "the Christian can point to nothing outside the Bible for verification of the Bible because the simple fact is that everything outside the Bible derives its meaning from the interpretation given it by the Bible." Jim S. Halsey, *For a Time Such as This: An Introduction to the Reformed Apologetics of Cornelius Van Til* (Nutley, N.J.: Presbyterian and Reformed, 1976), 38.

we may take the patriarch's representation that his wife was his sister. There are three narratives of this event. Doubtless there was an actual occurrence of this kind in the times of the patriarchs; but each one of these narratives shows the legendary embellishment.

The Ephraimitic narrative represents that Abraham was the patriarch and that the event took place at the court of Abimelech, king of Gerer. But the Judaic narrator already found two stories current in his time, one making Abraham the hero, the other Isaac; the one putting the event at the court of Pharaoh, the other at the court of Abimelech. Historical criticism cannot do otherwise than regard these as three legends of one and the same event.[87]

Enns shows no awareness of Briggs, but does in his recommended reading praise the work of J. Patterson Smyth, who, as it turns out, was not only a contemporary of Briggs, but one of his supporters.[88] However, Enns, who follows this recommendation with a reference to Warfield, likewise shows no awareness that Warfield reviewed Smyth's book (along with two others on the same subject). Warfield was fully aware of the angle from which Smyth was writing.

A copious literature on Inspiration is in process of production by the adherents of that lowered view of the Bible which the dominant school of Biblical Criticism is endeavoring to impose on the Churches. The three small volumes, the titles of which stand at the head of this notice, are very favorable specimens of this literature. The authors of all three books are men of devout spirit and of unquestionable attachment to the religion of the Bible; and they write with the earnest purpose of finding and commending to their fellow Christians some way by which, in what they suppose to be the new conditions of knowledge as to the origin, structure and contents of the Bible, as brought out by recent critical study, they may still retain reverence for the Bible as the depository of the saving truth of the gospel, and

---

87. Briggs, *General Introduction to the Study of Holy Scripture*, 557.

88. Enns writes of Smyth's work: "Written during the so-called modernist/fundamentalist controversy and addressing many of the same issues addressed here. What is perhaps most striking about Smyth's book, besides the honesty and spiritual sensitivity of the author (he was both a professor and pastor), is the reminder that an incarnational approach to Scripture was employed generations ago to address the problems introduced by the modern study of the Bible." *Inspiration and Incarnation*, 22. Actually, Enns has his chronology out of order. Smyth wrote this almost two decades before the fundamentalist/modernist controversy erupted.

deference to it as the supreme rule of faith and practice. They are all, therefore, dominated by what we may call a conservative purpose; they wish to save to the apprehension of Christian man the Bible as the foundation of religious doctrine and life.

These are therefore three very instructive little books. They exhibit to us the working of the new heaven in its mildest form; and advertise to us what is the least change in our attitude toward the Bible which will satisfy the most moderate adherents of the new views. As such, they are not reassuring. It becomes evident at once not only that an entire revolution in the doctrine of sacred Scripture incorporated in our creeds, and held indeed by the whole Christian past, will be required of us (which is a comparatively small matter); but also that on the new ground we can no longer occupy the same attitude toward Scripture that our Lord and His apostles occupied. The attempts of these books being taken as samples, it becomes equally evident also that no consistent doctrine of inspiration, conservative of the detailed divine authority of the Scriptures, can be framed on the basis of the new views. And we fear it also becomes evident that despite their earnest desire to serve the cause of God's truth in preserving the authority of the Bible, the really dominant note in the thought of these writers is an overweening confidence in the infallibility of the latest deliverance of "scientific study of the records," by which they are betrayed into subjecting the Word of God to the word of men. Naturally this note shows itself in different degrees and in different forms in the several writers, who naturally differ also in extent and accuracy of learning, critical acumen and constructive power. Their writings vary, therefore, not only in force and interest, but also in "light and leading." Of the three before us, that of Mr. Smyth is the least important and that of Mr. Rooke the most valuable. . . . Mr Smyth's little book, well meaning no doubt, but scarcely well conceived. . . . The *fact* of inspiration Mr. Smyth would hold fast to: but he expressed a doubt whether a *definition* of it can be attained. His own definition is that it is "a Divine inbreathing, a Divine influence"—which is certainly indefinite enough. He thinks it "best described by the simple statement that it is God's endowing of the writers, each as was needed for the work before him," which by defining by an undefined purpose, leaves a loophole of escape in every time of need. He rightly considers it impossible to draw the line between the divine and the human in the product of inspiration; but misleadingly illustrates by the staining of the pure light in its passage through a medium of colored glass. The ineradicable *a-prioriism* of this lowered view of inspiration is continually cropping out; the principle of construction is found in such questions as this: "Was it necessary for his purpose" that God should make the Biblical writers absolutely infallible? Why not frankly answer that we do not know? Why not really take our stand with Butler, and say that "we are in no sort judges beforehand how God would give a revelation," and hold the only question to be "whether Scripture be what it claims to be?" Why not, in a word, simply adopt the doctrine of Christ and His apostles? This is what we strive to do, and therefore we ask Mr. Smyth to note the clause *"but the Bible claims,"* in the passage which he quotes from us at p. 130 (doubtless at second hand, or he would not have neglected the essence of the statement), and to withdraw his unjustified strictures upon it. On the whole, we cannot think this little book likely to be helpful in the present distress; it will rather play into the hands of those who would destroy the credit of the Scriptures.[89]

Warfield obviously did not see Smyth's book in the same light that Enns does. One reason was that Warfield had reservations over the concept of the incarnation serving as the model for understanding the nature of Scripture. This he spelled out:

It has been customary among a certain school of writers to speak of the Scriptures, because thus "inspired," as a Divine-human book, and to appeal to the analogy of Our Lord's Divine-human personality to explain their peculiar qualities as such. The expression calls attention to an important fact, and the analogy holds good a certain distance. There are human and Divine sides to Scripture, and, as we cursorily examine it, we may perceive in it, alternately, traits which suggest now the one, now the other factor in its origin. But the analogy with Our Lord's Divine-human personality may easily be pressed beyond reason. There is no hypostatic union between the Divine and the human in Scripture; we cannot parallel the "inscripturation" of the Holy Spirit and the incarnation of the Son of God. The Scriptures are merely the product of Divine and human forces working together to produce a product in the production of which

89. B. B. Warfield, "Review of *How God Inspired the Bible*," by J. Patterson Smyth, *The Presbyterian and Reformed Review* 5 (1894): 169–71.

the human forces work under the initiation and prevalent direction of the Divine: the person of Our Lord unites in itself Divine and human natures, each of which retains its distinctness while operating only in relation to the other. Between such diverse things there can exist only a remote analogy; and, in point of fact, the analogy in the present instance amounts to no more than that in both cases Divine and human factors are involved, though very differently. In the one they unite to constitute a Divine-human person, in the other they cooperate to perform a Divine-human work. Even so distant an analogy may enable us, however, to recognize that as, in the case of Our Lord's person, the human nature remains truly human while yet it can never fall into sin or error because it can never act out of relation with the Divine nature into conjunction with which it has been brought; so in the case of the production of Scripture by the conjoint action of human and Divine factors, the human factors have acted as human factors, and have left their mark on the product as such, and yet cannot have fallen into that error which we say it is human to fall into, because they have not acted apart from the Divine factors, by themselves, but only under their unerring guidance.[90]

Briggs, on the other hand, argues that the human element in Scripture *necessarily* implies that the Bible is fallible, and as such subject to error. Enns wants to argue for the human element as well by implying that the Bible will reflect this in terms of limitation, in the sense that the Bible was written by men who were conditioned by their cultures and worldviews. According to Enns, this constitutes a concept of accommodation that accents the *human* element of Scripture,

90. B. B. Warfield, *Revelation and Inspiration*, vol. 1 of *The Works of Benjamin Breckinridge Warfield* (1927; repr., Grand Rapids: Baker, 1981), 108. Gerald Bray has correctly highlighted this point in Warfield's thinking: "In his understanding of biblical inspiration, Warfield claimed to be following the ancient tradition of the church, according to which the Spirit had superintended the authors' choice of words. This meant that the Bible was 'verbally inspired,' though in a less mechanical way than had normally been asserted in earlier times. Warfield wanted to give the human authors of Scripture as much intellectual autonomy as possible, which is why he rejected the Christological model as the basis for his doctrine of inspiration. To his mind, the Bible was not the fruit of hypostatic union between God and humanity, in which the only voice speaking would have been the voice of God. Instead, it was the fruit of a co-operative effort between God and humanity, in which both played their part in producing a divine-human work." Gerald Bray, *Biblical Interpretation Past and Present* (Downers Grove, Ill.: InterVarsity Press, 1996), 557.

one that highlights the human-nature of inspiration. Enns is not as blunt as Briggs, but he ends up advocating a very similar position. How so? Briggs contends that the Bible contains myth, legend, fable, and folklore. This is simply a matter of fact, and, he argues, must be recognized as such.

> The primitive sources of Biblical History are mythologies, legends, poems, laws, whether inscribed, written, or traditional, historical documents, and the use of historical imagination. There can be little doubt that there is a strong mythological element at the basis of Biblical History as well as of other ancient histories. The myth is indeed the most primitive historic form and mould in which that which is most ancient is transmitted from primitive peoples.[91]

Enns, in similar fashion, advances the notion that "myths" are embedded in the Old Testament, especially in the book of Genesis, where we find myths that are defined as "stories that are made up."[92] Yet Enns, like Briggs, does not feel that this in any way jeopardizes the doctrine of inspiration. Enns assures his readers with these words:

91. Briggs, *General Introduction to the Study of Holy Scripture*, 555.
92. Enns, *Inspiration and Incarnation*, 41. He goes on to add, "But this leads to a big problem for Christians today and their Bible. If the ancient Near Eastern stories are myth (defined in this way as prescientific stories of origins), and since the biblical stories are similar enough to these stories to invite comparison, does this indicate that myth is the proper category for understanding Genesis? Before the discovery of the Akkadian stories, one could quite safely steer clear of such a question, but this is no longer the case. We live in a modern world where we have certain expectations of how the world works. We neither understand the ancient ways—nor feel that we need to. To give a hint of where this discussion is going, it is worth asking what standards we can reasonably expect of the Bible, seeing that it is an ancient Near Eastern document and not a modern one. Are the early stories in the Old Testament to be judged on the basis of standards of modern historical inquiry and scientific precision, things that ancient peoples were not at all aware of? Is it not likely that God would have allowed his word to come to the ancient Israelites according to standards *they* understood, or are modern standards of truth and error so universal that we should expect premodern cultures to have understood them? The former position is, I feel, better suited for solving the problem. The latter is often an implicit assumption of modern thinkers *both conservative and liberal Christians*, but it is somewhat myopic and should be called into question. What the Bible is must be understood in light of the cultural context in which it was given."

The question I would ask Enns at this point is: How does your view differ from what Karl Barth called *Saga*? Are you attempting by introducing the category of *inspired myth* to move the so-called historical element of Scripture into some upper-story ghetto ("shadow land" is how Warfield described this in *Limited Inspiration*, 52), safe from the searching gaze of its critics? And given your position on accommodation, did Jesus and the apostles accommodate themselves to the cultural "errors" of their times?

The point I would like to emphasize, however, is that such a firm grounding in ancient myth does not make Genesis less inspired; it is not a concession that we must put up with or an embarrassment to a sound doctrine of Scripture. Quite to the contrary, such rootedness in the culture of the time is precisely what it means for God to speak to his people. This is what it means for God to speak at a certain time and place—he enters *their* world. He speaks and acts in ways that make sense to *them*. This is surely what it means for God to reveal himself to people—he accommodates, condescends, meets them where they are. The phrase *word of God* does not imply disconnectedness to its environment. In fact, if we can learn a lesson from the incarnation of God in Christ, it demands the exact opposite. And if God was willing and ready to adopt an ancient way of thinking, we truly hold a very low view of Scripture indeed if we make that into a point of embarrassment. We will not understand the Bible if we push aside or explain away its cultural setting, even if that setting disturbs us. We should, rather, learn to be thankful that God came to them just as he did more fully in Bethlehem many, many centuries later. We must resist the notion that for God to enculturate himself is somehow beneath him. This is precisely how he shows his love to the world he made.[93]

Briggs, in much the same fashion, puts it this way:

> All such errors are just where you would expect to find them in accurate, truthful writers of history in ancient times. They used with fidelity the best sources of information accessible to them: ancient poems, popular traditions, legends and ballads, regal and family archives, codes of law, and ancient narratives. There is no evidence that the Divine Spirit corrected their narratives either when they were lying uncomposed in their minds, or written in manuscripts. The purpose of the ancient historians was to give the history of God's redemptive workings.[94]

Briggs knew full well that this was something Warfield did not support, and yet now Enns would have us believe that what he is advocating is part of the Warfieldian tradition? Briggs would have

93. Ibid., 56.
94. Briggs, *General Introduction to the Study of Holy Scripture*, 632.

doubled over with laughter. Warfield would not have been amused, and his reaction may be gauged from one of his many reviews on the subject. Writing in reference to one of Briggs's staunchest supporters, the noted New School Presbyterian theologian Henry P. Smith, Warfield noted:

> It would seem that what Dr. Smith intends to affirm concerning the extent of inspiration is, that it does secure infallibility in matters of faith and practice, and that it does not secure errorlessness in any other matters. A further study of his views as to the effects of inspiration, however, will soon evince the fact that the negative side of this statement will very inadequately represent them. Take his exposition, for example, of the inspiration of the Chronicler. "His inspiration," he tells us, "which made him a source of religious edification to his contemporaries, and which makes his work still a part of the infallible rule of faith, did not correct his historical point of view any more than it corrected his scientific point of view, which no doubt made the earth the centre of the solar system." Now, what does Dr. Smith mean by such a statement? What can he mean but this: that inspiration was confined to making the Chronicler a "source of religious edification," and has nothing to do with him as historian or teacher of science? In other words, that the activity of God the Holy Ghost, which we call in theology inspiration, and which attends the whole process of the genesis of Scripture, influencing the collecting, choosing and arranging of the material, and the making of the book out of it, is confined to securing that this material shall be so collected, chosen and arranged that it shall subserve the purpose of religious edification. The scientific point of view of the writer may be absurd. The facts which he gives as natural facts may be the order of *the Oriental cosmogony*, which stands the earth on the back of an elephant and the elephant on the back of a tortoise and the tortoise on nothing. Inspiration has nothing to do with this. It only secures that what the writer deems to be facts shall be so collected, chosen and arranged as to edify religiously; and here it secures infallibility. The historical point of view of the writer may be equally deranged. He may be dominated by the spirit of his own day as to be incapable of reading himself back into a past era or of correctly representing it in history; his own prejudiced point of view may lead him to follow inexact, rather than accurate, predecessors; and thus the statements

which he sets down as historical facts may give a totally false view of the past, and may be historically useful to us chiefly as a betrayal of the unhistorical point of view of himself and of this times, so that by reading between the lines we may get from his exaggerated, deflected, falsified (but not *consciously* falsified) statements a vivid picture of the thoughts, aspirations, ideals of his own day and generation. Inspiration has nothing to do with this. It only secures that what such a faulty and, indeed, utterly untrustworthy historian should collect, choose and arrange as history shall serve the purpose of religious edification and here it secures infallibility.[95]

As mentioned earlier, Briggs also held a very peculiar view on justification that bears, in some ways, a striking resemblance to what is today being advocated in the so-called "New Perspective on Paul." Part of the controversy, especially among those evangelicals who identify with the Reformers' understanding of *sola fide*, is that the New Perspective advocates categorically claim that the Reformers were wrong on this issue. Justification, as argued by N. T. Wright, for example, is twofold: *initial* (by faith through grace) and *final* or eschatological (by maintaining covenantal fidelity).[96] This has also manifested itself in the teachings of Norman Shepherd[97] and in the representatives of

95. Warfield, *Limited Inspiration*, 36.
96. I earlier mentioned J. G. D. Dunn as a representative of the "New Perspective" (see note 68). Other representatives are E. P. Sanders and the noted Anglican bishop N. T. Wright. The literature here is immense. Cf. Guy Prentiss Waters, *Justification and the New Perspectives on Paul: A Review and Response* (Phillipsburg, N.J.: P&R, 2004).
97. I made reference to Shepherd earlier (see note 4). For another firsthand account of the Shepherd controversy, see A. Donald MacLeod, *W. Stanford Reid: An Evangelical Calvinist in the Academy* (Montreal & Kingston: McGill-Queens University Press, 2004), 257–79. Reid taught on the faculty of Westminster Theological Seminary during the Shepherd controversy. Shepherd taught that justification was twofold, by faith and works, and that one's initial justification could be lost. Shepherd has recently released a seven-page response to the Orthodox Presbyterian Church Report on Justification, particularly in reference to Professor Richard Gaffin of Westminster Theological Seminary in Philadelphia, who served on the committee. This is all the more significant because Gaffin was one of Shepherd's more vocal supporters during the controversy but has now come to disagree with Shepherd's views, particularly as they involve Shepherd's repudiation of the covenant of works and the imputation of Christ's active obedience. Furthermore Gaffin is uncomfortable with what he calls Shepherd's "recurring ambiguity" about the nature of justifying faith. Cf. "Some Comments on the OPC Justification Report" (2006) and Shepherd's two chapters, "Justification by Works in Reformed Theology" and "Justification by Faith in Pauline Theology," in Sandlin, ed., *Backbone of the Bible*, as well as Shepherd's paper "The Grace of Justification" (February 8, 1979), which was once available at the Westminster bookstore.

what is called the Federal Vision who want to define "faith" as "faithful obedience."[98] Briggs, as previously stated, found the Westminster divines' emphasis on the covenant of works "too scholastic." He also rejected the doctrine of the imputation of Christ's active and passive obedience,[99] something we find frequently in the followers of Norman Shepherd in the Federal Vision. Briggs's doctrine of justification bore little, if any, resemblance to that set forth by the Reformers or the Westminster divines.

Briggs became very disenchanted with the Reformers' understanding of justification, stating that their doctrine of original sin was defective. He also said that Luther was an *extreme* Augustinian in the matters of sin as well as grace, "and he led Lutherans into grosser views of original sin than the Catholic Church had ever sanctioned."[100] Briggs condemned the Reformers for following Augustine in their views on sin and grace, declaring that the Synod of Orange officially established the church's position in favor of a mild Augustinianism. "If only the Reformers had been content with the decisions of the Synod of Orange, a multitude of evils would have been averted."[101]

Briggs would go even further and write that Luther had done immense damage to the church and well-established Christian doctrines. Writing with an optimistic outlook on the possibility of a Protestant/Catholic reunion, Briggs would willingly offer up Luther as an ecumenical sacrifice. "It is possible that the German Reformers should have been more patient; that they should have gone on waiting as did their predecessors; that Luther might have served his generation better by dying at the stake rather than by rending the church."[102]

In addition to all of this, Briggs will indict Luther on one of the most cherished Reformation doctrines: the bondage of the will. "Luther asserted in the baldest form the bondage of the human will and waged

---

98. On this, see Waters, *The Federal Vision and Covenant Theology*, and his extensive bibliography.

99. Briggs, *Theological Symbolics*, 342.

100. Briggs, *The Bible, the Church and the Reason*, 81. Briggs also denied the doctrine of the immediate imputation of Adam's sin, *Theological Symbolics*, 375.

101. Briggs, *Theological Symbolics*, 338.

102. Briggs, *Church Unity*, 420.

a fierce war with Erasmus on this subject. Erasmus maintained the common doctrine of the Catholic Church before the Reformation."[103]

Since Briggs had argued that the official church doctrine had been established at the Synod of Orange, he likewise on this point proclaims that Luther was in the wrong. As noted, Briggs also rejected the Reformed doctrine of imputation of Adam's sin and of Christ's active and passive obedience; it should come as no surprise, then, to find Briggs making major revisions in the standard Protestant understanding of justification. After setting out the various views on the subject as expressed in the respective creeds, Briggs, in a very naïve fashion pronounces:

> There is thus no difference between the Churches as to the relation of Faith and the graces of hope and love, but only as to their relation to justification. There is no separation of Faith and these graces in fact or in time, but only in order. If justification is a work including sanctification, the Roman Catholic statement is certainly correct; if it is a momentary act, the Protestant position is correct. It cannot be doubted that in the New Testament, Justification is used in both senses; and therefore both Protestants and Catholics are correct, and they ought to get together and agree on their terminology.[104]

Briggs's understanding of justification led him to develop his own unique doctrine of "the Middle-state," a type of Protestant purgatory. Early in his career he tried to read this into the Westminster Standards. Later he contended that the Westminster divines were unclear on the matter, declaring, "Those who hold the doctrine of immediate sanctification at death do not really understand the Protestant doctrine of sanctification."[105] However, at the end of his career, he complained that the Reformers and the Westminster divines were all in the dark about the subject.[106]

---

103. Briggs, *Theological Symbolics*, 339.
104. Ibid., 316.
105. Briggs, *Whither?* 147.
106. Briggs, *Theological Symbolics*, 285. It should be noted that the well-known advocate of "open theism," Clark Pinnock, has proposed a similar view, suggesting that, "although not accustomed to thinking much about purgatory because I have shared the knee-jerk reaction against it in Evangelical thinking . . . I cannot deny that most believers end their earthly lives imperfectly sanctified and far from complete. . . . Obviously, Evangelicals have not thought

The Federal Vision advocates also share common ground with Briggs and his fully developed views on the sacraments. Briggs, however, never tried to read his views on the sacraments back into the Westminster Standards, something the supporters of the Federal Vision labor mightily to accomplish. He fully understood that this was something that the Confession could not be made to support. It was not until Briggs left the Presbyterian church that he began to develop his views on the sacraments. Briggs's position slowly evolved after he came under the influence of the noted church historian Philip Schaff, who closed his career at Union Theological Seminary in New York. Schaff had been instrumental in developing with John Williamson Nevin the Mercersberg Theology, with its distinctive understanding of the role of the sacraments. After Briggs was received into the priesthood of the Episcopal church, he became more and more "high church" in his views and embraced a position similar to that of Edward Pusey, the leader of the Oxford Movement in the Church of England. Like Briggs, Pusey labored to bring about a reunion with the Roman Catholic Church and expressed a view of the sacrament of baptism that said in effect that the sacrament, and not faith, was the deciding factor in a person's belonging to the true church: even hypocrites or blasphemers, if baptized, are members of the body of Christ; the church is not to be defined as a *societas Fidei et Spiritus Sancti*, but as a community of the *baptized*.[107] It comes as no surprise, therefore, given the similarities between the Federal Visionists and Briggs, that the Federal Vision proponents likewise frequently use Old Princeton as their foil in setting forth their views on the sacraments.[108]

---

this question out. It seems to me that we already have the possibility of a doctrine of purgatory. . . . Ask yourself, are you not going to need some finishing touches in the area of holiness when you die?" See his contributions in *Four Views on Hell*, ed. W. V. Crockett (Grand Rapids: Zondervan, 1992).

107. Cf. the discussion in the older work of one of Briggs's teachers in Germany: I. A. Dorner, *System of Christian Doctrine* (Edinburgh: T & T Clark, 1896), 4:284. Briggs's mature views on the subject are stated in his later works: *Theological Symbolics* (1914), *History of the Study of Theology* (1916), and *Church Unity* (1909). A helpful secondary source is M. S. Massa, *Charles Augustus Briggs and the Crisis of Historical Criticism* (Minneapolis: Fortress, 1990).

108. Both Douglas Wilson and Peter Leithart single out Warfield for criticism, while Mark Horne criticizes Samuel Miller, one of the founding faculty members at Princeton. Rich Lusk lumps Old Princeton into this statement: "For better and for worse, we have numerous popularizers of Reformed theology around today. The result is that what most of us think

Warfield's legacy is much easier to track. His works are continually reprinted and his views on a variety of subjects still carry significant weight in certain evangelical and Reformed circles. But as we have seen, he also has his critics. As noted in this book, Warfield's defense of biblical inerrancy has never lacked for critics, even in the evangelical camp. Recently he has become the object of animadversion from the Pentecostal/charismatic wing of evangelicalism. Warfield is considered the chief culprit in advancing the view known as cessationism—the idea that the apostolic gifts were unique to the infancy period of the church.[109]

It is not uncommon for those in charismatic circles to regularly make derogatory comments about Warfield. Vinson Synan, the dean of Pentecostal historians, credited Warfield with "quenching the Spirit in the lives of numerous clergy who in turn influenced their church members."[110] C. Peter Wagner shares that perspective in an endorsement he wrote for one of Jack Deere's books:

> One of the most severe historical setbacks to the full manifestation of the Kingdom of God in the U.S.A. was Benjamin Warfield's *Counterfeit Miracles* published seventy-five years ago. Jack Deere's new book, more than anything I have seen, has all the potential for neutralizing Warfield and his followers and opening the body of Christ to the full power of God's Holy Spirit.[111]

---

of as 'Reformed' is greatly truncated. American Reformed theology is like a bad cassette recording of the real thing. In this essay (and in this book as a whole), we are simply trying to recover nuances that were originally in the tradition, but have been lost." See Lusk's chapter "New Life and Apostasy: Hebrews 6:4–8 as Test Case," in *The Federal Vision*, ed. Steve Wilkins and Duane Garner (Monroe, La.; Athanasius Press, 2004), 297. The most troubling thing about Lusk's hubristic remarks is that they come from a person who has absolutely no formal theological training or a degree in a remotely related field. For Wilson, Leithart, and Horne's comments, see the extended discussion in Waters, *The Federal Vision and Covenant Theology*, 72, 198.

109. The volume of Warfield's that has attracted their attention is *Counterfeit Miracles* (New York: Charles Scribner & Son, 1918). This is reprinted by the Banner of Truth and was issued under the title *Miracles: Yesterday and Today: True and False* by Eerdmans in 1953. The pagination is the same.

110. Synan wrote the article "Presbyterian and Reformed Charismatics" in *The Dictionary of Pentecostal and Charismatic Movements*, ed. Stanley M. Burgess and Gary B. McGee (Grand Rapids: Zondervan, 1988), 724.

111. Wagner wrote this as an endorsement for the first book of Jack Deere listed in note 112 below.

Jack Deere and William DeArteaga produced books that are highly critical of Warfield, but both end up either distorting or misrepresenting his views.[112]

While the efforts of Deere and DeArteaga were designed to appeal to a popular audience, Jon Ruthven's work first appeared as a Ph.D. dissertation written at Marquette University. Ruthven is highly critical of Warfield and contends that Warfield not only went astray on cessationism and pneumatology but was likewise in error on the doctrine of inspiration, and that "his Christology, ecclesiology and eschatology warrants [*sic*] substantial review."[113] Ruthven's thesis is that Warfield's cessationism created a fault line that affects every aspect of Warfield's thought. This is a very astounding claim.

Ruthven charges that Warfield's polemic is motivated by a sense of fear; for example, Warfield's fear that ongoing miracles posed a threat to institutional Protestantism. Ruthven fails to demonstrate this. In fact, he fails to present any convincing arguments to that effect. It is difficult to determine how he arrives at this charge, but one comes away with the impression that Ruthven seems so determined to overthrow Warfield's cessationalist position that he gets carried away in his zeal. Ruthven complains that Warfield's concept of miracle is inconsistent and is traceable, so he contends, to Warfield's commitment to Reformed theology and (by implication) to Warfield's careless scholarship.[114] Warfield may be faulted

112. See, for example, Jack Deere, *Surprised by the Power of the Spirit: A Former Dallas Seminary Professor Discovers That God Speaks and Heals Today* (Grand Rapids: Zondervan, 1993). To his credit, Deere does refer to Warfield as "the greatest of the cessationist scholars" (268), but then proceeds to misrepresent Warfield's assessment of Augustine's position on miracles (74). This book was followed by Deere's *Surprised by the Voice of God: How God Speaks Today Through Prophecies, Dreams, and Visions* (Grand Rapids: Zondervan, 1996). See also William DeArteaga, *Quenching the Spirit: Examining Centuries of Opposition to the Moving of the Spirit* (Lake Mary, Fla.: Creation House, 1992).

113. Jon Ruthven, *On the Cessation of the Charismata: The Protestant Polemic of Benjamin B. Warfield* (Ph.D. diss., Marquette University, 1989), 179, 310. This was later published under the same title by Sheffield Press (1993).

114. Ruthven "speculates" that Warfield's cessationist position *may* have been influenced by Warfield's frustration over his wife, Annie's, semi-invalid condition (Ruthven, *On the Cessation of the Charismata*, 128). There is no evidence whatsoever that this was in any way a factor in Warfield's position, and Ruthven should have refrained from delving into that kind of Freudian psychohistory. Cf. David Hackett Fischer's description of this in his *Historians' Fallacies: Towards a Logic of Historical Thought* (New York: Harper & Row, 1970), 187–215. Both Deere and DeArteaga draw *uncritically* on Ruthven's work. These charismatic charges did not go

for any number of things, but sloppy or careless scholarship is not one of them![115]

In conclusion, Warfield's following remains somewhat restricted to what is often called the "Truly Reformed," while Briggs's views can be seen across the evangelical landscape, including those who self-consciously call themselves "Reformed."[116] I would argue, however, that it is not an exaggeration to claim that Warfield, not Briggs (and those today who mirror his views), stands fully in the Reformed tradition that traces itself back through the Westminster divines to the Protestant Reformers.

---

unchallenged. I critique Deere and DeArteaga (and indirectly Ruthven) in two extensive reviews in *Reformation & Revival: A Quarterly Journal for Church Leadership* 4, 1 (Winter 1995): 115–40, and *Reformation & Revival: A Quarterly Journal for Church Leadership* 8, 2 (Spring 1999): 179–83. Thomas R. Edgar wrote a very substantial critique of Jack Deere's position in *Satisfied by the Promise of the Spirit: Affirming the Fullness of God's Provision for Spiritual Living* (Grand Rapids: Kregel, 1996). For a rigorous defense of Warfield's Christology (contra Ruthven), see C. R. Trueman, "The Glory of Christ: B. B. Warfield on Jesus of Nazareth," in C. R. Trueman, *The Wages of Spin: Critical Writings on Historic and Contemporary Evangelicalism* (Ross-shire, Scotland: Mentor Imprints, 2004), 103–28. See also the contributions of Richard Gaffin to the book *Are Miraculous Gifts for Today? Four Views*, ed. Wayne Grudem (Grand Rapids: Zondervan, 1996), esp. 28–33.

115. Colin Brown, who writes critically of Warfield's position, nonetheless says, "Warfield's book was marked by the solid erudition and commitment to Reformed evangelicalism that characterized his other writings." Colin Brown, *Miracles and the Critical Mind* (Grand Rapids: Eerdmans, 1984), 198.

116. Briggs's colleague at Union, the Old School Presbyterian theologian W. G. T. Shedd, whom I have referenced already, strongly felt that Briggs's revisionist attempts were dishonest. Shedd no doubt had Briggs in mind when he wrote these words shortly before his death: "But heresy is not so great a sin as dishonesty. A heretic who acknowledges that he is such, is a better man than he who pretends to be orthodox while subscribing to a creed which he dislikes, and which he saps under pretence of improving it and adapting it to the times." W. G. T. Shedd, *Calvinism: Pure and Mixed* (New York: Charles Scribner's Sons, 1893), 152.

❧ 9 ❧

Warfield and the Briggs Trial:
A Bibliography

BARRY WAUGH

Benjamin Breckinridge Warfield, former professor of systematic and polemic theology at Princeton Theological Seminary, is generally believed to have been rarely involved in the work of the Presbyterian church's judicatories. It is thought that his absence was due to his remaining close to his Princeton campus home so that he could care for his homebound wife, Annie. Despite limited attendance, he kept himself informed about issues facing his presbytery, synod, and the General Assembly by means of ecclesiastical periodicals, judicatory documents, and conversations with his Princeton colleagues. One issue that particularly interested Dr. Warfield was the heresy trial of Charles Augustus Briggs, D.D., of Union Theological Seminary in New York. Warfield and Briggs served as co-editors of *The Presbyterian Review* for a turbulent period of about one year; the fundamental differences between the views of Union and Princeton regarding the inspiration and infallibility of Scripture contributed substantially to their conflict.[1] So, despite his failure to attend the General Assembly, B. B. Warfield

---

1. For an extended study of their views on Scripture see Trevor W. J. Morrow, "Infallibility as a Theological Concept: A Study in the Use of the Concept 'Infallible' in the Writings of B. B. Warfield and C. A. Briggs" (Ph.D. diss., University of Edinburgh, 1983). See also Channing R. Jeschke, "The Briggs Case: The Focus of a Study in Nineteenth-Century Presbyterian History"

kept abreast of the issues involved in the Briggs case by gathering and reading publications concerning the trial. He not only gathered and read these books, articles, and pamphlets, but also bound them together in four large volumes.

The purpose of this bibliographic study is to provide a listing of the items Dr. Warfield collected in his volumes. However, before looking at the listing, a short summary of the Briggs case will orient the reader regarding the context of the collection and the issues involved in the heresy trial of C. A. Briggs.

A Summary of the Briggs Case

Briggs began his service at Union Theological Seminary, New York, in January 1874 as a provisional professor; in 1875, he assumed the chair of Hebrew and cognate languages. In 1890 he was transferred to the Edward Robinson Chair of Biblical Theology, but he had already been teaching courses in the biblical theology discipline that included: The Religion of Israel, The Old Testament Doctrine of Redemption, Theology of the Old Testament, and New Testament Theology.[2] Briggs's inaugural address, "The Authority of Holy Scripture," delivered January 20, 1891, declared that "the reason, the church, and the Bible" were three complementary sources of authoritative, divine guidance for the Christian.[3] The inaugural lecture was published that same year, and in the following year, he explained his views further in *The Bible, the Church and the Reason*.[4] Professor Briggs's views on inspiration, inerrancy, the sufficiency of Scripture, and other theological issues evidenced his higher critical presuppositions and led to his trial by the Presbyterian church for heresy.

(Ph.D. diss., University of Chicago, 1966), which deals less with Dr. Warfield and more with Dr. Briggs.

2. George L. Prentiss, *The Union Theological Seminary in the City of New York* (New York: Anson D. F. Randolph, 1889), 49, 81, 89, 92.

3. C. A. Briggs, *The Edward Robinson Chair of Biblical Theology in the Union Theological Seminary, New York* (New York: Printed for the Union Theological Seminary, New York, 1891); this is the first edition of the speech. See also Briggs, *The Authority of Holy Scripture: An Inaugural Address*, 2nd ed. (New York: Charles Scribner's Sons, 1891).

4. C. A. Briggs, *The Bible, the Church and the Reason* (New York: Charles Scribner's Sons, 1892).

Issues pertinent to Dr. Briggs and Union Seminary came before the General Assembly through the report of the Standing Committee on Theological Seminaries given to the 1891 General Assembly.[5] Sixty-three presbyteries referred to the Standing Committee overtures relevant to Dr. Briggs's teaching at Union Seminary. Francis L. Patton of Princeton Seminary, chairman of the Committee on Seminaries, presented the committee report to the Assembly, which resolved, by a vote of 449 to 60, to veto the appointment.[6] In 1870, as a part of the reunion of the Old and New Schools, Union Seminary had agreed to abide by the same rules as the other seminaries of the Presbyterian church, including the rule allowing the General Assembly to veto faculty appointments.[7] There was a difference of opinion regarding the interpretation of the rules governing the Presbyterian church's oversight of Union. The seminary's leadership believed that Dr. Briggs was being *transferred* within the seminary to the new position and that his appointment, therefore, was not subject to veto, since he was not new to Union; the resolutions adopted by the Assembly contended that he was *elected* to the chair, whether new to Union or not, and the Assembly therefore could veto his appointment. Union's response to this decision was clear when its board of directors voted in June to retain Professor Briggs in his newly appointed position despite the General Assembly's veto.[8]

This was not the end of the case. In October 1891, the New York Presbytery returned two charges of heresy against Dr. Briggs. The first charge contended that his teaching conflicted with the Westminster Standards and Scripture because he denied that the Bible was the only infallible rule of faith and practice, and because he believed in progressive sanctification after death. His response to the charges was given in November and he pled that the accusations against him were not specific

5. While the report of the Standing Committee on Theological Seminaries was being presented, an unusual tragedy occurred: "The Hon. Samuel Miller Breckinridge, LL.D., took the floor, and after speaking twenty minutes in favor of the Report of the Committee, closed his speech with the words, 'I have discharged my duty,' and turning to leave the platform, fell dead." *Minutes of the General Assembly of the Presbyterian Church in the United States of America, New Series, Vol. XIV, A.D. 1891, 103rd General Assembly* (Philadelphia: Stated Clerk, 1891), 92. These minutes will be documented henceforth as: *Minutes*, year of meeting, and page number.

6. *Minutes*, 1891, 94, 97.

7. *Minutes*, 1870, 60–64, 148, 149; *Minutes*, 1871, 581.

8. Max G. Rogers, "Charles Augustus Briggs," in *Dictionary of Heresy Trials in American Christianity*, ed. George H. Shriver (Westport, Conn.: Greenwood Press, 1997), 49.

enough. The Presbytery voted to dismiss the charges against Professor Briggs by a vote of 94 to 39. The minority expressed its intention to appeal to the Synod of New York, but it instead went directly to the General Assembly.[9] The 1892 Assembly, which met in Portland, Oregon, sustained the appeal of the minority by a vote of 431 to 87, and the case was "remanded to the Presbytery of New York for a new trial."[10]

Before the new trial by the Presbytery of New York, Union's board met and adopted a resolution rescinding the Assembly's right to veto faculty appointments and ended the 1870 agreement that gave the Presbyterian church oversight of Union.[11] When the Presbytery of New York convened in November, it planned its method of operation for the impending trial and received amended charges, which had increased from two to eight. The charges against Dr. Briggs included: believing that "the Reason and the Church" are fountains "of divine authority"; not believing in the inerrancy of the autographs of Scripture; teaching that Old Testament prophecies were inaccurate; denying Mosaic authorship of the Pentateuch; denying Isaiah's writing of some of Isaiah; and believing that sanctification is not complete at death. The trial took place in December, and Dr. Briggs's presbytery acquitted him of all charges.[12] The prosecution announced its intention to appeal to the 1893 General Assembly.

The historic New York Avenue Presbyterian Church in Washington, D.C., was the site for the 1893 General Assembly. Before dealing with the issues concerning Dr. Briggs, the Assembly heard a communication from Union Seminary notifying the court of the board's termination of the 1870 agreement regarding the Assembly's oversight of the seminary.[13] Consideration of the Briggs case began on May 23, continued through extensive debate, which at some points was interrupted by other business, and was concluded late in the evening of May 31. The vote was taken by roll call and the appeal of the minority of the New York Presbytery was sustained by a vote of 379 to 116—Dr. Briggs was convicted of heresy and then suspended from the ministry in a

9. Rogers, "Charles Augustus Briggs," 50.
10. *Minutes*, 1892, 141, 152.
11. Rogers, "Charles Augustus Briggs," 51.
12. Ibid., 51–52, 53.
13. *Minutes*, 1893, 158.

later General Assembly action.[14] The tension that existed between Union and Princeton seminaries had increased with the failure of their joint publication of *The Presbyterian Review*, and the Briggs decision stretched the relationship to the breaking point.

C. A. Briggs later became an Episcopal minister while continuing his teaching at Union Seminary. In 1904, he resigned the Edward Robinson Chair and continued his service at Union by teaching symbolics and irenics. Dr. Briggs's work in publication was extensive and included editing of the International Critical Commentary series, writing of the *Critical Commentary on the Psalms*, and publication of a Hebrew lexicon with S. R. Driver and Francis Brown. He died of pneumonia in 1913.[15]

Warfield's Collection of Materials on the Briggs Heresy Case

The materials in the following bibliographic listing may be found at the Luce Archives of Princeton Theological Seminary, Princeton, New Jersey. This four-volume set is cataloged as SCC #2429.[16] The entries are annotated in some cases, but others have extended, self-explanatory titles requiring no annotation. Dr. Warfield has written personal annotations in some of these publications.

Volume 1, *The Briggs Heresy Case: Documents Published by Dr. Briggs*

(1) A book that covers the establishment of the biblical theology chair at Union, why Briggs was chosen, the inaugural service (Jan. 20, 1891),

---

14. Ibid., 70–140; pages 164–65 detail the final judgment.

15. Biographical information from: B. J. Longfield, "Briggs, Charles Augustus (1841–1913)," in *Dictionary of the Presbyterian and Reformed Tradition in America*, ed. D. G. Hart and Mark A. Noll (Downers Grove, Ill.: InterVarsity Press, 1999); Robert Hastings Nichols, *Presbyterianism in New York State*, ed. James Hastings Nichols (Philadelphia: The Westminster Press, 1963), 187–95; James H. Moorhead, "Briggs, Charles Augustus (1841–1913)," in *Encyclopedia of the Reformed Faith*, ed. Donald K. McKim and David F. Wright (Louisville: Westminster John Knox Press, 1992); Bruce L. Shelley, "Briggs, Charles Augustus (1841–1913)," in *The New International Dictionary of the Christian Church*, ed. J. D. Douglas (Grand Rapids: Zondervan, 1978); *New 20th-Century Encyclopedia of Religious Knowledge*, 2nd ed., ed. J. D. Douglas (Grand Rapids: Baker, 1991).

16. The author expresses his appreciation to Robert Benedetto, director of special collections at Princeton Seminary, for providing access to the four volumes on the Briggs case and for the use of the Luce Archives reading room.

the charge by Rev. David R. Fisher, Briggs's inaugural address on the authority of Scripture, and the position and importance of biblical theology. 84 pages.

(2) Briggs, Charles A. *The Authority of Holy Scripture and Inaugural Address*, 2nd ed. New York: Scribner's, 1891. 111 pages. This includes a preface and appendix containing additional notes and explanation.

(3) *The Case Against Professor Briggs*. New York: Scribner's, 1892. 171 pages. Includes: the charges submitted to the presbytery (Oct. 5, 1891); Briggs's response to the charges (Nov. 4, 1891); the Presbytery of New York's dismission of the case; the complaint of the Synod of New York against the presbytery for its decision (Nov. 13, 1891); the appeal of the Prosecuting Committee to the General Assembly (Nov. 13, 1891); Dr. Briggs's argument at the Assembly against its entertaining the appeal (May 26, 1892); the entertainment of the appeal (May 27, 1892); Briggs's argument against the Assembly sustaining the appeal (May 27, 28, 1892); and the action of the Assembly in sustaining the appeal and reversing the presbytery's dismissal of the case.

(4) *The Case Against Professor Briggs, Part II*. New York: Scribner's, 1893. 161 pages. This includes: Briggs's preliminary objections to the use of the Committee of Prosecution (Nov. 2, 1892); the action of the Presbytery of New York upon those objections; the complaint of Briggs to the Synod of New York regarding the presbytery's action on those objections; amended charges and specifications submitted to the presbytery (Nov. 9, 1892); Briggs's preliminary objections to the amended charges and specifications (Nov. 9, 1892); the action of the Presbytery of New York on these preliminary objections; the complaint of Briggs to the Synod of New York; evidence submitted by Briggs in his defense; Briggs's exceptions to new material introduced by the prosecution; and the final judgment of the Presbytery of New York (Dec. 30, 1892 and Jan. 9, 1893).

(5) *The Defense of Professor Briggs Before the General Assembly, The Case of Professor Briggs, Part III*. New York: Scribner's, 1893.

311 pages. This includes the appeal of the Prosecuting Committee to the General Assembly; the argument of Briggs before the General Assembly against entertaining the appeal; the entertainment of the appeal; Briggs's argument before the Assembly against sustaining the appeal; the action of the Assembly in sustaining the appeal; and the final judgment of the General Assembly (June 1, 1893).

Volume 2, *The Briggs Heresy Case: Trial in Presbytery*

(1) *The Presbyterian Church in the United States of America, Against the Rev. Charles A. Briggs, D.D. Report of the Committee of Prosecution, with Charges and Specifications Submitted to the Presbytery of New York, Oct. 5th, 1891, by the Committee of Prosecution.* There is no publication information provided. 45 pages.

(2) Briggs, Charles A. *Response to the Charges and Specifications Submitted to the Presbytery of New York.* [n.p.]: Charles A. Briggs, 1891. 34 pages.

(3) *One Hundred and Fourth General Assembly of the Presbyterian Church in the United States of America. Portland, Oregon, May, 1892. The Presbyterian Church in the United States of America against the Rev. Charles A. Briggs, D.D. Record of the Case. Including the Appeal to the General Assembly, and All Papers Pertaining to the Case. From the Minutes of the Presbytery of New York.* New York: PCUSA, 1892. 272 pages.

(4) Brown, Francis. *The Question of the Original Party, in the Case of Dr. Briggs. Argument Prepared for the Synod of New York, October, 1892, on a Complaint of 114 Ministers and Elders Against the Presbytery of New York, by Prof. Francis Brown, D.D.* New York: [n.p.], 1892. 51 pages.

(5) This item is described in Warfield's notation as: "Proofs of Amended Charges Against Dr. Briggs: handed me by Dr. Lampe on Oct. 13, 1892." This item is on six printed proof sheets of 8" x 22" folded paper.

(6) "Proposed paper for the General Assembly to pass *in re* Dr. Briggs. Drawn up May 7 [1892]—for Dr. Green by B. B. Warfield." This item constitutes sixteen sheets of manuscript by Warfield that express his reasons for convicting Dr. Briggs of heresy.[17]

(7) *Presbytery of New York. The Presbyterian Church in the United States of America. Against the Rev. Charles A. Briggs, D.D. Amended Charges and Specifications.* New York: PCUSA, [n.d.]. 36 pages. There is a "Note" that lists amendments to the charges before the charges were declared to be in order.

(8) *Presbytery of New York. The Presbyterian Church in the United States of America. Against the Rev. Charles A. Briggs, D.D. Amended Charges and Specifications as Delivered to Dr. Briggs by the Moderator in Open Session of Judicatory, Nov. 9th, 1892.* New York: PCUSA, [n.d.]. 36 pages.

(9) *Presbytery of New York. The Presbyterian Church in the United States of America. Against the Rev. Charles A. Briggs, D.D. Extracts from the Proceedings of Nov. 28th, 1892. Dr. Lampe's Reply to Objections Filed by Prof. Briggs under Section 22 of Book of Discipline.* New York: Presbytery of New York, [n.d.]. 16 pages.

(10) *Presbytery of New York. The Presbyterian Church in the United States of America. Against the Rev. Charles A. Briggs, D.D. Extracts from the Proceedings of Nov. 29th, 1892. Objections presented by Mr. McCook to the Motion to Strike Out Charges IV. and VII. from the Amended Charges and Specifications.* No publication information. 11 pages.

(11) *Presbytery of New York. The Presbyterian Church in the United States of America. Against the Rev. Charles A. Briggs, D.D. Argument of Rev. W. F. Birch, D.D.* No publication information. 74 pages.

---

17. A transcription of this manuscript was published in the fall 2004 issue of *The Westminster Theological Journal* on pp. 401–11.

(12) *Presbytery of New York. The Presbyterian Church in the United States of America. Against the Rev. Charles A. Briggs, D.D. Argument of John F. McCook.* No publication information. 49 pages.

(13) *The Defense of Professor Briggs Before the Presbytery of New York December 13, 14, 15, and 19, 1892.* New York: Scribner's, 1893. 193 pages.

(14) Briggs, Charles A. *Who Wrote the Pentateuch?* [n.p.]: Charles A. Briggs, 1892. 162 pages.

(15) *Presbytery of New York. The Presbyterian Church in the United States of America against the Rev. Charles A. Briggs, D.D. Argument of the Rev. Joseph J. Lampe, D.D.* No publication information provided. 146 pages.

Volume 3, *The Briggs Heresy Case: Trial in Assembly*

(1) *The Presbyterian Church in the United States of America against the Rev. Charles A. Briggs, D.D. Notice of Appeal and Appeal to the General Assembly from the Decision and Final Judgment of the Presbytery of New York rendered January 9th, 1893.* New York: PCUSA, 1893. 34 pages. This item notes on the title page that the members of the Prosecuting Committee were: George W. F. Birch, D.D., Joseph J. Lampe, D.D., Robert F. Sample, D.D., John J. Stevenson, and John J. McCook.

(2) *One Hundred and Fifth General Assembly of the Presbyterian Church in the United States of America, Washington, D.C. May 1893. The Presbyterian Church in the United States of America against the Rev. Charles A. Briggs, D.D.* New York: PCUSA, 1893. 165 pages. This item includes, on pages 139–57, a listing of how the commissioners voted.

(3) *One Hundred and Fifth General Assembly of the Presbyterian Church in the United States of America, Washington, D.C. May 1893. Appellant's Argument Before the General Assembly in Support of the*

Motion to Entertain the Appeal, May 25, 1893. Argument of John J. McCook, A Member of the Prosecuting Committee. New York: PCUSA, 1893. 71 pages.

(4) *One Hundred and Fifth General Assembly of the Presbyterian Church in the United States of America, Washington, D.C. May 1893. Appellant's Argument in Support of Motion to Sustain the Appeal. Argument of Rev. Joseph F. Lampe, D.D. A Member of the Prosecuting Committee.* New York: PCUSA, 1893. 85 pages.

(5) *Some of Dr. Charles A. Briggs' Views. Published Since His Suspension by the General Assembly.* No publication information. 14 pages.

Volume 4, *The Briggs Heresy Case: Illustrative Documents*

(1) McCosh, James. *Whither? O Whither? Tell Me Where.* New York: Scribner's, 1889. 47 pages. This is Professor McCosh's perspective on the Briggs case.

(2) *The Main Issue. A Straight Question to Professor Briggs.* Saratoga Springs, N.Y.: The Saratoga News Co., 1890. 25 pages. This item contends that the Briggs case is of greater concern to Presbyterians than the debate about creed revision.

(3) McPheeters, William M. "A Recently Proposed Test of Canonicity." This is the inaugural address of the author as the Professor of Biblical Literature in the Theological Seminary at Columbia, May 1890, and it is found on pages 33–55 of an unnamed periodical. Warfield's copy was given to him by McPheeters "with the author's compliments."

(4) Morris, Edward D. *A Calm Review of the Inaugural Address of Professor Charles A. Briggs.* New York: Anson D. F. Randolph and Co., 1891. 50 pages. The conclusion says of Briggs's views that there is "too much that is defective in doctrine or in statement."

(5) Sixtus. *A Review of Professor Briggs' Inaugural Address*. New York: Charles L. Webster and Co., 1891. 45 pages. Dr. Warfield's annotation says that Sixtus is "Said to be a Roman Catholic author." The pseudonymous author does not support Briggs's views because of his "attacks upon the authenticity and authority of the Inspired Scriptures" (44).

(6) Chambers, F. W. *The Inaugural Address of Professor Briggs*. This address is found on pages 481–94 of an unnamed periodical. The author ends his article by stating his belief that "the duty of Christian rebuke is imperative, however unpleasant. Hence we have done what in us lies to hinder any from being carried away by diverse and strange teachings."

(7) Warfield, B. B. "The One Hundred and Third General Assembly." *Presbyterian and Reformed Review* 2 (July 1891): 495–99. Dr. Warfield gives his perspective on the actions and events of the recent General Assembly, including the Briggs case.

(8) Beattie, Francis R. "Inauguration of Dr. Charles A. Briggs, at Union Seminary, New York." Warfield attributes this to: *The Presbyterian Quarterly* (April 1891): 270–83. Beattie says that Briggs's perspective on Scripture "undermines the very foundation of a supernatural revelation from God, such as the Bible purports to be, and as we believe it to be" (283).

(9) *The Report of the Standing Committee on Theological Seminaries in the Matter of the Appointment of the Rev. Charles A. Briggs, D.D., as Professor of Biblical Theology in Union Theological Seminary, New York City*. There is no publication information provided for this three-page article. Professor Warfield dated this item May 1891.

(10) Warfield, B. B. "An Answer to Dr. Briggs' 'Shortest Catechism.'" *Detroit Free Press*, May 27, 1891. 7 pages. Warfield noted that this is a "corrected copy." It is a pamphlet reprint that includes several corrections and notations in Warfield's hand.

(10a) Warfield, B. B. *The Shortest Catechism*. This is a twelve-page proof copy. The introduction to the article says this edition was "furnished to The Free Press by Mr. John J. McCook, an elder in the Fifth Avenue Church, New York (Dr. John Hall, pastor), a commissioner from the Presbytery of New York to the General Assembly." A footnote comments: "The subjoined paper was written by Professor Warfield on May 21st, and placed in the hands of a friend for his personal information, but with liberty 'to make whatever use of it he chose.' In the exercise of this liberty, and in the desire not to commit Professor Warfield without consultation with him, it was printed anonymously in *The Detroit Free Press* of May 27th. On the issue of this reprint, Professor Warfield has expressed a desire to have the anonymous removed, as he has no unwillingness to assume the responsibility of the entire contents of the paper" (1).

(11) Watts, Robert [of Belfast]. "Dr. Briggs's Biblical Theology Traced to its Organic Principle." Richmond: Whittet and Shepperson, 1892. 30 pages. This selection was reprinted from *The Presbyterian Quarterly*. Cites Briggs for "lack of clear definition of terms" (26) and his statement that the church is one of the "three great fountains of Divine authority," and discusses Briggs's view of progressive sanctification after death (16ff.).

(12) "The Crisis in the Presbyterian Church." 15 pages. Notation by Warfield says: "By the Revd. Dr. John Duffield, Princeton College. Reprinted from *The Independent* for April 13 or April 27th, 1893." Given to Warfield by the author with his regards.

(13) *How Josh worked up a Concept, By Josh Senior*. New York: Fleming H. Revell, 1891. 8 pages. The author writes against the hermeneutical principle that it is the concept behind the particular words of Scripture that is inspired rather than the words themselves. This is accomplished by using a story in which a business transaction goes awry when the second party goes by the *words* of the contract, but the first party proclaims that the wording that the second party understood was not the *concept behind the words* of the contract.

(14) McDougall, Thomas. *The General Assembly of 1893 and the Case of Dr. Briggs*. Cincinnati: Elm Street Printing Co., 1893. 24 pages. The author gives his perspective on how the case was conducted and his belief that Briggs's views struck at the fundamentals of the faith.

(15) *Third Edition, The New Theology in the Nursery*. Author unknown. New York: John I. Covington, [n.d.]. 15 pages. A conversation between a mother and her children about issues related to the Briggs case.

(16) *A Review by Thomas McDougall of Certain Statements in a Book, Entitled: "The Trial of Dr. Briggs Before the General Assembly; A Calm Review of the Case by a Stranger, who Attended all the Sessions of the Court."* Cincinnati: Elm Street Printing, 1894. 27 pages.

(17) Sample, Robert F. *The Higher Criticism, An Address*. New York: [n.p.], [n.d.]. 33 pages. The author is against higher criticism and warns of its dangers.

(18) Schaff, Philip. *Other Heresy Trials and the Briggs Case*. Warfield notes: "The Forum, January 1892. [Pages 621–33.] Dr. Schaff contends that the Presbyterian Church 'should have room to spare for such scholars as Dr. Briggs. She is orthodox and conservative enough, and can afford to be tolerant and liberal without running any risk.'" (633).

(19) Briggs, Charles A. "Theological Education and its Needs." Warfield noted: "The Forum Jany. 1892." Pages 634–45.

(20) Briggs, Charles A. "Redemption After Death." *The Magazine of Christian Literature* 1, no. 3 (Dec. 1889), 105–16. This copy of the article is very fragile and deteriorated. Dr. Briggs elaborates on his view of further sanctification after death.

(21) Briggs, Charles A. "Have the Quakers Prevailed?" *Bibliotheca Sacra* [in Warfield's hand], 1890, 325–52. Briggs concluded that

253

the Presbyterian church and Congregational churches of his day had abandoned the views of both the Boston ministers of 1690 and the Westminster divines of 1646 and adopted the views of the Quakers.

(22) Briggs, Charles A. "Church and Creed." Warfield noted that this is from *The Forum*, June 1891, 367–78. Briggs concluded that the aim of Christianity is to progress to the realization of the Christian ideal, and for this to occur, it is necessary to construct a new "consensus creed" that will express the Christian faith better than the old creeds.

(23) Briggs, Charles A. "The Theological Crisis." Warfield noted that this is from the *North American Review*, either July or January [which month is unclear], 1891. Pages 99–114. Briggs concluded that the evolution of Christian theology that brought about the crisis involving him was preparing the way for a new Reformation.

(24) Briggs, Charles A. "The Future of Presbyterianism in the United States." *North American Review* 440 (July 1893): 1–10.

(25) Briggs, Charles A. "The Alienation of Church and People." Warfield noted: "*The Forum*, Nov. 1893. Pages 366–78." Briggs opened his article by stating that he was living in the ebb tide of the church and that he saw his generation as being led by "dogmaticians, ecclesiastics and traditionalists" (366).

(26) Briggs, Charles A. "The Sunday-School and Modern Biblical Criticism." Warfield noted that this came from *The North American Review*, Jan. 1894, pages 64–76. Briggs contended that a great amount of false and erroneous material was used in Sunday school to illustrate everything but the lesson itself. He believed, further, that to teach Sunday school without taking into account modern biblical criticism would result in "a mass of material" that would have to be unlearned in a few years (76).

Conclusion

The massive collection of materials gathered by Dr. Warfield exemplifies two aspects of his involvement in the Briggs heresy case. The first is Warfield's extensive reading and familiarity with the sources pertaining to the charges brought against C. A. Briggs, while the second looked to the future and preserved these sources for the use of succeeding generations—the collection of these materials reflects Warfield's conviction that the Briggs case was an adjudication with importance for his own generation and generations to come. Dr. Warfield's polemic and apologetic efforts were often concerned with the doctrine of Scripture. This collection concerning the Briggs trial shows his belief that higher criticism, inspiration, and infallibility would continue to be points of contention within the Presbyterian church. Looking at the issues from a twenty-first century perspective and remembering the inerrancy/infallibility conflicts of the twentieth century, it seems that B. B. Warfield's understanding of the foundational nature of the doctrine of Scripture may actually be the hinge upon which religion turns.

It is hoped that the bibliographic information provided here will be helpful to those desiring further study of B. B. Warfield, C. A. Briggs, the doctrine of Scripture, or the Briggs trial itself. The many publications contained in Dr. Warfield's four-volume set provide a substantial resource for academic investigation.

Index